Ocean yacht navigator

Ocean yacht navigator

Kenneth Wilkes

DAVID McKAY COMPANY, INC.
NEW YORK

Ocean Yacht Navigator

First American edition, 1976

Library of Congress Catalog Card Number: 76-338
ISBN: 0-679-50636-5

Printed in Great Britain

Contents

1. Where are we?

The weather has been clear for most of the ocean passage, but for the past two days the sky has been overcast and it is now blowing quite hard. Evening is approaching and you estimate the position is about 50 miles off the coast, which you see from the chart is rocky and will be a lee shore. You are by no means certain of your position as your last reliable sights were taken three days ago. Is it safe to stand on, or should you heave to and wait for daylight?

As you weigh up the situation there is a brief clearing and you see the moon, a planet and a couple of stars. Out with the sextant, and in a short time you have an up-to-the-minute observed position. As all four position lines form only a small 'cocked hat' on the chart you know the position is reliable. You can now shape a course for your destination, and can make a fairly accurate prediction of when you should make your landfall, and where. You can get your head down for a few hours, safe in the knowledge that you will not finish up on the rocks in the middle of the night.

This is the sort of situation every navigator faces from time to time. The more he knows about deep-sea navigation the safer and quicker the passage, and the sounder he—and his crew—will sleep.

In any ship or yacht safe navigation depends on the navigator knowing where he is at any time. When within sight of landmarks he uses these to fix his position. On a coastal passage, when no landmarks are visible, the position arrived at by dead reckoning can often be checked by using coastal radio beacons, provided these are well within range. Sometimes confirmation may be obtained by taking soundings. However, as soon as a yacht is about 40 or so miles from two or more radio beacons and out of sight of land having identifiable landmarks the position soon becomes in some doubt. There are of course other radio navigational aids such as Consol and Decca. The former only operates over limited areas and is insufficiently accurate for making landfalls, and the latter, though very accurate, requires equipment beyond the means of most yachtsmen. There are also long-range radio systems which cover the world, such as Loran, Omega, and the computer-controlled satellite systems, but these have little application for most yachtsmen.

When we yachtsmen plan being well offshore or making ocean passages we must rely on celestial navigation—by observations of heavenly bodies, and this is what we shall be investigating first. It is interesting to note that every mercantile marine deck officer is required to know how to take celestial sights, and that many captains still insist on the position being checked daily by sextant sights even though the ship is equipped with the most sophisticated radio aids. It is no exaggeration to say that no yacht should attempt a long offshore passage without having someone aboard with the equipment—and the ability—to take celestial sights. The sextant is the traditional instrument used throughout the world for finding the position and is likely to be used for the foreseeable future, even though other methods may become more available.

Many years ago there may have been some excuse for yachtsmen not being too competent with a sextant. The tables and books then available and the methods used needed a good deal of study and a fair knowledge of trigonometry. Now that has changed, and modern methods, using 'rapid sight reduction' tables, have vastly simplified the necessary work. No knowledge of trigonometry is required—simply the ability to follow a set pattern (which a blank 'sight form' will provide), to look up a few figures in tables, to add and subtract, and to plot the resulting position line on the chart.

The best approach to deep sea navigation is to learn how to work out sights in comfort at home, to check the working with exercises, then to practice with the sextant, taking sights from a known position to verify the accuracy of both the sights taken and the position arrived at. Sights taken from the beach can be most useful for this purpose.

There is really nothing difficult in getting good celestial sights and positions, but it must be admitted that—to start with at least—it is easy to make mistakes. Taking and working out celestial sights is like riding a bicycle. Anyone can do it, but not the first time. Practice makes perfect—or next door to it. This is not to say that it takes as long to learn as to ride a bicycle, but some practice is essential, and as with most things, what seems difficult at first soon becomes simplicity itself after

a little practice. In the explanations that follow a number of examples are given. It is strongly recommended that the reader checks every figure given. He should then work out the exercises, checking his results with the answers given at the end of this book. The extracts from the Nautical Almanac and sight reduction tables given at the back of this book will enable all the examples and exercises to be checked.

There are several types of 'rapid sight reduction' tables available. The merits of each are discussed in Appendix 1, together with notes on their use. We shall be working on the 'Air Navigation Tables' AP 3270 as these are the simplest to use and the least bulky aboard a yacht. The identical tables are published in U.S.A., HO 249. Sights can also be worked up by calculation, and the Marcq St Hilaire Haversine method is explained in Appendix 3 for those interested.

All celestial sights hinge on the solution of a spherical triangle on the surface of the earth, commonly called the PZX triangle. For those interested, notes on this are given in Appendix 3, but it is stressed that it is not necessary to master this in order to be able to use the sextant for position finding anywhere in the world.

The following books are recommended for navigational work :

Sight Reduction Tables AP 3270 (Vols, 1, 2 & 3) (HMSO) or HO 249 (Vols, 1, 2 & 3) (USN)

Norie's (or Burton's) Nautical Tables

Nautical Almanac for current year (HMSO & U.S. Government Printing Office)

(Only the Nautical Almanac requires replacing annually—the others last indefinitely.)

Other equipment required :

Sextant

Deck Watch (chronometer) or other accurate timepiece

Radio for receiving time signals

Compasses and dividers (about 6 in.)
Straight edge or parallel rule
Protractor ('Douglas' 5 in. preferred)
Pad of squared paper (pref. 1 in. & 1/10ths or
    2, 10, 20 mm)
    Pencils (soft, BB) sharpener, soft rubber.
    Perhaps rather surprisingly, the most difficult part of celestial navigation work is not in remembering what to do—a simple 'pro forma' or blank sight form will solve this—nor HOW to do it. It is to be ACCURATE. Inevitably, a number of figures have to be looked up, written down and added or subtracted. This is where the beginner tends to fall down. He knows what to do, and how to do it, but makes mistakes in simple arithmetic. There is a golden rule which I recommend to every navigator, whether novice or experienced:

CHECK every figure, check every addition or subtraction and every 'name', (N or S, E or W) and every sign (+ or −), and TICK every item checked. Then do not use the answer till you have ensured that every figure, sign etc. has been ticked as checked. This may sound tedious, but it only takes a few moments if done while the book or table is open on the chart table. It is maddening when a sight makes nonsense and it is found, on checking, to be due to a simple mistake right at the beginning.

Further points worth making are:

(a) Write all figures down—do not rely on memory or attempt mental arithmetic. What is easy at home is not quite so easy at sea, when one may be wet, cold, hungry, or sleepy—or all four together.

(b) Be methodical. Follow a regular sequence of working and don't try short cuts. Always insert a caption or 'label' against a figure, and put in the 'name' (N, S, E or W) e.g. 10^h 25^m 18^s GMT, 24°48′ N. This greatly helps checking.

(c) Write all figures neatly, boldly and clearly so that there is no risk of their being misread. Write figures accurately under each other, so that adding and subtracting is made easy.

(d) Check all subtractions by 'adding up backwards'

e.g.   35°05′   Check by adding 10′ to 34°55′ and
      −34°55′   ensuring it makes 35°05′.
      ─────
      =   10′

(e) If a mistake is made, do not try and write over a figure, but cross out and put in the new correct figure.

(f) Having done a calculation, whenever possible 'stand back' and ask yourself 'does it LOOK sensible?' If it does not, it is almost certain to be wrong, and needs re-checking.

(g) If you have followed these precepts, HAVE CONFIDENCE in the final result.

Sight Reduction Tables NP 401 (HMSO) or the identical HO 229 (USN). Each of the six volumes covers a band of latitudes of 15° (0°–15°, &c) and tabulates all Declinations 0°–90°. Four volumes are required to cover all bodies between 60° N and 60° S, but stars are less easily reduced than if using Vol. 1 (Selected Stars) of AP 3270 or HO 249. The tables are fractionally more accurate than AP 3270 and HO 249 but are a little less easy to use. Any error using AP 3270 or HO 249 is usually less than 1′ and this is well within the accuracy to which sights can be taken from a yacht at sea.

2. Signposts in the sky

Where are we? When in coastal waters we can usually fix our position—at suitable intervals—by reference to landmarks of one sort or another, such as prominent headlands, lighthouses, navigational buoys, light vessels, and so on. When crossing an ocean or making any long sea passage there will be periods of several days—and often weeks—when we are out of sight of any landmark, and beyond the range of coastal radio beacons. However, there are still 'landmarks' for us to use —if we know how to use them. These are the sun, moon, planets and the stars. Except only when the sky is overcast or the horizon is not visible, we can always use one or more of these splendid 'signposts in the sky' to establish our position.

When using a landmark for fixing our position in coastal waters we have to identify the landmark we see, find its geographical position (by finding it on the chart) and find our position in relation to it—perhaps by taking a compass bearing of it. To use any heavenly body we must also identify it, find its position and determine our position in relation to it with the sextant. The sun's identity is obvious, as is also the moon's. Planets are easily distinguished, and it is not difficult to locate a fair number of prominent stars. The geographical position of any heavenly body is found from the nautical almanac, for any required moment, bearing in mind that it is changing all the time as the earth makes its daily revolution. Our position

in relation to any heavenly body is found by observing it with the sextant.

In coastal navigation a single observation of a single landmark will provide us with a position *line*—a line somewhere on which our position must lie. (Fig. 1)

If two (or more) suitably situated landmarks can be observed more or less simultaneously, each will provide a position line, and our position or 'fix' will be at the intersection of the two (or more) position lines. (Fig. 2)

Where only one landmark is available, a fix can be obtained by the 'Transferred position line' method, commonly referred to as the 'Running fix'. The bearing of the landmark is taken and a first position line drawn on the chart. When the yacht has moved a suitable distance a second observation is made and a second position line drawn in. The first position line is then 'transferred forward' the distance and direction the yacht has moved over the ground in the interval. The transferred position line, transferred parallel to the first position line, will cut the second position line, and where the two intersect will be the yacht's position when the second observation was made. This is straightforward coastal navigation. (Fig. 3)

When out of sight of land the only objects available will be heavenly bodies. The sun is the most useful since it is visible, in clear weather,

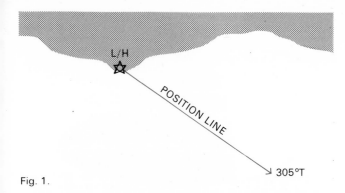

Fig. 1.

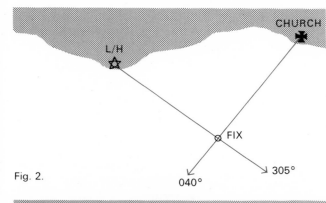

Fig. 2.

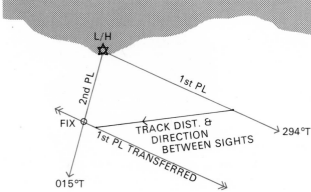

Fig. 3.

throughout the day. A single observation of the sun (or of any heavenly body) will only provide a position *line*, somewhere on which is the position when the sight was taken, exactly as will a single observation of a landmark. If a second observation of the sun is made when the sun's position in the sky has changed substantially, a second position line can be established. The first position line can be transferred forward, in the direction and distance sailed in the interval, as in a 'running fix'. The intersection of the second position line and the first position line transferred forward will be the position when the second sight was taken.

If however two (or more) heavenly bodies are observed more or less simultaneously, then each will provide a position line, the point of intersection of the two (or more) being the observed position at the time. Again, this is similar to position fixing by compass bearings of two (or more) landmarks.

Simultaneous observations are possible:
(a) By day, when both sun and moon are visible, and (occasionally) a planet.
(b) At dawn or dusk twilight, when two or more stars, planet or moon are visible.
This is why it is so useful to be able to take sights of heavenly bodies other than the sun.

What are the broad principles involved in finding a position line from any heavenly body? To save repetition, only the sun will be referred to now, though the same principles apply to any other heavenly body (planet, star or moon).

In the same way that we must know the position of a landmark if we are to use it for position finding, so we must know the position of the sun at the moment we observe it. We shall shortly see how we find the sun's geographical position, but before that, let us refresh our memory on a few points.

ocean yacht navigator

Angles and circles

There are 360 degrees (360°) in a circle, 60 minutes (60′) in a degree. Fractions of a minute of arc are now normally recorded in decimals of a minute. (The second of arc, 1/60th of a minute, is too small to be of practical value.) E.g. 50°25½′ is written 50°25′·5.

Meridians

The equator is a great circle girding the earth exactly midway between north and south geographic poles. Any straight line which runs between north and south poles is a meridian. It cuts the equator at right angles, and is half a great circle (a circle or disc which cuts the centre of the earth). The meridian which passes through Greenwich is termed the Prime Meridian, and is named 0°. (Fig. 4)

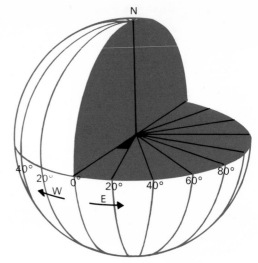

Fig. 4.

Any number of meridians can be drawn, at any desired angular distance from the Prime Meridian measured either at the centre of the earth, or along the equator, or at either pole (all give the same figure). Any meridian is identified by this angle, in degrees and minutes, and is named East or West, and can be any angle up to 180°E or 180°W.

Parallels of latitude

A parallel of latitude is a line drawn parallel to the equator and is a circle girding the earth. Any number of parallels can be drawn, cutting every meridian at a right angle, and each passing through a given point on every meridian measured from the equator along any meridian. The angular distance of any parallel of latitude is measured along a meridian, or at the centre of the earth, from the equator towards the nearer pole, and is named North or South, and may be any angle up to 90° N or 90° S. (Fig. 5)

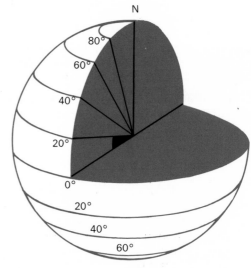

Fig. 5.

14

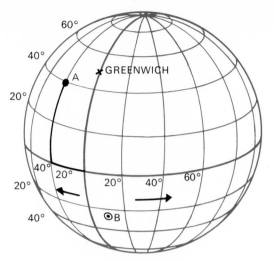

Fig. 6.   Naming a point by latitude and longitude. In this diagram position A is 40° North, 20° West. Position B is 25° South, 10° East

Position

Positions are defined by a form of grid reference, the co-ordinates being latitude and longitude. A position's latitude is the number of degrees and minutes it is north or south of the equator, measured along the meridian on which it lies. Its longitude is the degrees and minutes which the meridian on which it lies is east or west of the prime meridian 0° (the Greenwich meridian). (Fig. 6)

Nautical mile

The definition of a nautical mile (M) is the distance between two points on the earth's surface which subtend an angle of one minute of arc ($1' = 1/60°$) at the centre of the earth. (Strictly, at the centre of curvature of the earth. As the earth is not a perfect sphere the distance varies fractionally, but is taken as the mean value,

6,076 ft.) The nautical mile is divided into ten cables (roughly 200 yds each), normally written as decimals of a mile. The term cable is usually only employed for distances of less than a mile, a distance of say $10\frac{1}{2}$ miles being referred to and written as 10·5 M. Note that whenever a mile is referred to in navigation or nautical matters, this is invariably a nautical mile, which differs appreciably from the statute mile of 5,280 ft used on land. (Fig. 7)

A meridian is one half of a great circle, so a minute of arc, measured along any meridian, is one mile. But note on the other hand that the only parallel of latitude which is a great circle is the equator: all others are 'small circles' since their centres are not at the centre of the earth. See how they become progressively smaller as they approach either pole. For this reason a minute of longitude is *not* a mile (except only when measured along the equator). See how the meridians taper together as they approach the

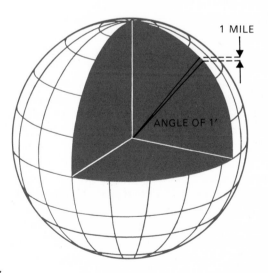

Fig. 7.

15

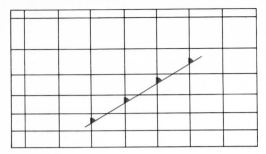

Fig. 8.   Mercator projection. Note that longitude is equally spaced, but latitude, although parallel, is spaced further apart as it approaches the Pole.

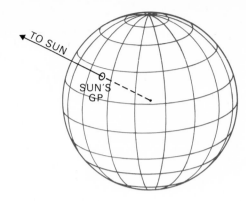

Fig. 9.

poles. (Fig. 4) This is why we must always use the chart's latitude scale (vertical left- or right-hand borders) for scaling off distances on a mercator projection chart, and *never* the longitude scale (horizontal borders). (Fig. 8)

The Sun's position

We know that the earth revolves on its N–S axis daily, and travels round the sun once a year. For navigational purposes it is simpler to assume that the earth is stationary and that the sun (and other bodies) goes round the earth, always moving from east to west. At any instant throughout the day and night there is, somewhere on the earth's surface, a spot where the sun is exactly overhead. An imaginary line drawn from the centre of the earth to the sun would cut the earth's surface at this point. This is called the sun's geographical position, or GP. (Fig. 9)

This spot, the GP, is travelling continuously round the earth, always moving from east to west, making a complete circuit once every twenty-four hours. The track of this spot is also changing in a north–south direction, but very much more slowly, according to the season of the year. At the spring equinox, March 21st, the daily track of the sun's GP is around the equator, and slowly spirals

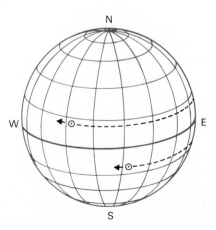

Fig. 10.   The sun's GP moves round the earth as it rotates.

16

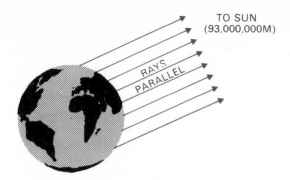

TO SUN
(93,000,000M)

RAYS PARALLEL

Fig. 11.   Sun's rays are parallel at all points of the earth's surface.

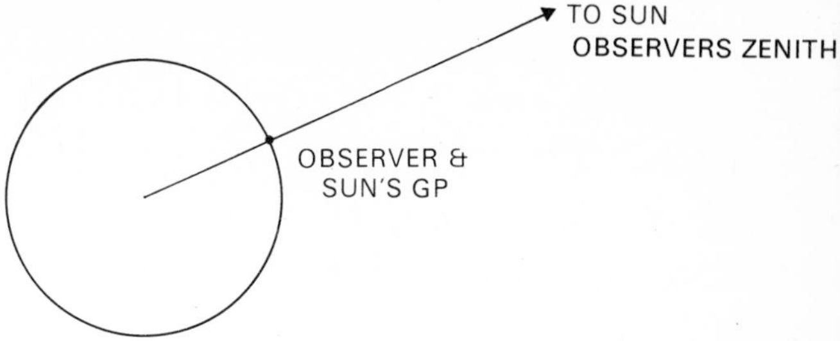

TO SUN
OBSERVERS ZENITH

OBSERVER &
SUN'S GP

Fig. 12.

northwards till midsummer day in the northern hemisphere, when it is tracking round in latitude approximately 23°N. Then it starts spiralling southwards, crossing the equator on September 23rd and on south till it reaches about 23° S on December 22nd, when it starts spiralling northwards once more. (Fig. 10)

The sun's GP is thus moving in an east-to-west direction extremely fast, and much more slowly in a north-to-south or south-to-north direction. It is necessary to find out the exact position of the sun's GP at the instant a sight is taken. For this, all we need is a nautical almanac for the current year. This gives the sun's GP at any instant throughout the year. We shall shortly see how this is found.

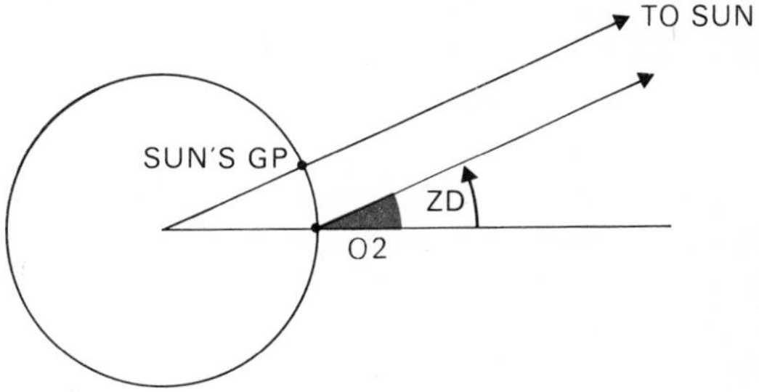

TO SUN

SUN'S GP

ZD

O2

Fig. 13.

Circle of position

The sun is some 93,000,000 miles away. For practical purposes we can say that the sun's rays, striking anywhere on the earth's surface, are parallel to each other. (Fig. 11)

The sun's GP is the position where (at any given moment) the sun is directly overhead. The point in the heavens exactly over an observer's head is called his Zenith. So an observer standing

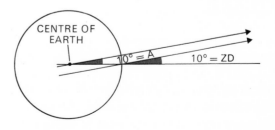

CENTRE OF EARTH

10° = A   10° = ZD

Fig. 14.

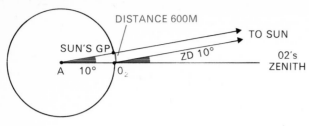

Fig. 15.

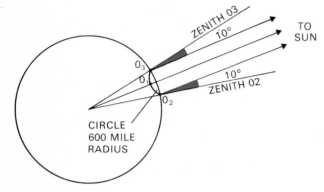

Fig. 16.

at the sun's GP would see the sun in his zenith. (Fig. 12) If an observer (0_2) were standing some distance from the sun's GP he would find that the sun was not at *his* zenith, but some angle away from it. The angle ZD, is called the sun's Zenith Distance. (Fig. 13) From elementary geometry we know that a straight line which crosses two other lines which are parallel to each other will cut each line at the same angle. (Fig. 14) So the angle A, at the earth's centre, will be the same as the angle ZD.

We can now see that the sun's zenith distance, measured at the observer's position 0_2 is the same as the angle A at the earth's centre. By definition of a mile, a minute of arc at the earth's centre subtends a mile on the earth's surface. So a zenith

distance of, say, 10° at a point 0_2 equals 10° at the earth's centre, so the point 0_2 is 10° or 600' = 600 miles from the sun's GP. (Fig. 15)

Imagine a ring of observers standing in a circle of exactly 600 miles radius around the sun's GP. Each would find that the sun's zenith distance at his position was the same 10°. They would all be standing on a 'circle of position'. If each had no other evidence, none would know just where on this circle he was, but each could say with certainty that he was 600 miles from the sun's GP. (Fig. 16)

If then we can measure the sun's zenith distance we can establish our distance from the sun's GP (the centre of the circle of position). If we could now mark the sun's GP on our chart, we could describe a circle round it, of radius the number of miles equal to the sun's zenith distance in minutes of arc. This would give us a circle of position, and we could say that our true position was somewhere on the circumference of this circle. (Fig. 17)

The intercept

We now see that IF we could mark the sun's GP on our chart we could draw a circle of position round it. But the sun is very, very seldom nearly overhead, indeed only occasionally when we are in the tropics and then only near midday. As we shall see later, we shall frequently wish to observe the sun when it is quite low in the sky, say for example, 20° above the horizon.

The angular distance between the zenith and the horizon is a right-angle, 90°, so the zenith distance is always the compliment of the altitude. If the altitude were 20°, the zenith distance would be 70° (90° − 20°). (Fig. 18.)

A zenith distance of 70° = 70° × 60 = 4,200', so that when the sun's altitude is 20° her GP will be 4,200 miles away. We shall find that the

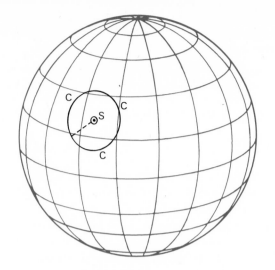

Fig. 17. S is the sun's GP. CCC is the circle of position. The dotted line radius is the sun's zenith distance in minutes of arc.

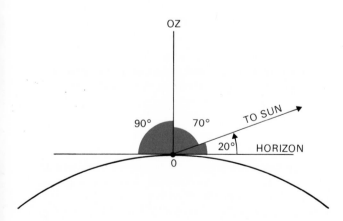

Fig. 18. The observer is at O. His zenith is OZ. The angle 70° is the sun's zenith distance. The angle 20° is the sun's altitude.

distance will seldom be less than many hundreds of miles. From this it follows that the sun's GP will very, very seldom be on the chart we are using to plot the yacht's position, because normally we use a chart which spans at most a few hundred miles or so. As we can seldom mark the sun's GP on our chart, we must tackle the problem in a different manner.

If the latitude and longitude of two points on the earth's surface are known, the distance between them can be found by calculation. Thus if a position is selected on the chart and the position of the sun's GP is known, the distance between them can be calculated. Better still, we can find this distance from our sight reduction tables without any calculation. We can also find the bearing of the sun's GP from the same chosen position. So we can proceed.

We choose a position on our chart, near where we believe we are. We could, if we wish, choose the position by DR. If we are going to use our sight reduction tables we choose a position whose lat. and long. suit our tables, and which is within half a degree of the DR's lat. and long. (We shall see how we decide on the precise position shortly.) We call this the chosen position (CP) and we note its lat. and long. We mark this on our chart. (Fig. 19.)

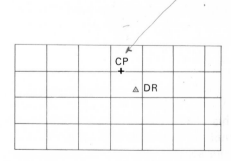

Fig. 19.

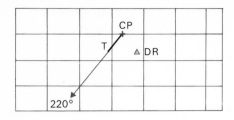

Fig. 20. The line CP to T is 8 miles towards the sun's GP, which is 220° shown by the arrow.

CP = CHOSEN POSITION

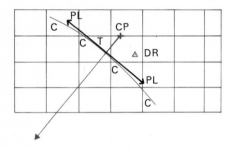

Fig. 21. CCC is the circle of position and the line PL is the position line.

Either by calculation, or from our tables, we find what is the distance between our CP and the sun's GP, and the bearing of the sun's GP from the CP. Let us assume we found this to be 3,620 miles, bearing 220°. We draw a line from the CP in the direction of the sun's GP (220°). If this line could be extended far enough it would strike the sun's GP, but this is almost certain to be miles off the chart. This line therefore represents the outer end of a radius from the sun's GP. (Fig. 20.)

With our sextant we have found that the sun's zenith distance at our true (but yet unknown)

position was, say, 60°12'. Converted into minutes, this shows that our true position was 3,612 M from the sun's GP. Comparing:

Distance from Chosen Pos'n to sun's GP	3,620 M
Distance from True Position to sun's GP	3,612

Shows our True position to be nearer the sun's GP than is the CP by 8 M

Measure off 8 M along the bearing line, from CP in the direction *towards* the sun's GP to point T. The line CP–T is called the INTERCEPT. (Fig. 20.)

We now know that we must be on a circle of position drawn round the sun's GP, of radius 3,612 M. We might, by pure chance, be at T, but we could equally well be anywhere on the circumference of this circle, for at any point on this circumference we should find that the sun's zenith distance was the same 60°12'. We want the small part of the circumference of this circle of true position which, if we could draw it, would be on our chart. As it is a very large circle we can assume that a small piece of the circumference would, for practical purposes, be a straight line, or a tangent to the circle. We shall get this if we draw a straight line through T, at right angles to the direction of the intercept. This is because the intercept is a radius of a circle which, if projected far enough, would strike the sun's GP. (Fig. 21.)

The line PL is therefore a position line, somewhere on which our true position lies. Note that our position may be *anywhere* along the PL, and that the PL may be extended in either direction. We have a position *line* but not yet an observed position on that line. This is analogous to the single compass bearing of a single landmark which also gives a position line only.

The foregoing is only given to illustrate the principles involved. In practice we can simplify the work a great deal. In the explanation just given we found the distance between the sun's GP and the true position by converting the zenith distance angle found by sextant into miles (in the example, 3,612 M). But we are really not interested in this distance. We want to know how many miles the circumference of our true circle of position is from the chosen position marked on our chart (in the example, 8 M). So it is only necessary to compare the zenith distance as at the chosen position (found by calculation or by tables) with the zenith distance at our true (but unknown) position, found by sextant.

Again, in practice, it is not feasible to measure with our sextant the sun's zenith distance at our true position, for we cannot readily pinpoint our own zenith—the point exactly overhead—there is nothing there to measure from. Instead, we measure the sun's ALTITUDE—the angle between the horizon and the sun. Refer back to Fig. 18.

Since we are now going to use the sun's altitude at our true position (instead of its zenith distance), the tables we shall use are also computed to give the angle of the sun's altitude (not zenith distance) as if measured at the CP at a given moment, when we take the sight. Now we can make a direct comparison between:

Sun's Alt. at CP (lat. and long. known), found by tables, in degrees and minutes, and
Sun's Alt. at True position (lat. and long. unknown), found by sextant, in degrees and minutes.

and our tables will also give us the bearing of the sun's GP from the CP so that we can draw the intercept in the correct direction.

As we are now dealing with two altitudes instead of zenith distances we must be careful that we mark off the intercept the number of miles in the correct direction from the CP, either towards or away from the sun's GP. In our example:

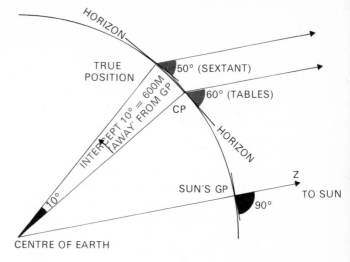

Fig. 22.

To sun's GP from CP	3,620 M	— ZD 60°20′,	or alt. 29°40′
To sun's GP from true pos.	3,612 M	— ZD 60°12′,	or alt. 29°48′
Intercept, TOWARDS	8 M	8′	8′

So the rule is:

TRUE ALT. GREATER than CP Alt., Intercept 'TOWARDS' GP

TRUE ALT. LESS than CP Alt., Intercept 'AWAY from GP'

In Fig. 21 the curvature of the circle of position has been greatly exaggerated to make the point. In practice the sun's GP would be so far away that the circumference would be much more nearly a straight line or tangent to the circle.

Fig. 22 may make the matter clearer. It also is much exaggerated to show the principles—in practice the intercept would only be a few miles, not hundreds. Assume our tables (or calculations) tell us that, at a given moment, the sun's altitude at the CP we have selected would be 60°. This is called the 'Tabulated altitude'. With our sextant we find that at our true (but unknown) position the altitude is 50°. We call this the 'True Alt.' Our true position must therefore be 10° or 600 M from the CP. (Because 10° = 600′, and a minute = a mile, along any great circle.) In this case the true alt. is less than the tabulated alt., so the true position is from the CP in the direction away from the sun's GP. Had the true alt. been more than the tab. alt., the intercept would have been from the CP in the direction *towards* the GP.

Summary

We are finding a point on our chart through which a position line will run, and the bearing of this PL. To do this we compare two figures:

(a) The altitude the sun WOULD BE if measured at a chosen position on the chart—found by tables, and

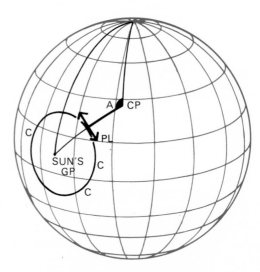

CP = CHOSEN POSITION

Fig. 23. The angle at A is the bearing of the sun's GP from the CP.

(b) The altitude the sun ACTUALLY IS at our
     true (but unknown) position—found by
     sextant.

We find the bearing of the sun's GP from the
CP by tables, which gives us the direction or
bearing of the intercept. The difference between
(a) and (b) above in minutes of arc gives the
length of the intercept in miles. This distance
measured along the intercept from the CP gives
the intercept terminal point. A line through this
point at right angles to the intercept gives the
Observed Position Line. (Fig. 23.)

3. How the sextant works

The sextant does something quite simple. It is an instrument, designed for measuring (in degrees and minutes), the angle subtended at the observer between two objects. In celestial navigation this is always the angle between the visible horizon and a heavenly body. In coastal work, the horizontal angle between two objects or landmarks can be measured, or the vertical angle between top and bottom of an object of known height, such as a lighthouse, can be measured from which the distance from the object can be obtained very easily. Although simple in principle (Fig. 24), the sextant has to be extremely accurate and made to very fine limits. So it is delicate and its accuracy may be impaired by rough handling.

A telescope which is fixed to the frame of the sextant points at a mirror which is also fixed to the frame. This mirror, called the horizon mirror, is bisected vertically, the left half being plain glass and the right half silver-backed to form a mirror. The horizon mirror is fixed at such an angle that, when looked at through the telescope, one is looking at a second mirror, called the index mirror.

The index mirror is mounted on the index arm which can pivot over a wide arc. Movement of the index arm along the arc of the sextant causes the index mirror to be turned on the axis of the index arm. If the sextant telescope is directed at the horizon immediately below, say, the sun, one will see the horizon through the plain glass half of the horizon mirror. If now the index arm is moved along the arc a point will be reached where the sun will also be seen in the telescope, reflected from the index mirror, into the silvered part of the horizon mirror, and into the telescope. Thus one will see the horizon through the plain glass part of the horizon mirror and, superimposed on it, the reflection of the sun coming from the index mirror. The angle between horizon and sun may now be read on the engraved arc, opposite the arrow on the index arm.

Movement of the index arm is made in two stages. Firstly, a bold movement in order to 'find' the sun (or other heavenly body)—to get the sun into the telescope at the same time as the horizon. This is done by disengaging the worm wheel under the index arm from the toothed rack fixed to the back (or on some sextants, the edge) of the arc. A quick-release button or trigger (or on old models, a screw) is provided for this purpose. When so moving the index arm, make sure the quick-release is fully pressed so that the worm wheel does not drag or grate across the teeth of the arc. Having 'found' the sun (and horizon) somewhere in the telescope, release the quick-release so that the worm re-engages with the rack. Fine adjustments can now be made to cause the sun to touch the horizon very accurately. This is done by turning the micrometer wheel,

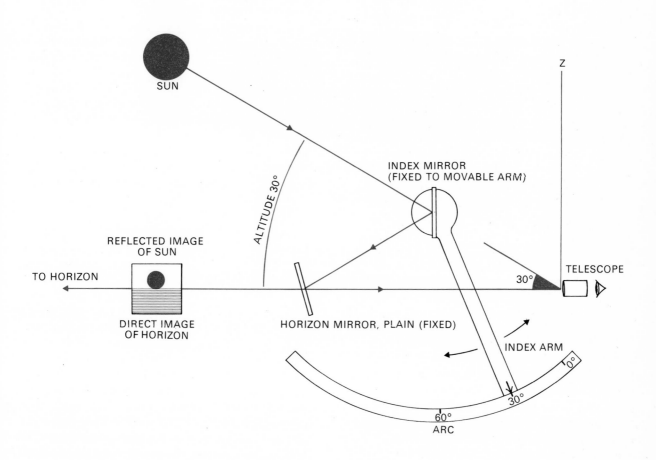

SUN

INDEX MIRROR
(FIXED TO MOVABLE ARM)

Z

ALTITUDE 30°

REFLECTED IMAGE
OF SUN

TELESCOPE

TO HORIZON

30°

DIRECT IMAGE
OF HORIZON

HORIZON MIRROR, PLAIN (FIXED)

INDEX ARM

0°

30°

60°

ARC

Fig. 24.

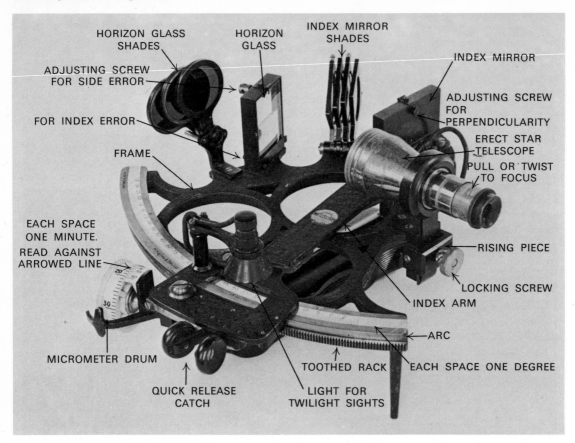

Parts of a micrometer sextant

which causes the worm wheel to screw slowly along the rack on the arc, thus fractionally altering the tilt of the index mirror. The moment exact coincidence has been made, instantly read and note the exact time, and read the angle shown on the sextant.

The sextant angle is read in two stages:

1. Read the number of degrees of arc by noting where the arrow on the index arm touches the engraved arc. If, as is most frequently the case, the arrow points to between two degree marks, naturally read the lower.

2. Read the number of minutes on the micrometer edge, and either interpolate to the nearest 0'·2 or use the small vernier adjacent to the engraved arrow.

When reading the degrees on the main arc, if the arrow is very close to an engraved degree line, it is best to read the MINUTES on the micrometer FIRST, then to decide whether to take the degree as that nearest to the arrow, or to take the one lower. (Fig. 25.)

Looking now at the photograph of a modern sextant, note that there are four shade glasses in front of the index mirror, and three near the horizon glass. Those covering the index mirror should all be swung downwards, out of the way, and those for the horizon mirror swung upwards out of the way. The index mirror shades filter the light received from the sun to a suitable brilliance. Before using the sextant for the sun, ALWAYS swing one shade up to cover the index mirror. Failure to do so could damage the sight as the sun will be magnified two or more times by the telescope. The shades for the horizon mirror are provided to dim down the light from the sea and are usually only needed when the sun is low and there is excessive sparkle from the sea.

Telescopes

Sextants are available with a variety of telescopes. The most common, and that most practical for yacht use, is an erect star telescope. This is slightly bell-shaped (object glass larger than eyepiece), shows the images the right way up, and usually has a magnification of $2\frac{1}{2}$ times. Others have a prismatic monocular (half a binocular) which gives magnification of 4 or more, and a wider field of view. Though capable of more accurate sights, they weigh—and cost—more. The long, narrow 'inverting' telescope occasionally found has certain uses, but presents the objects viewed upside down, and has a very narrow field of view which makes it difficult to use. It is not recommended for yacht use. Special telescopes and lenses are made for particular purposes but are chiefly of use where extreme accuracy, from a stable platform, are required,

such as in surveying. The lenticular lens is an interesting example. When used for sighting a star, the lens splits the light into a fine horizontal line instead of a pinpoint of light.

All good sextants have provision for the telescope holder to be raised or lowered, away from or towards the plane of the sextant's frame. This is referred to as the rising piece. By adjusting the telescope with this, the telescope's axis may be brought more over the plain glass side of the horizon mirror, or more over the mirror side. Usually the half-way position gives good results, but if it is desired to brighten one image more than the other, the telescope can be raised or lowered. The telescope has provision for focusing —either by screwing the eyepiece in or out, or simply by push and pull. Naturally, the telescope should be focused to suit the observer's eyesight. This is done by sighting any clearly defined, distant, object and adjusting the telescope to give the sharpest image. Once this position is found, it is a good idea to make a mark on the tube so that it can be re-set if it is disturbed.

Sextant adjustment

The sextant is a solidly made instrument which, with reasonable care, will last a lifetime. However, the mirrors, on which accuracy depends, are mounted so that their rake and angle can be adjusted should they move slightly. Apart from focusing the telescope, these are the only parts that may need adjustment. Checks for accuracy of alignment of the mirrors should be made periodically. The errors, and the corrections which can be made, are three in number:

1. *Perpendicularity.* This is to check that the index mirror is exactly at right angles to the plane of the instrument. To check, remove the telescope. Set the index to about 45° on the arc. Hold the sextant flat, mirrors upwards and handle

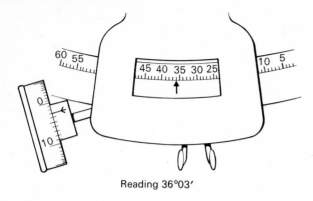

Reading 36°03′

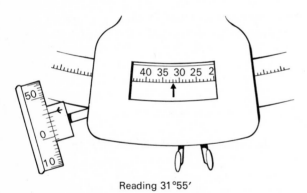

Reading 31°55′

Fig. 25.   Micrometer readings.

downwards, the plane of the frame almost level with the eye, the arc away from you and the index mirror towards you. Fold the index mirror shades down out of the way. Look in the index mirror and move the eye sideways till the arc can be seen reflected in the mirror. Move the eye till this is seen in the mirror AND a portion of the arc can ALSO be seen, direct, adjacent to the reflection of the arc. If the two pieces of arc (reflected and direct) are absolutely coincident—make one straight line— no adjustment is necessary. If the two are not level, the index mirror is not truely vertical. Adjust by a *fractional* turn of the adjusting screw at the top of back of index mirror. (Fig. 26.)

2. *Side error.* Index mirror and horizon mirror not parallel to each other in a vertical plane. To check, replace the telescope. Set index arm to approximately 0° on the arc and sight any distant, clearly defined vertical line, such as chimney, flagstaff or building. If the vertical edges of direct and reflected images coincide there is no side error. The best check is to point the telescope at any bright star with the index set to 0°. Two stars will usually be seen, close together, the reflected and direct image. If the sextant is adjusted by the micrometer so that the stars, when they rise and fall relative to each other, cross exactly, there is no side error. If the stars cannot be made to coincide, adjust fractionally the screw on the back of the horizon mirror which is at the top edge (furthest from sextant frame). This rocks the mirror in a vertical plane. (Fig. 27.)

3. *Index error.* Mirrors not parallel to each other when sextant set to exactly 0°0′. To check, set to approximately 0° and sight any sharp, distant object more than about three miles away. The line of a clear horizon is excellent for this. Adjust the sextant by micrometer till both direct and reflected images exactly coincide vertically (horizons make one straight line). Read the sextant. (Fig. 28.)

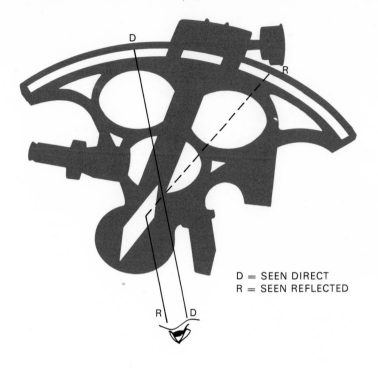

D = SEEN DIRECT
R = SEEN REFLECTED

AS SEEN WHEN CHECKING

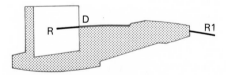

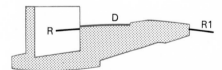

O.K. PERPENDICULAR
ARCS IN LINE

NEEDS ADJUSTMENT NOT PERPENDICULAR
ARCS NOT IN LINE

R = REFLECTION OF ARC ABOUT R1
D = SEEN DIRECT

Fig. 26.

Checking a sextant for perpendicularity. Hold the sextant so
that it faces this way.

Perpendicularity. Line up in the index mirror both the reflected
and direct image of arc. In this picture they are both in line
so that there is no error.

If the index is above 0°, or micrometer above 0′, the sextant is reading 'high'—too big an angle (with no error it would read 0°0′). The amount that it is above 0°0′ is the error 'on the arc'. If the arrow is below 0°0′, the error is said to be 'off the arc'—the instrument is registering too low. An index error of, say, 2′ ON the arc is recorded as −2′·0 and this must be subtracted from every sextant reading. If the error is 2′ OFF the arc it is recorded as +2′·0 and this must be added to every sextant reading.

If the error is less than about 5′ or 6′ it is advisable to make no adjustment but to record the error and to apply it whenever reading the sextant. If the error is excessive it may be removed by fractionally turning the screw on the back of the horizon mirror which is nearest to the sextant's frame.

There is a point to watch. If the arc reads about 0° and the micrometer reads, say, 56′, remember that this is 4′ OFF the arc, and not 56′—it is only 4′ below 0°, and is therefore recorded as +4′·0. This figure must be ADDED to every sextant reading.

It is advisable to check for index error every time a sight is taken—it only takes a moment if the horizon is used.

If either perpendicularity or side error is adjusted it is essential that all three errors are checked and if necessary adjusted *in the order given here*, because each may well affect the others.

To take a sight

Sun. Focus telescope and check for index error, note if any present. Put one shade glass in front of index mirror (swinging others down).

Set index arm to approximately 0°. Hold sextant in right hand: place left hand fingers on the quick-release button on the index arm.

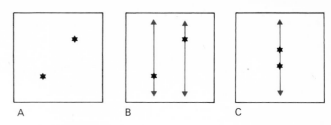

Fig. 27.   A. Reflected and direct images of a Star. B. Images when micrometer is turned; side error is present here. C. Images crossing when the micrometer is turned; here there is no side error.

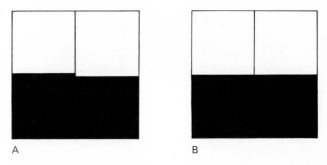

Fig. 28.   A. Appearance when the sextant is set to 0°; horizons are not in line. B. Appearance after micrometer has been turned until horizons come into line: the reading on the micrometer, if any, is then the error of the sextant.

Direct telescope at horizon immediately below the sun. Disengage index arm by quick-release button and slowly move index arm away from you, keeping the horizon steady in plain glass side of horizon mirror.

Sun should presently appear in mirror side of horizon glass. If it fails to appear you have swept past it to one side or the other. Reset to 0° and repeat.

When sun appears in telescope, release quick-release button. Now transfer left hand to micrometer drum. Turn drum slowly to cause image of the sun to sit on the horizon. Adjust so

THE SUN

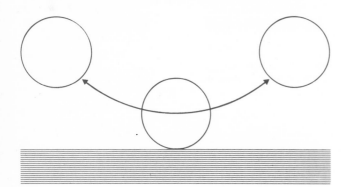

Fig. 29.

that edge (lower limb) of sun just 'kisses' the horizon—no gap between, no overlap.

Rock whole sextant laterally, pivoting it round the telescope so that the sun appears to swing like a pendulum. Find the position where the sun is at the lowest point of swing. This ensures that the sextant is vertical. Ensure exact coincidence at this point, then immediately note the exact *time*, and record, then read angle on sextant, and record. (Fig. 29.)

A star or planet. Check for index error. Swing all shades away. Set sextant to 0°0'. Point telescope up at the star or planet. Both direct and reflected images will be seen, very close together. Press quick-release button and very slowly slide the index bar away from you, and simultaneously slowly depress the sextant. The direct image of the star will disappear upwards—keep the other, the reflected image, steady in the telescope. Continue opening the sextant and depressing it in step with the movement of the index bar while still keeping the reflected star in the telescope. Presently the horizon will appear from below. Release the quick-release button and make fine adjustments with the micrometer as before.

Stars have no visible diameter, and planet diameters are extremely small, so place both on the horizon. Rock sextant to ensure it is vertical, as for the sun. Note exact *time*, and read and record sextant altitude.

An alternative method for picking up a star which some navigators prefer is as follows:

Set sextant to approximately 0°. Hold sextant in *left* hand and upside down, the telescope below and the micrometer above. Tilt the sextant up and through the telescope sight the star in the plain glass of horizon mirror. Now, keeping the sextant quite stationary and keeping the direct image of star in the telescope, slowly 'open' the sextant by moving the index arm away, along the arc.

Taking a sight. Here the quick release catch is used to 'find' the sun.

The next stage in taking a sight. An exact coincidence is obtained by using the micrometer drum.

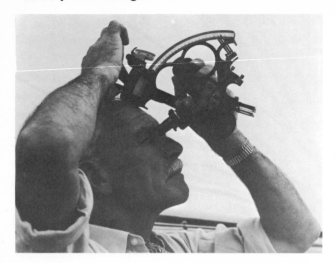

Using the sextant reversed. Here the horizon is 'brought up' to a star.

PLANET

STAR

Fig. 30.

HORIZON

HORIZON

LOWER LIMB

UPPER LIMB

Fig. 31.

Presently the horizon should appear (reflected image) in the mirror of horizon glass. Release the quick-release button. Now transfer the sextant to the right hand and correct way up and (without disturbing the setting) sight the horizon below the star. The star's reflected image should appear in the mirror of horizon glass. With the micrometer make exact coincidence of star and horizon, rock laterally to ensure sextant is vertical, note exact time, and read sextant. (Fig. 30.)

Moon. Except when it is full moon, a portion of the moon is always in shadow and invisible. Note whether the lower or upper limb (edge) is visible, and use this limb to 'kiss' the horizon. (Fig. 31.)

At twilight the moon can usually be picked up in the same way as the sun (as described earlier). By day, when the moon, if above the horizon, may be very pale, it may be necessary to 'bring it down to the horizon', as is done for a star. Rock for verticality, when satisfied with coincidence note exact *time*, and read and record sextant altitude, and note whether lower or upper limb was observed.

To record time
All sextant observations of heavenly bodies require the exact time, by GMT, to be recorded at the instant the sight is taken. The time must be correct to within about five seconds for accurate observations. The only exceptions to this are observations for meridian altitudes and observations of Polaris, where accuracy to within a few minutes is sufficient. These sights are explained later.

If an assistant is available, he can be detailed to read and record the exact instant of a sight, and to record the sextant altitude given him by the observer. When almost ready, give him a preparatory warning—'Ready'. He should then watch the chronometer or deck watch

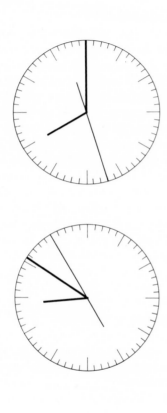

Fig. 32. Top shows wrong way to set deck watch with minute hand exactly on hour when second hand well away from 0. Bottom shows error that can occur with uncertainty about whether time is 8.49.55 or 8.50.55.

Fig. 33. Shortly before time signal set the minute hand exactly on a minute mark when second hand is at 0. Middle shows clock at time signal, showing it is 34 sec. fast. Bottom shows sight taken at 10.57.40, therefore real time is 10.57.06 (minus 34 seconds).

continuously. The instant you establish exact coincidence on the sextant, call 'Stop'. He then reads the time shown, and records it. Check this yourself unless you have 100% confidence in your timekeeper—it is remarkably easy to make a mistake of a whole minute.

If a reliable person to act as timekeeper is not available, proceed as follows:

At each radio time signal, listen in and record error of watch.

Sling stopwatch round neck, have deck watch ready on chart table.

Take sight and *immediately* start stopwatch. Return to chart table and replace sextant in box, taking care not to disturb setting.

Observe deck watch till the second hand comes round to 0. Minute hand should then be on (or very close to) a minute gradation. Instantly stop the stopwatch.

Read and write down the time by deck watch (hours and minutes).

Under this reading, write down the time elapsed by stopwatch, and deduct.

Adjust answer for deck watch error, determined by radio time signal. If watch was recording Summer Time, deduct one hour for GMT.

	h	m	s	
Thus: Deck or wrist watch	09	14	0	GMT
Stopwatch—deduct			−35	
	09	13	25	
Deck watch error, slow +		+1	17	
	09	14	42	GMT

Do not try to set the chronometer or deck watch correct at frequent intervals, but leave alone, recording the error daily at least, if within radio distance.

When resetting, ensure that when the second hand is at 0, the minute hand is set as close as possible to a minute gradation. This reduces the risk of mis-reading by a full minute, which is a common cause of error if this point is overlooked. (Figs. 32 and 33.)

Care of the sextant

When not actually in use, the sextant should always be kept in its box. There should be one specific place aboard a yacht where the box can be securely stowed, preferably fixed so that it cannot get thrown out when the going is rough. Ideally, the stowage should be so arranged that the lid can be opened and the instrument removed without having to take the box from its stowage, but this is not always possible. Immediately after use, the sextant should always be carefully replaced in its box, and *never* left on chart table, seat or berth where it could fall off or be sat on. To drop the sextant is to risk damaging it irreparably. When placing in the box, make sure it is snugly in and no portion where the lid might foul it on being closed (watch the shades, and telescope).

Always remove the sextant from its box by the left hand, avoiding picking it up by the index bar, and promptly transfer it to the right hand, grasping it by its handle. Replace in the reverse sequence. Never put the sextant down mirrors downwards— for obvious reasons.

The only maintenance necessary is to keep the mirrors and telescope lenses clean by lightly rubbing with a soft cloth, and very occasionally lubricating the rack and gears with a drop of light oil, and wiping over the scale with a lightly oiled cloth. Avoid polishing the arc, and particularly with a vernier sextant resist the temptation to clean the arc with metal polish. This will soon rub out the finely engraved gradations.

Aboard a yacht it is almost inevitable that at some time a dollop of salt spray will fly over the sextant. When this happens, promptly immerse the whole instrument in clean fresh water to remove all salt, shake gently and dry with a soft, dry cloth. Salt left on the instrument will rapidly get behind the silvering on the mirrors and render them useless. One has to be strong-minded about this.

Types of sextant

A wide variety of sextants is available, at prices varying from as little as about £15 up to £200 or more. Second-hand ones can sometimes be found. A micrometer sextant in good condition may cost about 75% of the price of an equivalent one new.

All modern sextants are of the 'micrometer' type (as described earlier). The arc is inscribed with degrees only, the micrometer drum with minutes, some having a small vernier scale on the micrometer permitting readings to the nearest 0'·2 of arc. A full-size micrometer sextant usually has an arc of radius about $6\frac{1}{2}$ in (162 mm). Smaller ones are also available with arc radius about $4\frac{1}{2}$ in (114 mm). These can be just as accurate as full-size ones, can certainly be read to within 1' of arc, and have the advantage of taking up less space and being handy to use. Some sextants can be supplied with a light to illuminate the arc and micrometer when required. This is a great help when taking twilight star or planet sights.

A sextant should have four shades to the index mirror and three to the horizon glass, all of varying densities. Older ones are tinted different colours; the newer ones are neutral shades of grey. The latest idea is a single glass made up of a pair of polarized glasses—the further one glass is turned the more light it cuts out, thus providing an infinitely variable opacity. Telescope magnifications vary from $2\frac{1}{2}$ times to 4 times or more. Some have a prismatic monocular

The Ebbco plastic sextant.

A modern sextant of German manufacture made for use on yachts.

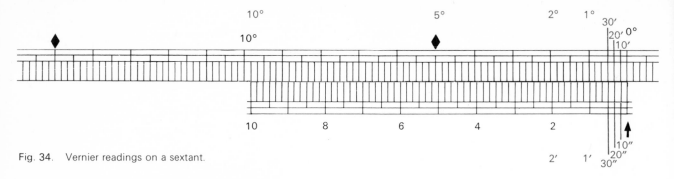

Fig. 34.   Vernier readings on a sextant.

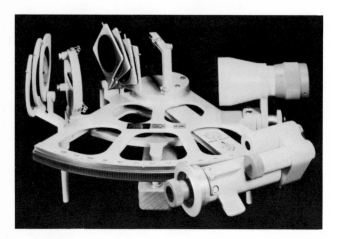

A German drum sextant which has particularly easy adjustment
to the micrometer.

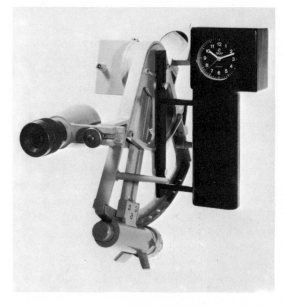

A drum sextant combined with a timing device. At the
instant the sight is taken the clock can be stopped and
subsequently read off. After a short interval the clock
starts again at the correct time, catching up for the
period while stopped.

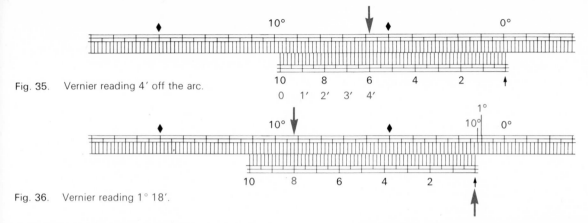

Fig. 35.   Vernier reading 4' off the arc.

Fig. 36.   Vernier reading 1° 18'.

This is a bubble sextant. It can be used for practice on dry land, but is of no use on board a yacht at sea.

magnifying 7 times. A fairly high magnification helps accuracy, provided the mirrors are of suitably large size to give a good angle of vision. A small angle of vision means you see only a small piece of sky and may have to 'seek' for the star (or even the sun) for some time before finding it in the telescope.

The most vulnerable parts of a sextant are the two mirrors. Salt-laden air can soon blemish the fine silvering of the mirrors. A good modern sextant has mirrors specially sealed against the ingress of moisture.

Good second-hand vernier sextants are sometimes available. If such a sextant has been looked after, even though it could be fifty or more years old, it may be quite reliable. A vernier sextant differs from a micrometer sextant, basically only in the method of indicating and reading the angle. Instead of a quick-release catch for making the initial movement, a screw underneath the index arm is loosened to free the arm, being tightened again when the object viewed is 'found'. Fine adjustment is made by a knurled knob instead of a micrometer drum. The whole reading is taken from the divisions on the arc, supplemented by a vernier scale.

Fig. 34 is a very much enlarged diagram of a portion of the arc, and the vernier. First study the main arc divisions, note that only every fifth, or maybe tenth, degree is named (sextants vary). In the illustration only every 10° is named, a diamond indicates each intermediate 5° mark. Note next that each whole degree space is subdivided into six small spaces, each of which is 10′, (10′ × 6 = 60′, = 1°). Having taken a sight as usual, we first read on the main arc, opposite the arrow or zero point on right-hand end of the vernier scale, the whole degree and the 10′ line which lies immediately to the right of the vernier arrow. We then run the eye along the vernier scale till we find a division which exactly corresponds with a division on the arc. In Fig. 36 the vernier arrow (or zero) is above 1°, and above the first 10′ line, nearly but not quite up to the next, the 20′ line. Now looking along the vernier scale (Fig. 36) we see that the vernier 8 is exactly opposite a line on the arc, but no other vernier line corresponds exactly with another line on the arc. So the full reading in this case is 1°18′—1°10′ from the arc, plus 8′ from the vernier. (If we wanted to split hairs, we might find that perhaps one fine line on the vernier to the left of the vernier 8 line fitted better. As the vernier scale has each 1′ divided into six small spaces, each space represents 10″ (seconds of arc, 60″ = 1′), and the reading would be 1°18′10″. However, as no sight we are able to take on a yacht can be guaranteed to be much more accurate than 1′ we can forget this refinement.)

A vernier sextant usually has a small moveable magnifying glass to enable the fine gradations to be read. This can be swivelled over the length of the vernier scale. Because of the large number of engraved lines on the arc, a vernier sextant is usually a good deal larger than a micrometer one, the arc radius being perhaps $7\frac{1}{2}$ in. Apart from its size, the only disadvantage of a good vernier model is that it takes a little longer, and a little more care, to read accurately, but practice largely overcomes this problem.

Another sextant well worthy of mention is the plastic sextant made by Ebbco. This is far cheaper than any 'traditional' sextant, costs under £20, and is accurate to within 2′·0 of arc—which is as accurate as most sights taken aboard a yacht.

Even if a traditional sextant is preferred, it is comforting to have an Ebbco as a stand-by. On a long voyage I would rather carry two good plastic sextants than only one expensive one. There is always the risk of the sextant being damaged, lost or stolen in port, and if this happened far from civilization one would be in deep trouble.

If you buy a second-hand sextant, do so from a reputable instrument supplier. Wherever you get it, check it carefully yourself, paying particular attention to:

(a) If a vernier model, are the fine engraved divisions on arc and vernier still clear? Check by reading at various settings. (Repeated cleaning may have almost levelled-off the fine lines.)

(b) Are the two mirrors unblemished, specially round the edges?

(c) Are both mirrors firm, adjusting screws not loose nor seized-up?

(d) Check for perpendicularity and side error, as well as index error, but do not condemn unless the errors cannot be removed.

(e) Check that main frame shows no signs of distortion.

(f) Check telescope—can it be focused, appears to be parallel to plane of frame, and is of adequate magnification and angle of vision.

4. True altitude

The first step in using a sextant observation of a heavenly body is to determine the body's true altitude. The altitude we read on our sextant is called the sextant altitude, and this angle has to have some adjustments made to it before it becomes the true altitude. We have already seen that, if there is any index error on our sextant, this must be taken into account. This is one of the five items to be dealt with before we can arrive at the True Altitude. Fortunately they are all very easily found and applied, and require no calculation. The corrections to be made are those for:
1. Index Error—found by the observer for his particular sextant.
2. Dip—found in the Nautical Almanac.
3. (a) Semi-diameter ⎫
   (b) Refraction   ⎬ found in a single figure in the Almanac.
   (c) Parallax   ⎭

Index error
Few sextants have absolutely no index error—any more than a watch corresponds, to the second, with exact GMT. Every reading of the sextant must be corrected by the index error (if any), if the sight is to be accurate. Finding the index error was described in chapter 3. The error so found should be noted on a card or paper kept in the sextant box for reference, and it is advisable to check the error before each fresh set of sights is taken. It only takes a moment if the horizon is used, and

does guard against an undetected error which might arise if, for example, a mirror had been accidentally knocked.

Dip
This is the angle between the horizontal plane through the observer's eye and the *visible* horizon. It occurs because the eye is always above sea level, so that the observed altitude is always greater than the altitude as measured from a point at sea level, where the horizon would be, theoretically, in a true horizontal plane. (Fig. 37.)

The amount of the correction depends entirely and only on the observer's height of eye above sea level, and is always to be subtracted from the observed altitude of *any* heavenly body. A table on the inside cover of the Nautical Almanac lists* the correction for any required height of eye, in minutes of arc. It is sufficient to gauge the height of one's eye when taking a sight to the nearest foot (or say 25 cm).

Semi-diameter
The true altitude which we require is the angle between the true horizon and the *centre* of the body being observed. Stars have no visible diameter, but both the sun and the moon have very appreciable diameters. It is much more accurate to measure with our sextant the angle to one edge or 'limb' of sun or moon rather than to

* See Extracts from Nautical Almanac, first sheet, at end of this book, p. 147.

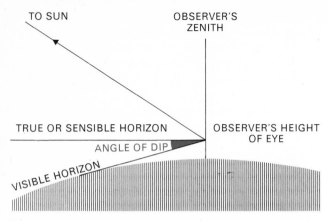

TO SUN

OBSERVER'S ZENITH

TRUE OR SENSIBLE HORIZON

ANGLE OF DIP

OBSERVER'S HEIGHT OF EYE

VISIBLE HORIZON

Fig. 37.

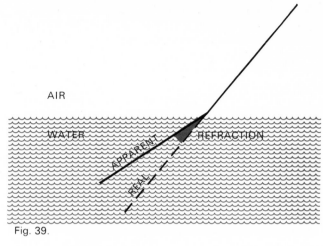

AIR

WATER

APPARENT

REAL

REFRACTION

Fig. 39.

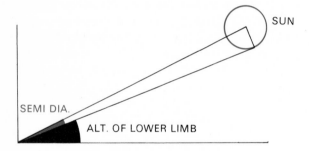

SUN

SEMI DIA.

ALT. OF LOWER LIMB

Fig. 38.

APPARENT DIRECTION

REAL DIRECTION

HORIZON

AIR OF VARIOUS DENSITIES

ANGLE OF REFRACTION

Fig. 40.

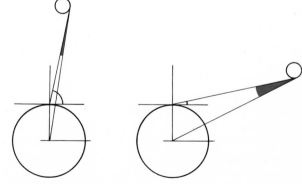

Fig. 41.   Parallax angles (shown in red).

the centre. A correction must therefore be made for the semi-diameter (or half-diameter) of the sun or moon. The necessary correction is incorporated in a single figure, found in the Nautical Almanac, which takes care of this correction, AND the two corrections which follow. This is called the 'Total Correction'. (Fig. 38.)

Refraction

This arises due to the bending of light rays as they pass from one medium to another of different density. The phenomenon of the stick which appears to be bent when a part is put in water at an angle, is well known. (Fig. 39.) Light passing from outer space into the earth's atmosphere is similarly refracted. Refraction is at a maximum when the body viewed is low down, near the horizon, diminishing to zero when the body is overhead. (Fig. 40)

Parallax

The altitude of a body as measured from the surface of the earth differs from that which would be found if it were measured from the centre of the earth, which is the condition required for a True Altitude. (Fig. 41.) Parallax is greatest when the altitude is low, and it diminishes gradually to zero when the body viewed is overhead. Parallax also varies as the distance between the earth and the body changes. The moon's parallax can be up to 61' in arc because the moon is, relatively, quite near the earth. The amount therefore depends on the moon's altitude and her distance from the earth, which varies during the year. The sun's parallax is fractional, never exceeding 0'·15. Parallax of all other heavenly bodies is so small as to be negligible.

Total correction

These three factors, semi-diameter, refraction and parallax, are all taken care of in a single correction, given in the Nautical Almanac for the particular body being observed, for its particular altitude, and in the case of the sun, given either for summer or winter, as required. The moon's parallax changes so markedly that it is given as a separate correction according to the changing apparent diameter of the moon. The simple correction table to be used for the moon is fully explained in chapter 10.

Application of corrections to sextant altitude

An example will show how the necessary corrections are applied to a sextant altitude of the sun, to arrive at the true altitude. When adjusting the sextant for index error it is convenient (though not essential) to leave any small residual error 'on the arc'. The index error will then be a minus, to be subtracted, and this can be combined with the correction for dip, which is *always* a minus, to give a single subtraction.

Example. A sight of the sun, taken in November, gave a sextant reading of 34°25'·0. The sun's lower limb was observed and the observer's height of eye was 2·5 metres.

First, write down the Sextant Angle, as read on the sextant, and note down which limb was used. The three corrections required are

Index Error—IE
Height of Eye—Dip
Correction—Cor.

The figures should be arranged as shown below. IE is that previously found for the particular sextant. Suppose this is −2'·0. Look on the inside of the front cover of the Nautical Almanac.* On the right hand side of the left page is a panel headed *dip*. In the column headed 'Ht of Eye' find the pair of heights which 'straddle' our 2·5 metres. These are 2·4 and 2·6m. Against this pair extract the − 2'·8 shown. Note this where shown below. Combine IE with dip and place under the sextant altitude. Subtract, and we have the 'apparent altitude' (app. alt.).

Sextant alt. LL		34°25'·0
IE	−2'·0	
Dip.	−2'·8	−4'·8
App. alt.		34°20'·2

Note that the dip correction for small heights of eye (2 ft to 10 ft) are given half-way down the right hand column in the dip panel in the Nautical Almanac.

We now only need the correction, found in left-hand panel on left-hand page, headed 'Sun'. This panel has two columns headed respectively 'Oct—Mar' and 'Apr—Sept'. Each of these columns shows 'app. alt.', and against each, the correction to be made for, alternatively Lower limb (all are +) or upper limb (all are −). We are in November, so we use the 'Oct—Mar' column. Run eye down 'app. alt.' column till a pair is found which 'straddles' our app. alt. of 34°20'·2. These are 34°17' and 36°20'. In the column headed 'Lower limb' we find, half-way between these two figures, +14'·9. This is the correction for any altitude between these two figures.

Sextant alt. LL		34°25'·0
IE	−2'·0	
Dip.	−2'·8	−4'·8
App. alt.		34°20'·2
Cor.		+14'·9
TRUE ALT.		34°35'·1

We have now found the True altitude at the position where we took the sight. We must now decide on a Chosen Position, and find out what the altitude WOULD be, if measured there at the same time. We can then compare the two altitudes, which will give us our Intercept—the distance our true position line is from the chosen position.

Exercise No 1 (Answers on p. 177)
a) − e)
All questions are based on 1975.
  Find sun's true altitude:
(a) On 1975 Aug. 31st, Sextant alt. LL 10°43'·5 IE −1'·9 HE 8 ft.
(b) On 1975 Feb. 17th, Sextant alt. LL 19°57'·1 IE −3'·0 HE 8 ft.
(c) On 1975 May 20th, Sextant alt. LL 28°47'·3 IE −2'·0 HE 6 ft.
(d) On 1975 Aug. 30th, Sextant alt. UL 20°54'·0 IE −2'·6 HE 6 ft.
(e) On 1975 Aug. 30th, Sextant alt. LL 48°31'·7 IE −2'·6 HE 6 ft.

5. Tabulated altitude

Altitude and bearing from the chosen position

From chapter 2 it will be recalled that finding a position line from a sight resolves itself into our making a simple comparison between two angles:

The altitude of the sun at our true (but unknown) position, found by sextant.

The altitude the sun would be if measured at a chosen position (near where we believe we are), the lat. and long. of which we know.

It also involves finding the bearing of the sun from the chosen position.

In chapter 4 we saw how to find the sun's true alt. In this chapter we shall discover how to find the sun's altitude if measured at the chosen position, and her bearing from that CP. As both these figures are found in our Tables (AP 3270), we call this the *tabulated altitude* (tab. alt.). We shall also see how we choose a suitable Chosen Position (CP).

The first step is to find the sun's geographical position (GP) at the moment we took our sight with the sextant. This is given in the Nautical Almanac. Open the almanac at any page in the main part of the book.* Note that both pages (left- and right-hand) are headed with the same three dates—year, month, and three dates. Both pages are divided horizontally over the three days. The left-hand page has columns headed 'Aries' and each of the four planets of navigational use. The

right-hand page has columns headed 'Sun' and 'Moon'. The panel for each date and day has the 24 hours in the day listed downwards, 00^{hrs} being midnight. Note that the layout of every page throughout the year is identical—only the figures are different.

The Sun's position

Positions on the earth, or on a chart, are expressed in terms of their latitude and longitude. (Fig. 42.) The terms used to define the sun's position in the heavens—and hence its GP—are Declination (Dec.) and Greenwich hour angle (GHA).

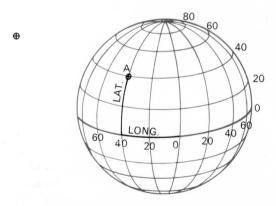

Fig. 42.   Position A is latitude 40° North, Longitude 40° West.

Declination corresponds exactly with latitude, giving the number of degrees and minutes which the sun's GP is N or S of the equator at any given time. Greenwich hour angle is like longitude, but differs in that it is always measured *westward* from the Greenwich meridian, 0°. The GHA at any instant may be anything from 0° to 359° (unlike long. which is measured westward *or* eastward from the Greenwich meridian and can never exceed 180° W or 180° E). The sun appears to travel round the earth once a day, and her GP therefore moves approximately (but not exactly) 360° in 24 hours, 90° in 6 hours, 15° in one hour, and so on. The 'longitude' of the sun's GP can therefore be expressed either in hours since it crossed the Greenwich meridian, or in degrees and minutes of arc. It is more convenient to use degrees and minutes, but this explains why it is called Greenwich hour angle.

The GHA of the sun is therefore the angular distance between the meridian passing through Greenwich (0°) and the meridian on which the sun's GP lies at any given instant, always measured *westward* from Greenwich meridian. (Fig. 43.)

The Nautical Almanac gives the sun's position in terms of its GHA and Declination at any required moment.

Example. Find the sun's GHA and Dec. on 1975 May 19th at $07^h 52^m 15^s$ GMT.

On Nautical Almanac p. 103 headed May 19, 20, 21 (right-hand page) is a panel headed 'Sun', and under this, 'GHA' and 'Dec.' In left margin the hours from 00^h (midnight) to 23^h are listed, with the GHA and Dec. adjacent. These are the figures for exactly 'on the hour' each hour. Note that the GHA continuously increases each hour, round the circle (because the sun is always travelling E to W). At 11^h the GHA has nearly made a full circle, and starts another circle around

12^h (midday). Dec. on the other hand may be increasing each succeeding hour (as in May), that is, going further N hour by hour. But in February when its Dec. is S, the figure is reducing each hour that passes—it is travelling slowly northward and is a little LESS S each hour. The small 'd' at the bottom of the column (May 19th, d = 0'·5) is the amount the Dec. is changing each complete hour. We can now write:

	GHA	*Dec.*
May 19th 07^h	285°54'·1	N 19°38'·9

and the change in Dec.
each succeeding hour
(d, at foot) is   d, + 0'·5
It is + because at 08^h it
will be greater.

Now we must find the amount by which these figures change because the time we are concerned with is $07^h 52^m 15^s$. Turn to the buff pages in the Nautical Almanac headed 'Increments & Corrections', see buff page xxviii (Extracts p. 156). This has one large panel headed '52^m' and another '53^m'. Down the left-hand edge of each panel are seconds (s). In the 52^m panel against our 15^s we find, in the column headed 'Sun—Planets', 13°03'·8. This is the increase in our GHA for our extra $52^m 15^s$. We add this (always +)

	GHA	*Dec.*
May 19th 07^h	285°54'·1	N 19°38'·9
Incr. for $52^m 15^s$	13°03'·8	d, + 0·5
	298°57'·9	

The same panel for 52^m also gives us the change in Dec. for our extra 52^m. All we have to do is to find our d, 0'·5 in the column headed 'v. or d.' and against this in the column headed 'Corr.' is 0'·4. As the Dec. to-day is increasing hour by hour the correction must be plus. (Note that the Dec. changes so slowly that it only needs

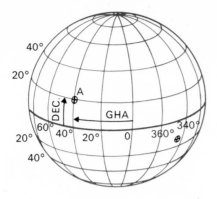

Fig. 43.   At A the sun's GHA is 40° and DEC is 20° North.

Date & Time: 1975 Aug. 30th at 10ʰ 53ᵐ 38ˢ GMT.

	GHA	Dec.
Aug. 30th 10ʰ	329°48'·3	N 9°09'·5
Incr. 53ᵐ 38ˢ	13°24'·5 d. − 0·9	−0'·8
	343°12'·8	N 9°08'·7

To find the Tabulated Altitude we have to find the angle between the Chosen Position and the sun's GP measured between the two meridians on which they lie. (Fig. 44.) This is called the *local hour angle* (LHA), to differentiate it from the GHA of the sun, and it is always measured *westward* from the CP to the sun's GP. If we know the sun's GHA, and the longitude of the CP, it is a simple matter to deduce the sun's LHA. (Fig. 45.) In this example the sun's GHA is shown as 60°, i.e. 60° westward from 0°. The CP is shown as on long. 40° W. Therefore the LHA of the sun (from the CP) is the difference between the two, namely

correcting for the extra minutes—in our case 52ᵐ—and we can disregard our seconds (15ˢ)

	GHA	Dec.
May 19th 07ʰ	285°54'·1	N 19°38'·9
Incr. for 52ᵐ 15ˢ	13°03'·8 d. + 0·5	+0'·4
	298°57'·9	N 19°39'·3

Remember, when extracting GHA and Dec. from the daily page, to note all *three* figures (GHA, Dec. and d factor), to give Dec. its name (N or S), and the d factor its sign (+ or −) according to whether Dec. is increasing or reducing. Here are two more examples:

Date & Time: 1975 Feb. 17th at 18ʰ 55ᵐ 50ˢ GMT.

	GHA	Dec.
Feb 17th 18ʰ	86°29'·0	S 12°00'·8
Incr. 55ᵐ 50ˢ	13°57'·5 d. − 0·9	−0'·8
	100°26'·5	S 12°00'·0

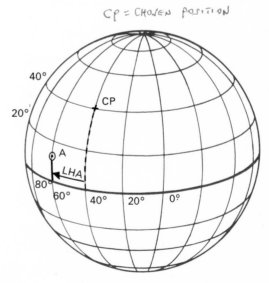

Fig. 44.

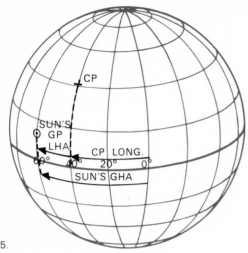

Fig. 45.

CP = CHOSEN POSITION

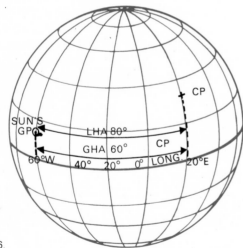

Fig. 46.

20°. Suppose the CP had been 20° *E*, the sun's LHA would have been the *sum* of its GHA and the E long. of the CP, namely 80°. (Fig. 46.)

So the formula is

$$\text{GHA} \begin{Bmatrix} +\text{E long. of CP} \\ -\text{W long. of CP} \end{Bmatrix} = \text{LHA}$$

Sometimes it is necessary either to add or to subtract a full circle of 360° to carry out the little sum. The following diagrams, which represent a bird's eye view of the earth from over the N pole, will clarify this. (Fig. 47.)

Remember whether to add or subtract the CP's long. by the rhyme: 'Longitude *east*, Greenwich is *least*, longitude *west* greenwich is *best*.'

(Meaning, long. E, *G*HA is less than *L*HA, long. W, *G*HA is more than *L*HA.)

The chosen position

A chosen position is marked on a chart to find out what the sun's altitude WOULD be, if measured from such a position. It should be near the supposed position so it could be the position by DR. However, a DR position is very likely to have both degrees and minutes in both its lat. and long., e.g. DR 48°10′ N, 5°35′ W. If we wish, we can calculate the sun's altitude and bearing from such a position if we know the sun's GHA and Dec. But it is much easier, quicker and less liable to error if, instead of calculations we use our Tables (AP 3270) to give us the answer, namely the Tabulated Alt. and the bearing of the sun.

The Tables are entered with three factors:

    Lat. of Chosen Position

    LHA of observed body (say the sun)

    Dec. of observed body (say the sun)

In order to keep the tables of manageable size they give the required answer against WHOLE degrees of Lat., and WHOLE degrees of LHA e.g. Lat. 48°, LHA 344° (no minutes). For this

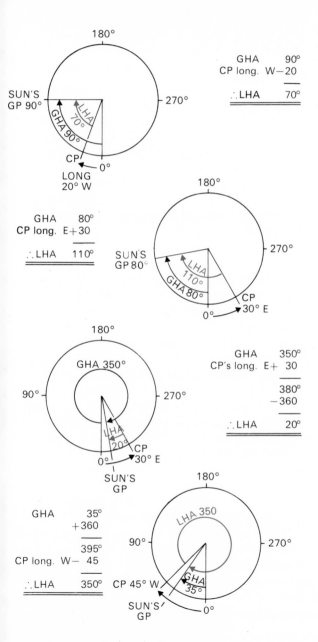

EARTH AS VIEWED FROM OVER N. POLE   Fig. 47.

```
GHA          90°
CP long.  W−20

∴ LHA        70°
```

```
GHA          80°
CP long.  E+30

∴ LHA       110°
```

```
GHA         350°
CP's long.  E+ 30

            380°
           −360

∴ LHA        20°
```

```
GHA          35°
            +360

            395°
CP long.  W− 45

∴ LHA       350°
```

CP = CHOSEN POSITION

reason we do not use our precise DR position, but choose a 'Chosen Position', as near our DR as possible, which will be such that it will have a lat., and give a LHA in whole degrees, without minutes.

The lat. of the CP presents no problem: we simply choose a round degree of lat. nearest to the DR lat. If our lat. by DR were 51°23′ N, we should make our CP lat. 51° N. If 48°51′ N, then 49° N would be the nearest whole degree.

To get the LHA in whole degrees needs a little thought. Remember, LHA was arrived at by applying the CP's long. E or W, to the GHA. So we must choose a long. for the CP which, when either added to, or subtracted from, the GHA will yield a LHA in round degrees, e.g. DR long. 21°34′ W.

```
GHA                    93°45′
Make CP long. W    −21°45′

LHA                    72°
```

or DR long. 22°50′ W.

```
GHA                    86°15′
Make CP long. W    −23°15′

LHA                    63°
```

In each case the CP's long. is the nearest figure to the DR long. which will yield a LHA in whole degrees, without minutes.

The same principle applies where the long. is E, but now we must use the compliment of the

ocean yacht navigator

minutes in the GHA (60 − minutes), e.g.

DR long: 33°18′ E.

GHA	284°45′	
Make CP long. E	+33°15′	(60′ − 45′)
LHA	318°	

or DR long. 43°10′ E.

GHA	286°11′	
Make CP long. E	+42°49′	(60′ − 11′)
LHA	329°	

If this presents any difficulty at first, proceed as follows:

(a) If DR long. is W, *first* put in the CP long. *minutes*, the same as the GHA's minutes, *then*, put in the CP long. degrees which make the whole CP long. nearest to the DR long.

(b) If DR long. is E, *first* put in the CP long. *minutes* space the compliment of the GHA minutes (60-mins.) THEN enter the CP long. degrees which make the whole CP long. nearest to the DR long.

Eg. DR 54° N 6°15′ E, GHA 290°10′

First, enter the minutes (60′ − 10′)

GHA 290°10′
CP long. E 50′
now put in the degrees,
GHA 290°10′
CP long. E +5°50′

LHA 296°

Note that we have used 5° because 5°50′ is nearer the DR 6°15′ than 6°50′ would have been. It may be necessary either to add in, or to subtract, 360°, as in the following examples:

Long. by DR 45°20′ W, GHA 24°25′.

We cannot subtract 45° from 24°, so we add 360°:

GHA	24°25′
	+360°
	384°25′
CP long. W	−45°25′
LHA	339°

or
Long. by DR 61 °E, GHA 348°20′
CP long. E +60°40′

	409°
	−360°
LHA	49°

The chosen position, from which we shall work our sight, will now be:

CP long. in Degrees & Minutes (to give a round-degree LHA)

Lat. in WHOLE degrees (nearest to lat. of DR) and we shall have a LHA in round degrees (no minutes). The next step is to use tables for finding the tabulated alt. and the sun's bearing. We now have the necessary data to do so, namely:

LHA, degrees only
CP's Lat., degrees only
Sun's Dec., degrees and minutes

Let us work through an example:

LHA 30°
CP Lat. N 50°
Dec. N 12°30′

Note first that Lat. and Dec. are both N, i.e. *same name.* (If one had been N and the other S, they would have been *contrary names.*) (Table extracts pp. 160–171.) All are headed 'LAT. 50°'. Turn the Tables sideways and note that the pages are headed:

'Declination (0°–14°) SAME name as Lat.'
'Declination (0°–14°) CONTRARY name to Lat.'
'Declination (15°–29°) SAME name as Lat.'
'Declination (15°–29°) CONTRARY name to Lat.'

50

The pattern is now clear, and the pages covering each lat. (40° to 89°) all follow the same sequence. (AP 3270 Vol. 2 gives lats. 0° to 39°.)

Find the page headed 'Lat. 50°' and (longways) headed 'Declination SAME name as Latitude'. With book sideways, run eye along the top and find Dec. 12°. Run eye down left edge under LHA column and find 30°. At the intersection we find three figures, and at the top of the column, their designations, viz:

> Hc   d.   Z.
> 44°44′ +53   137°

Hc is the Tabulated Alt. and Z is the Azimuth, or bearing from N or S.

This tab. alt. is for a declination of exactly N 12°, but our Dec. is N 12°30′. The 'd' is the factor (53) which governs the small change in the tab. alt. necessary for our extra 30′ of Dec. Refer now to the last page of Tables* AP 3270 (or to the loose card), both headed 'Table 5.— Correction to tab. alt. for minutes of declination.' This prints the 'd' factors across the top of the columns, and the 'extra minutes' down the sides. Find our 'd 53' at the top, and our extra 30′ Dec. down the side. At the junction we find '26'. This is the 'extra minutes' required. Note particularly that the sign was +, so

> Hc   44°44′
> d, +53 =   +26′ (from table 5)
> ──────
> TAB. ALT. 45°10′

d may be plus or minus—always check.

On every page of the tables, at top and bottom of left-hand side, small 'precepts' are printed, to convert the azimuth (Z) into true bearing in 360° notation, (Zn). Our lat. 50° was N lat., so read the *top* precept. Our LHA was 30°, i.e. *less* than 180°, so we must subtract our Z, (137°) from 360°:

> 360°
> Z,   −137°
>   ──────
> Zn = 223°, the *true* bearing of the sun's GP
>   ────── from the CP.

EXERCISE No. 2

Find sun's GHA and Dec.

(a) On 1975 May 20th at 08-53-15 GMT.
(b) On 1975 Aug. 31st at 20-55-40 GMT.
(c) On 1975 Feb. 17th at 19-52-32 GMT.
(d) On 1975 Feb. 16th at 05-55-25 GMT.
(e) On 1975 May 20th at 15-54-40 GMT.

EXERCISE No. 3

Find suitable CP long. and lat.; LHA & Dec. (to nearest minute).

(a) 1975 May 20th at 08-53-15 GMT when in DR 50°15′ N 18°25′ W.
(b) 1975 Aug. 31st at 20-55-40 GMT when in DR 49°45′ S 165° E.
(c) 1975 Feb. 17th at 19-52-32 GMT when in DR 50°25′ S 41°50′ W.
(d) 1975 Feb. 16th at 05-55-25 GMT when in 49°36′ S 165°31′ E.
(e) 1975 May 20th at 15-54-40 GMT when in DR 49°50′ N 127°40′ W.

EXERCISE No. 4

Find lab. alt. and Bearing (Zn) for the following:

(a) LHA 296° CP lat. N 50°, Dec. N 19°53′.
(b) LHA 299° CP lat. S 50°, Dec. N 8°38′.
(c) LHA 73° CP lat. S 50°, Dec. S 11°59′.
(d) LHA 71° CP lat. S 50°, Dec. S 12°32′.
(e) LHA 292° CP lat. N 50°, Dec. N 19°56′.

6. Plotting the sight

We have now found both the true altitude, and the tabulated altitude—the altitude as at the chosen position—and the bearing of the sun's GP from the chosen position. All we have to do is to compare the true and the tab. alt. and the difference between the two will give us the *intercept*—the distance between the chosen position and a point on our (true) position line.

Assume the two altitudes were:

True alt.	34°45′
Tab. alt.	34°30′

Intercept, Towards   15′, Bearing (Zn) = 095°T.

(We note 'Towards' as, in this case, True is greater than Tab. Alt.) Assume also that our chosen position was 50° N 2°15′ W.

We are now ready to plot the sight on our chart. The steps are shown in Fig. 48.

1. Mark the CP on the chart.
2. From the CP draw a line in the direction of the sun's bearing (Zn).
3. Along this line, mark off a point 15 miles from the CP, Towards the sun's GP, using the lat. scale. This is the *intercept terminal point.*
4. Through the intercept terminal point draw a line at right angles to the intercept. This is the position line, somewhere along which is our true position.

Note that this is only a Position *line*, and that our position may be anywhere along the line—or indeed on an extension of the line in either direction.

We may find that our true alt. is *smaller* than our tab. alt., as in the following case. This indicates that our true position line is further away from the sun's GP than is the CP, so this time we must measure our intercept *away from* the sun's GP.

Example:
CP 50° N 3°53′ E

True alt.	28°20′
Tab. alt.	28°28′

Intercept, AWAY   8′ Bearing 175°T (Fig. 49.)

If ever in doubt as to whether to draw the intercept from the CP towards or away from the bearing of the sun (or other body), draw a thumb-nail sketch. (Fig. 50.)

'TRUE GREATER than tab.—TOWARDS' (greater number of letters in 'Towards').

'TRUE LESS than tab.—AWAY.' (less letters than 'Towards').

A complete sight

It takes a great deal longer to explain how to work up a sight than to do it. Let us now tackle one. It pays handsomely to set out the figures in a consistent order. To start with, a sight form

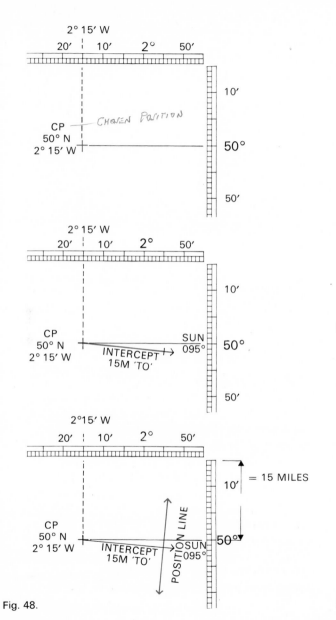

2° 15′ W
20′ | 10′ 2° 50′
CP
50° N
2° 15′ W — CHOSEN POSITION
10′
50°
50′

2° 15′ W
20′ | 10′ 2° 50′
CP
50° N
2° 15′ W — INTERCEPT 15M 'TO' → SUN 095°
10′
50°
50′

2°15′ W
20′ | 10′ 2° 50′
CP
50° N
2° 15′ W — INTERCEPT 15M 'TO' → SUN 095° POSITION LINE
10′ = 15 MILES
50°

Fig. 48.

3° 53′ E
40′ 50′ 4° 10′ 20′
POSITION LINE
INTERCEPT 8M 'AWAY'
CP
50° N
3° 53′ E
SUN 175°
20′
10′
8M
50°
50′

Fig. 49.

TRUE LESS THAN TAB ALT
TAB. ALT.
TRUE ALT. GREATER THAN TAB. ALT.
INTERCEPT TP
CP
INTERCEPT TP
SUN'S GP

FROM CP
DIRECTION AWAY FROM SUN'S GP
DIRECTION TOWARDS SUN'S GP

Fig. 50.

reminds one of the steps to be taken, but it is surprising how quickly one remembers the sequence after a little practice. The form given in App. 5 Fig. 94 p. 144 will be found convenient.

Let us assume we took a sight on 1975 May 19th, using the sun's lower limb. Our sextant read 27°01′·3 and the exact time was 07^h 52^m 15^s GMT. Our index error was 2′·0 on the arc, and our height of eye above sea level about 6 ft. Our approximate position by DR was 50°15′ N 9°40′ W.

First enter all this data at the top of the sight form in the spaces provided. (Still in Appendix 5.) One can either work down from 'sext. alt.' to 'true alt.', or start on the left, to find tab. alt. and Bearing. If we start on 'sext. alt.', enter the index error, find the Dip for our Height of Eye (cover of Nautical Almanac), arrive at Apparent alt. Then find the Correction (cover of Naut. Almanac) in panel 'SUN', Apr.–Sept., lower limb, and we have our true alt.

In Nautical Almanac find our date page, our 07^h and write in the GHA and Dec. AND the d factor at foot (noting whether Dec. is increasing or reducing each hour). In buff pages, find our minutes and seconds Increment, and the correction to Dec. for our d factor. Sum up GHA and Dec. Select a CP long., eliminating minutes and arriving at LHA without minutes. Write in CP lat. (nearest whole degree to DR lat.). Write in Dec. from above. We now have the three figures to find in our sight reduction tables.

In the tables, find our CP lat. pages, selecting the page which shows 'DEC. SAME NAME as LAT.' and our Dec. 19°. In right-hand edge (p. 71) find our LHA of 289°. Extract Hc, d, and Z. Check the precept (top left corner) and apply it to give Zn, the bearing of the sun's GP.

In table 5, or loose card, find our d, 44 and our extra minutes of Dec. (39′). The resultant 29′ is

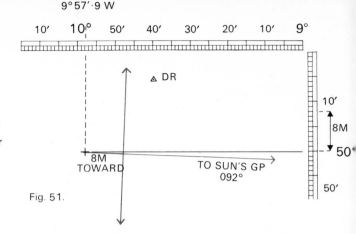

Fig. 51.

entered under Hc, the sign (+ or −) applied, summed up and we have our tab. alt.

Re-write the tab. alt. under true alt., subtract the smaller from the greater and we have the intercept. Name the intercept either 'TO' or 'AWAY', according to the rule 'True greater than tab., TOWARDS'.

We now have the necessary information to plot the position line, namely—CP lat. and long. is 50° N 9°57′·9 W. Intercept, direction and length is bearing 092° T, 8 M towards. (Fig. 51.)

EXERCISE No. 5

Give the CP lat. and long., Intercept distance and bearing from these sun observations:

(a) 1975 Aug. 31st 20-55-40 GMT in DR 49°45 S 165° E. Sextant alt. LL 10°43′·5 IE −1′·9, H of E 8ft.

(b) 1975 Feb. 17th 19-52-32 GMT in DR 50°25′ S 41°50′ W. Sextant alt. LL 19°57′·1 IE −3′·0 H of E 8 ft.

(c) 1975 Feb. 15th 17-54-10 GMT in DR 49°50′ N 130° W. Sextant alt. LL 16°08′ IE −2′·1 H of E 8 ft.

(d) 1975 May 20th 15-54-40 GMT in DR 49°50′ N 127°40′ W, Sextant alt. LL 28°47′·3 IE −2′·0 H of E 6 ft.

7. The Latitude by sun and pole star

Latitude by Sun's meridian altitude

This is by far the easiest of all sights to take, as no tables are required, and even the time is not critical. We do not have to plot the sight on the chart as a simple calculation provides the latitude.

The sight is taken at noon, local time. The sun's GP is then crossing the meridian on which our position lies and will then be bearing due S, if we are N of the sun's GP. The only data required is the sun's true altitude (found by sextant), sun's declination (from the Nautical Almanac).

The steps are :

1. Observe Sun's alt., correct this to True Alt.
2. Subtract True Alt. from 90°, thus obtaining true zenith distance. (TZD). ← *[handwritten: TRUE ZENITH DIST.]*
3. Reverse 'name' of sun's bearing (S to N, or N to S).
4. Find sun's Dec. from Nautical Almanac.
5. Combine TZD with Dec. (same names, add ; contrary names, subtract smaller from greater and name as the greater).

The result is the latitude at the time of the sight.

Example 1. Sun's true alt. 60° (bearing S), Dec. 20° N. (Fig. 52.)

True alt.	60° S (bearing from observer)
from	90°
TZD	30° N (bearing reversed)
Sun's Dec.	20° N
LATITUDE	50° N

Example 2. Sun's true alt. 40° bearing N (in S hemis.), Dec. 20° N. (Fig. 53.)

True alt.	40° N
from	90°
TZD	50° S (bearing reversed)
Sun's Dec.	20° N
LATITUDE	30° S

On ships the traditional method is to start observing the sun about 15 minutes before midday local time, to follow it up with the micrometer or tangent screw as it rises until it ceases to climb, and to observe the moment it starts to dip down. The maximum angle obtained is read and logged as the sextant altitude at meridian passage.

Aboard a yacht it is more practical to work out, in advance, the time by GMT when the sun will be on the meridian of the yacht's position by DR, and to observe the sun just before this time by chronometer. Very exact time is not essential as a few minutes is unlikely to affect the accuracy of the latitude by any significant amount. Note that meridian altitude sights (and Polaris sights) are the ONLY ones where exact GMT is not essential.

To find the GMT when the sun will be on the meridian at the DR position, and thus due S or N, we use the Nautical Almanac. First find the page on which the month and day appear. In bottom right-hand corner will be found a box with the caption 'Sun'. From the column headed 'Mer. Pass.' extract the time shown against the date (day). This is the GMT when the sun will cross the GREENWICH meridian on that day, and will then be at its maximum altitude to an observer who is anywhere on the Greenwich meridian (long. 0°).

If our DR position is W, the sun will cross our meridian AFTER it crossed the Greenwich meridian; if our DR long. is E, it will reach us *before* it reaches the Greenwich meridian. We must therefore convert the long. of our DR position from arc (degrees and minutes) into time, using the Nautical Almanac's 'Conversion of Arc into Time' table (the first of the buff pages). See extracts. Note that the table gives whole degrees from 0° to 359°, and any additional minutes of long. in the panel on the right-hand side, e.g. 85°19'.

$$85° = 5^h \ 40^m$$
$$19' = \underline{1^m \ 16^s}$$
$$\underline{5^h \ 41^m \ 16^s}$$

Write the long. in *time* under the time of Mer. Pass. GMT just found.

If W long.—ADD

If E long.—SUBTRACT.

Example 1. 1975 February 17th, DR 37°15' N 27°30' E.

Sun, mer. pass.	12 14 GMT (at Greenwich merid.)
DR long. 27°30' E	−1 50
Mer. pass. at DR	10 24 GMT

Example 2. 1975 May 20th, DR 50°20' N 9°10' W.

Sun, mer. pass.	11 56 GMT (at Greenwich merid.)
DR long. 9°10' W	+37
Mer. pass. at DR	12 33 GMT

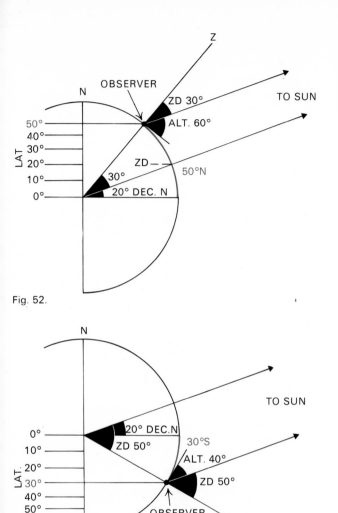

Fig. 52.

Fig. 53.

TRUE ZENITH DIST.

We should start observing the sun a few minutes before the GMT at DR just found (in case the DR long. is not quite correct). If the sun is still moving upwards, we follow it up, keeping it just 'kissing' the horizon, with the micrometer (or tangent screw) till the altitude steadies and then starts to fall. We do NOT adjust the sextant downwards, but catch it at its highest point. We read the sextant and note the time, GMT, which we shall need for the sun's Dec. (to the nearest minute is enough).

All that remains to be done is to:

Correct sextant alt. to true alt. in the usual way; subtract true alt. from 90° to give TZD, and reverse name of sun's bearing (N or S); find sun's Dec. at the GMT of the sight; the algebraic sum of TZD and Dec. gives the latitude.

Example 1. (Fig. 54.) On 1975 May 20 when in 51°30′ N 9°10′ W by DR a meridian altitude of sun's lower limb was 57°50′·5 bearing S. Index error was −2′·0, Height of eye, 6 ft.

Mer. pass.   11 56 GMT at G. Merid.
DR long. 9°10′ W   +37

Mer. Pass.   12 33 GMT at DR

Sextant Alt. LL		57°50′·5 brg. S
IE	−2′·0	
Dip.	−2′·4	−4′·4
	App. alt.	57°46′·1
	Cor.	+15′·4
True Alt.		58°01′·5
from		90°
TZD		31°58′·5 N

Dec. 12ʰ 19°54′·4 N
d, + 0·5 33ᵐ +0′·3   19°54′·7 N

LATITUDE   51°53′·2 N

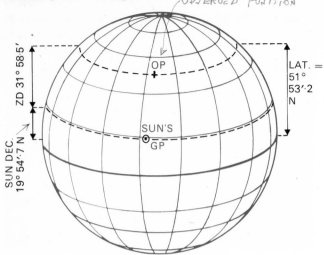

Fig. 54.

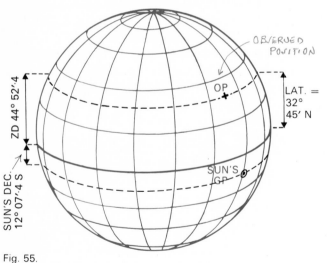

Fig. 55.

Example 2. (Fig. 55.) On 1975 February 17th in DR 33° N 27°30′ E. Meridian alt. sun's LL 44°57′·4 bearing S. Index error —2′·4, Height of eye, 8 ft.

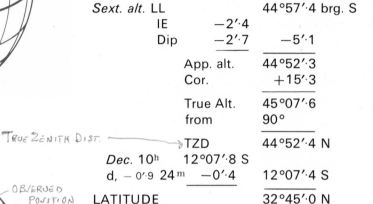

		IL 74
Mer. Pass.	~~12 14~~	GMT (at G. Merid.)
DR long. 27°30′ E	—1 50	
Mer. Pass.	10 24	GMT at DR

Sext. alt. LL		44°57′·4 brg. S
IE	—2′·4	
Dip	—2′·7	—5′·1
App. alt.		44°52′·3
Cor.		+15′·3
True Alt.		45°07′·6
from		90°
TZD		44°52′·4 N
Dec. 10ʰ	12°07′·8 S	
d, — 0′·9 24ᵐ	—0′·4	12°07′·4 S
LATITUDE		32°45′·0 N

EXERCISE No. 6

Find approx. GMT of sun's Mer. Pass. and the observed latitude:

(a) 1975 Feb. 16th DR 49°40′ S 165° E, sextant alt. LL 52°58′ brg.N. IE —2·6 H of E 8 ft.

(b) 1975 May 20th DR 49°50′ N 127°40′ W, sextant alt. LL 60°15′·8 brg.S. IE —2·0 H of E 6 ft.

(c) 1975 Aug. 30th DR 50°27′ N 6° W, sextant alt. LL 48°31′·7 brg. S. IE —2·6 H of E 6ft.

Latitude by polaris (the pole star)

Most people know the Pole Star, Polaris. It is almost (but not exactly) directly over the north pole. Whenever one wants to know which way one is facing at night, one has only to locate Polaris—it is almost exactly due north. But it has a more important use for the navigator.

When in the northern hemisphere, a sight of Polaris taken at dawn or dusk twilight can be very useful in providing the yacht's latitude, without any plotting. As will be seen later, it can be 'crossed' with a position line found from a sight of another star to provide an immediate position (as opposed to only a position line). Like a meridian altitude, the exact time is not necessary.

Polaris is most easily shot in the morning twilight. It is not a very bright star, so it is best to identify it, by reference to the constellation Ursa Major (the Plough), before dawn, while the sky is still quite dark. Polaris should then be shot as soon as the horizon becomes visible but before the star becomes indistinct in the gathering light. If attempted in the evening, by the time Polaris is seen and identified the horizon may have disappeared. (Fig. 56.)

Polaris can often be picked up in the sextant telescope when not clearly visible to the naked eye. To do so, all that is necessary is to set on the sextant the latitude of the yacht's position by DR and to sweep the horizon due N. Polaris is useless when the yacht's position is near or south of the equator, as it will then be on or below the horizon.

Polaris is very close to the 'elevated N pole', i.e. very nearly vertically above the (true) N pole. If it were exactly there, a measurement of it's true altitude would give the exact latitude of the observer, without any calculation at all. (Fig. 57.)

In fact, it describes a small circle round the elevated N pole of about $1\frac{1}{2}°$ in diameter. A small adjustment therefore has to be made to Polaris's true altitude, according to where on this small circle round the elevated pole it is at the time the sight is taken. (Fig. 58.)

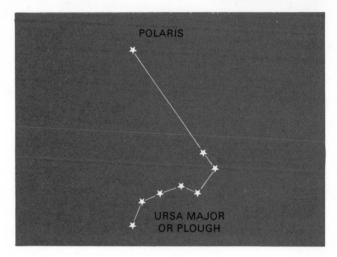

Fig. 56.

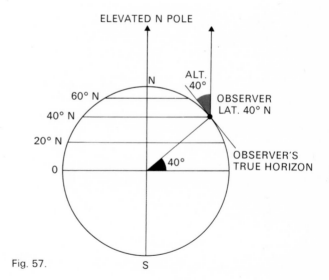

Fig. 57.

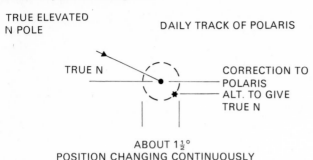

TRUE ELEVATED
N POLE

DAILY TRACK OF POLARIS

TRUE N

CORRECTION TO
POLARIS
ALT. TO GIVE
TRUE N

ABOUT 1½°
POSITION CHANGING CONTINUOUSLY

Fig. 58.

The necessary adjustment is found in the
Nautical Almanac on pp. 274–276, immediately
before the buff pages. To use the table we need
two figures only:

    LHA of Aries at the time of the sight
    Approximate lat. of yacht's position by DR.

Aries is an invisible point in the heavens,
calculated by the astronomers, used as a datum
point for finding the position of stars. This will be
explained later. For the purposes of this
explanation, Aries can be imagined as being an
invisible star. The GHA of Aries is tabulated in the
Nautical Almanac for every day and hour, in the
left-hand column of every page. The GHA of
Aries must be converted into LHA Aries by
applying the long. of the DR, as was done for the
sun's LHA. But note that we do not require a CP
—we use the long. as worked up by DR.

Example: 1975 Feb. 17 at 06^h 55^m in DR.
50°20′ N 8°40′ W.

GHA Aries 06^h	236°35′·9
Incr. 55^m	13°47′·3
	250°23′·2
DR long. W	−8°40′
LHA Aries	241°43′·2

Note that the increment for 55^m is extracted
from the column headed 'Aries' in the buff pages.

Next, we convert the sextant alt. of Polaris into
its true alt. Apply IE and Dip. as usual, but as
Polaris is a star, use the central panel of the
Altitude Correction Table (front cover of NA)
headed 'STARS and PLANETS'.

The Polaris correction to be used is in three
parts, called a_0, a_1 and a_2. Enter the Polaris Table
(NA p. 274–276)* with LHA Aries (just found) to
find the correct column. Each column refers to a
10° range. In our example, LHA Aries is 241°43′·2.
We select the first column, headed 240°–249°
(p. 276). Against the units of degrees (1°), shown
on the left, extract the a_0 degrees and minutes. We
interpolate between 1° and 2° because our LHA
is 241°43′·2, and use 1°43′·1. This is the a_0
correction.

Run down the *same* column into the second
panel headed a_1. Opposite our DR lat. 50° we
find 0′·6. This is the a_1 correction. Run down the
SAME column to opposite our month, which is
February, and extract 0′·3. This is the a_2
correction.

Enter the three corrections, a_0, a_1 and a_2 under
the true alt. and add up (all are always positive).
Lastly, *subtract one degree* from the total. This is
necessary because all the corrections are so
calculated that they are always additive, to
simplify the tables. The answer is the yacht's
latitude when the sight was taken.

The same tables also give the azimuth or
bearing of Polaris, at the foot of the column used.
For our lat. of 50° the bearing is 0°·7, so Polaris
bears within one degree of true north. Unless very
exact plotting is essential, this can be
disregarded for practical purposes. It simply
means that the position line is not an exact
parallel of latitude 50°29′·3 N, but is strictly a
line drawn through 50°29′·3 N 8°40′ W, bearing

* See extracts

090°·7–270°·7.

Example: 1975 Feb. 17th at 06^h 55^m when in 50°20′ N 8°40′ W by DR the sextant alt. of POLARIS was 49°50′·5, i.e. −2′·0, Ht of eye, 6 ft.

GHA Aries 06^h	236°35′·9
Incr. 55^m	13°47′·3
	250°23′·2
DR long. W	−8°40′
LHA Aries	241°43′·2

Sext. Alt. Polaris	49°50′·5
IE −2′·0	
Dip. −2′·4	
	−4′·4
App. alt.	49°46′·1
Cor. (star)	−0′·8
True alt.	49°45′·3
a_0	1°43′·1
a_1	·6
a_2	·3
	51°29′·3
	−1°
LATITUDE	50°29′·3

EXERCISE No. 7

(a) Find yacht's latitude by POLARIS:
1975 May 19th 03-54-08 GMT DR 49°40′ N
6°25′ W. Sextant alt. 49°29′·5 IE −2′·6. H of E 6 ft.
(b) On 1975 Aug. 31st when in DR 29° N 45° W
Polaris is observed at 21^h 53^m GMT. Sextant alt.
28°24′·0. IE −3·0, H of E 8 ft. Find latitude of
the position.

8. Where on the Chart?

Plotting the position by sun sights

The sun is the heavenly body most commonly used for navigational purposes. The reason is, of course, because in clear weather the sun is visible from dawn till dusk, and needs no identification. Sights can be taken over many daylight hours, and indeed the sun can be observed at any time during the day when its altitude is preferably more than about 15°.

However, we have already noted that a single observation of a single heavenly body can only provide a position LINE but not a position. If the sun only is used for sights, then two (or more) observations must be made at suitable intervals of time during which the sun's position will have markedly changed. If an interval elapses between the sights, then the yacht will have moved her position during this interval, and this must be allowed for (unless of course the yacht happened to be completely becalmed and was subject to no current). This is taken care of by the application of the principle of the 'running fix', used in coastal navigation when observing, say, a single landmark. An example will show the method using two sights with a run between.

Example: On August 8th a morning sun sight at 0750 GMT gave a chosen position of 50° N 2°15′ W. Intercept: 6 miles 'Away', sun bearing 096° T. This is plotted on the chart. (Fig. 58.)

Yacht then steered 220° T a distance (by log)

of 21 miles, when a meridian altitude sight was taken. From any point on the first position line, say A, lay off the run, 21 miles (from lat. scale) in the direction 220° T to B. Transfer the first position line through B with parallel rule, and mark the new PL with double arrows to show it is a transferred PL. (Fig. 59.) The latitude found by the meridian altitude was 49°41′ N. Draw this PL. (Fig. 60.)

Where the second PL crosses the first PL transferred forward is the *observed position* at the time of the second sight. Ring this point and record the lat. and long. of this position, and date and time, as shown.

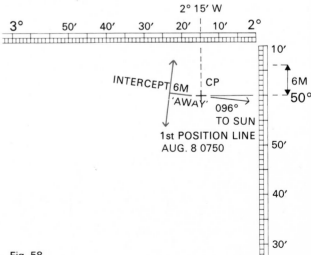

Fig. 58.

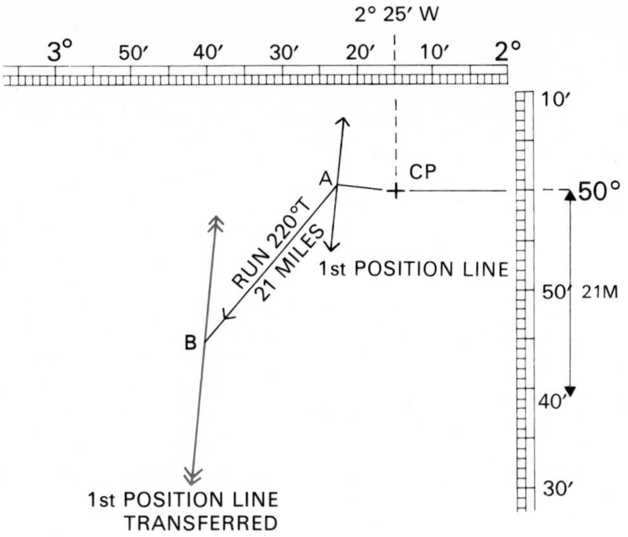

Fig. 59.

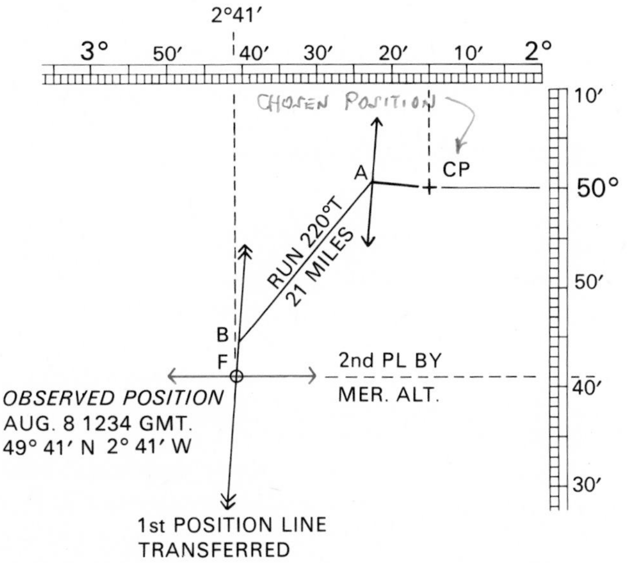

Fig. 60.

Closing dangers

In Fig. 61 we have worked up our position by DR to be 53°15′ N 9°55′ W. We take a morning sight with the following results: CP 53° N 10°05′ W, Intercept, 6 M 'towards', sun 102°. We plot this and produce the first PL.

Suppose the course to our destination is about SW (say 230° T). We know that, if our sight was right, we are on, or very near, our observed first PL. Now, if we assume we are at A, we might be tempted to continue on course say 230° T. Suppose we did so, and after sailing 25 miles on this course we took a second sight which gave us a lat. 52°56′ N. We transfer the first PL forward, through B and plot the second PL. This shows us that our position is now at F, 52°56′ N 10°21′ W. Now we can see that our actual course between the two sights was not A to B, but must have been A_2 to F—and it passed dangerously close to the rocks. (Fig. 62.)

If we are near any dangers, when we get our first PL the procedure should be to drop a perpendicular from the DR to the PL (A_1) and to plan the next course with this as a tentative position, but allowing a suitable factor for safety. Had we done so, as in Fig. 62, we should at once have seen that, if the DR was anywhere near correct (and we can see that in the example given, the DR was at least not far out for longitude) our proposed course 230° from A_1 would be dangerous if not disastrous.

In these circumstances the prudent action to take at the morning sight would be to alter course to steer along the P.L. (Co 192° T) until the noon sight gave us our latitude. If we have confidence in the morning sight we can see that this will run safely past the danger, and we can decide on a fresh, safe course when we have established our OP at noon sight.

Always bear in mind that the CP is only a

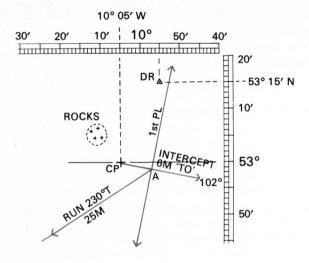

Fig. 61

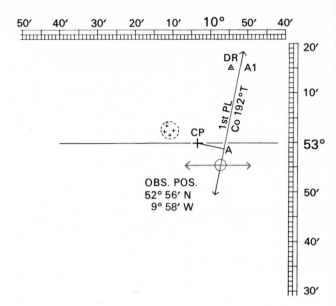

Fig. 63.

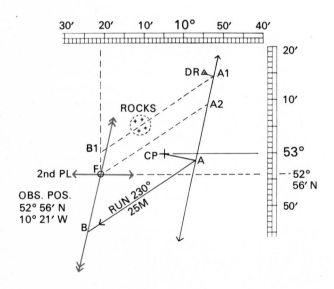

Fig. 62

datum point to enable us to plot a position line from a sight. One may therefore be anywhere along a PL, or on an extension of it, and the true position is more likely to be near the DR position, i.e. near a perpendicular dropped from the DR position, than near the CP.

The accuracy of an observed position arrived at by transferring forward an earlier PL—as in the example given—depends on the correctness of both the direction and the distance used to plot the 'run' between the sights, as well as upon the accuracy of each sight. A short run of a very few hours should not normally be much in error. But if sights cannot be taken for a day or more, or a current of doubtful rate or direction is present, or for any reason the accuracy of the run between sights is suspect, a position line depending on a transferred position should be treated with caution and only accepted as approximate. These are the conditions when simultaneous sights of two (or more) heavenly bodies are valuable, because then no run between sights has to be considered.

Simultaneous sights can be taken:

(a) By day when both sun and moon are visible. For several days during the moon's first and last quarters it will be visible when the sun is up. Occasionally it is possible to sight a planet in the sextant telescope by day when it will be invisible to the naked eye.

(b) At dawn or dusk twilight, when stars, planets, and sometimes the moon are visible.

(c) After dark, stars, planets, and sometimes the moon can very occasionally be observed by sextant when the night horizon happens to be clear enough to be used.

Sights can be treated as simultaneous when they are taken within a few minutes of each other, as a yacht will move an insignificant distance in this time. Note that the exact GMT of *each* sight must be taken and recorded. When accuracy is important, as when nearing land or any dangers, it is advisable to take sights of at least three stars, planet or moon at twilight (dawn or dusk). If then the position lines of all three (or more) cross almost at a point, or form only a small 'cocked hat', each observation tends to confirm the others and one can have a high degree of confidence in the resulting observed position. On the other hand, if the PLs do *not* so cross, or form a large 'cocked hat', one or more of the sights (or plots) must be wrong, and all should be re-checked. The ideal is to observe four (or more) stars or planet, all at suitable altitudes between about 20° and 50°, and located so that two are within about 60°–120°

(ideally, 90°), in azimuth apart in one direction, and two (or more) are similarly apart in the opposite direction. This will show up any error due to abnormal refraction, or index error.

When simultaneous sights are taken, the lat. of all the CPs will of course be the same, since we use the whole degree of lat. nearest to the DR lat. But each of the sight's CPs will have a different long. because the exact long. of each CP depends on the LHA used for each. Having picked up the correct parallel of lat. we mark on this the long. of each CP and against each, note the name of the star. From each CP we lay off the respective intercept, draw a line at right-angles through each intercept terminal point and we have the several PLs. Where these intersect is the *observed position*.

Fig. 64 shows four stars plotted from the following data from the sights taken:

Star A CP 40° N 19°05′ W Intercept, 'Away' 8 M, brg. 173° T
    B   ,,   18°47′ W   ,,   'Away' 12 M, ,, 238°
    C   ,,   18°51′ W   ,,   'To'   12 M, ,, 083°
    D   ,,   19°00 W   ,,   'To'   14 M, ,, 011°

and the plot gives observed position, 40°11′ N 18°38′ W.

Note that two pairs of stars have been selected, one pair (stars A and B) to the S of the observer, one pair (stars C and D) to the N. Each star in a pair makes a good angle of cut with the other.

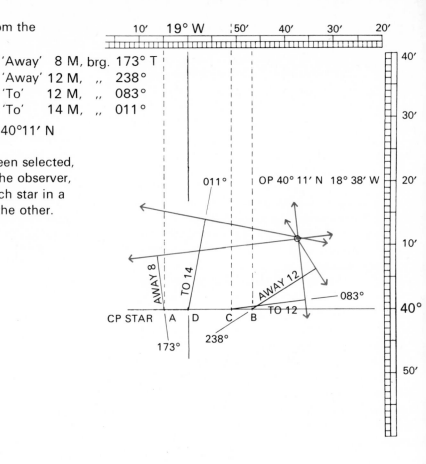

Fig. 64

EXERCISE No. 8

On 1975 Feb. 16th when in 50°10′ N 6°30′ W by DR the morning sun sight gave CP −50° N 60°21′ W, Intercept AWAY 3′·5, bearing 101°. Yacht then sailed 23·7 M on Co. 038°, when the latitude by meridian alt. was 50°25·5′ N.

Find the observed position when the mer. alt. was observed. (Plot on chart, squared paper or on Plotting Sheet.)

9. Keeping tabs on time

Time by GMT to an accuracy of better than about five seconds is necessary for working out celestial sights. For this purpose ships carry a chronometer, and often several, so that they can be checked against each other. For yachts a chronometer is not recommended as it does not take kindly to the violent motion and conditions likely to be experienced. A more serviceable timepiece is a good deck watch. This has a lever escapement, looks like a large pocket watch or 'turnip', and is housed in a padded box. If it is anticipated that radio time signals will be able to be picked up daily, then a really good pocket or wrist watch can be used as a deck watch. Such a watch to be used for GMT purposes should preferably not be worn, but kept stowed safely. On a long voyage it is most advisable to have at least two timepieces earmarked as deck watches, in case of failure of one. Without accurate GMT, only the latitude can be obtained.

A deck watch, or indeed any chronometer, seldom if ever corresponds exactly with GMT to the second, nor is it necessary that it should. All timepieces (except perhaps quartz-crystal clocks) inevitably have some 'error'—they run slightly fast or slow. This is dealt with by regularly recording the error (fast or slow), between deck watch time and GMT obtained from radio time signals. If this is done as a regular routine it is a simple matter to calculate the daily rate of the error. If then a time signal is unobtainable, due perhaps to radio failure, it is possible to calculate the additional error built up since the last time check, and thus to get the accumulated deck watch error (DWE) for example:

On June 26th the deck watch showed 8^h 48^m 16^s when a sight was taken. Earlier time checks showed the following DWEs—

| June 3rd | 2^m 30^s Fast |
| ,, 13th | 4^m 10^s Fast, |

then no more time checks obtained.

What was the correct GMT on June 26th?

DWE June 3rd	2^m 30^s F
,, 13th	4^m 10^s F
in 10 days	1^m 40^s gained.

= Daily rate, 10^s gain.

| DWE on June 13th | 4^m 10^s Fast |

June 13–26th = 13 days
at 10^s per day = 130^s
= 2^m 10^s Gain

| DWE on June 26th | 6^m 20^s Fast |

Time by deck watch 26th	8^h 48^m 16^s
DWE fast	— 6^m 20^s
Correct GMT	08^h 41^m 56^s

A note book should be kept in which the DWE of each timepiece is recorded at every time-check.

For more details about clocks, see chapter 15.

The deck watch (or watches) being used for exact GMT is not normally the timepiece used for everyday purposes aboard a yacht. It is more usual to have a 'ship's clock', mounted perhaps on the cabin bulkhead, giving the 'time of day' used for mealtimes, changing watches and so on. In the U.K. this will show the approximate GMT (except during summer time, when it will be one hour in advance of GMT). However, if the yacht is located in, or sails to, an area any appreciable distance east or west of the Greenwich meridian, it would be extremely inconvenient to keep the 'ship's clock' on GMT. If we were near New York we should of course find that when the ship's clock showed 12 midday, the clocks ashore would be showing 7 a.m.—five hours back. On land, the time used is the Standard Time kept in that country. This is usually an exact number of hours (in a few cases, half-hours) different from GMT, the difference corresponding (to the nearest hour or half-hour) to the longitude of the locality from Greenwich long., expressed in time.

The sun appears to make a complete circuit of the earth (360°) every 24 hours, so moves 15° each hour (360° ÷ 24). The standard times kept by all countries are given in the Nautical Almanac (pp. 262–5). To keep the ship's clock roughly to the time 'by the sun' it has to be altered as the ship moves east or west. To avoid making frequent alterations to the ship's clock, Time Zones have been devised, and these are used by all ships.

The world has been divided into 24 Zones of longitude, each 15° wide—the same number of zones as the hours in a day. The time 'by the sun' differs from one zone to the next. (Fig. 65.) Zero Zone (ZO) extends from 7½° E, through 0° to 7½° W, and the clocks of all ships in this zone should register GMT. Z + 1 extends between 7½° W and 22½° W, and all ships' clocks in this

zone should register one hour *earlier* than GMT. Similarly, ships' clocks in Z − 2 (long. 22½° E— 37½° E) should register two hours LATER than GMT. If we apply the zone number to Zone Time we get GMT.

Example 1. Time in Zone +5 (long. 67½° W— 82½° W).

```
  07 00 hrs Zone Time
Z +5
  ─────
  12 00 hrs GMT
```

```
Time in Zone −3 (37½° E—52½° E)
  14 00 hrs Zone Time
Z −3
  ─────
  11 00 hrs GMT
```

This rhyme helps:
Longitude EAST, Greenwich Time LEAST (less than zone time)
Longitude WEST, Greenwich Time BEST (more than zone time).

Whenever a passage may take a yacht much beyond say 8° E or 8° W longitude, it should be an invariable rule that the Zone to which the ship's clock is set is clearly written at the top of the Time column on every page of all log books. Normally, as the yacht's position reaches somewhere near a fresh time zone the ship's clock is altered one hour, preferably at midnight though this is not essential. A line is drawn across each log book and the zone number altered by one hour to correspond. Viz.:

Yacht sailing WESTWARD
In W long., clock put BACK and Z + increased one hour.
In E long., clock put BACK and Z − reduced by one hour.
Yacht sailing EASTWARD.
In W long., clock ADVANCED and Z + reduced one hour.

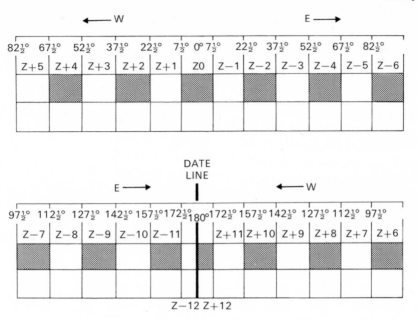

Fig. 65.

In E long., clock ADVANCED and Z — increased one hour.

Note that it is not vital that the ship's clock and Zone number are altered exactly when the yacht crosses a zone boundary—it is merely convenient. If for example one omitted to change clock and zone number for, say, 10° of long., all that would happen is that one would find the sun rising (and setting) perhaps half an hour or so earlier (or later, depending on E or W passage) than usual. What IS important is that log books should always indicate, by the Zone number and sign at the head of the time column, the number of hours by which ship's clock time (and thus very approximately the 'time by the sun') differs from GMT as shown by

deck watch or chronometer. Remember that the deck watch time is left *constantly* at GMT, wherever the yacht's position in the world—that is, it should give exact GMT after correction by the current deck watch error.

If the longitude of our position is anything more than say 10° E or W, then the deck watch (set to GMT) will read a different time from the ship's clock, the difference being of course the Zone number in use. If we are in, say, long. 30° W, log books should be headed Z + 2. If the ship's clock reads about 6^h, the deck watch will read about 8^h. This is quite straightforward. But remember that clocks only register 12 hours, not the 24 hours in the day, and (normally) do not say whether the time shown is a.m. or p.m. If we are in Z + 6 and it is morning and the ship's clock shows about 8^h, the deck watch will show about 2^h, but as the 24-hour notation is used for all navigational work we should take this as 1400 GMT (ZT 8^h, Z + 6 = 14^h GMT). But what if it is 8^h by ship's clock in the evening? We must of course read the ship's clock as 2000 hrs. Add Z + 6 to this and we get 26^h. Clearly this must be 0200 hrs GMT (approx.), but *the next day*. So there are times when we must check what is the *date* at Greenwich, called GD.

When it is late evening in San Francisco (by their standard time, which is Z + 8) it is early the *next* morning at Greenwich, London. In San Francisco an evening paper will be dated July 4th at the same time that a Londoner is reading his (morning) paper dated July 5th. When we extract data from the Nautical Almanac we must use not only the GMT (from the deck watch) at the moment we take our sight, but the GMT on the *date* at Greenwich at that moment. As was shown above, this *may* be a day different from the local date and day of the week. Whenever there can be any doubt as to whether the Greenwich date could be different from the local date, which will be shown in the log book, always make a rough check by applying the Zone number to the local date and time by ship's clock (or even by the sun), and compare the time so arrived at with the deck watch.

Example: On June 10th (local date and date in log) an evening star sight was taken, the ship's clock, set to Z + 10, showed 6^h 15^m. The deck watch, after correction for DWE, showed 4^h 13^m 20^s. What is the GD and GMT to be used for the sight?

As it is evening (local time) the ship's clock, reading 6^h 15m, is taken as

$$\text{June 10th} \quad 18^h \; 15^m \text{ Zone Time approx.}$$
$$\text{apply } Z + 10 \quad +10$$
$$\text{GD} \quad 11^d \quad 04^h \; 15^m \text{ approx. GMT.}$$

We now have the correct Greenwich date, and the deck watch should be taken as 04^h 13^m 20^s GMT (and not as 16-13-20). We shall therefore use for our almanac
June 11^d, 04^h 13^m 20^s GMT

Take another case. Assume the ship's clock has stopped. The deck watch is working and we have a recent GMT time check. The position by DR is 20° S 155° E. The (local) date is May 20th, and this is the log book date. We take a morning twilight sight when the deck watch (after correction for DWE) shows 7^h 35^m 45^s. What is the GD and GMT to use for the sight?

From the Nautical Almanac we find that civil twilight in our latitude is about 6 a.m. or 0600 hrs, local time. (This is found in right-hand top panel of the Almanac on this date, civil twilight, lat. S 20° = 0559.) We may be unsure of the Zone but we know our approximate long. (155° E). Convert this from arc into time by the table on first buff page in the Almanac, thus:

$$\text{Civil twilight, a.m. May} \quad 20^d \; 0600 \text{ approx. local time}$$
$$\text{Long. } 155° \text{ E in time } = \quad -1020$$
$$\text{GD} \qquad\qquad\qquad\qquad \text{GD} \quad 19^d \; 1940 \text{ approx. GMT}$$

The time by deck watch (7^h 35^m 45^s) must be 19-35-45, and the GD is 19^d (not 20^d), so we use for our sight—May 19^d 19^h 35^m 45^s GMT.

The date line

Not many of us cross the date line often, but when a yacht does, it is important to keep track of both date and Zone time. The date line is an arbitrary line in the vicinity of the 180° meridian. On either side of this line the date and day of the week differ by one day, the date on the eastern side being one day behind the day on the western side of the line. Let us see how this comes about.

Assume the yacht is sailing westward and approaching 180° by DR, say 179° W. Her log books will be headed Z + 12. It is not essential to change the ZT on the exact date that the yacht crosses the date line, but it is best to do so at midnight about that date. Just before midnight the log books might show the following entries:

```
LOG BOOK
(Local)     Time              15d 23  55  local time
 Date       Z + 12      Z      +12
--------------------------------------------------
July 15th   23  55     GD 16d 11  55  appx: GMT
```

Ten minutes later, date and Z sign altered, but ship's clock LEFT UNCHANGED (not the usual one hour back)

```
            Z − 12            17d 00  05
July 17th   00  05     Z       −12
--------------------------------------------------
                       GD 16d 12  05  appx: GMT
```

Note that the GMT has altered (right-hand figures) by the correct amount, 10 minutes, though the LOCAL date has jumped a whole extra day.

If the yacht were sailing eastward across the Date Line we should again alter the Z sign in all log books, but this time from Z − 12 to Z + 12, and would leave the date unchanged at midnight (instead of the usual advance of one day).

```
LOG BOOK
(Local)     Time              16d 23  55  local
 Date       Z − 12      Z       −12
--------------------------------------------------
July 16th   23  55     GD 16d 11  55  appx: GMT
```

Ten minutes later, only Z sign altered

```
            Z + 12            16d 00  05
July 16th   00  05     Z       +12
--------------------------------------------------
                       GD 16d 12  05  appx: GMT
```

Again, the GMT has altered by the correct 10 min.

Again, the GMT has altered by the correct 10^m.

Further points worth noting in the use of the deck watch or chronometer are:

(a) Wind up once every day, preferably about the same time each day, irrespective of whether the deck watch is a 2-day or an 8-day clock. This helps the clock to maintain a steady rate.

(b) Do not alter the setting of the deck watch unless or until the error (from exact GMT) becomes excessive. There is bound to be some error, and the amount (unless excessive) is immaterial. The less the deck watch is disturbed the more reliable it will remain.

(c) When it becomes necessary to re-set the deck watch (because it has stopped or the DWE is unacceptably large), set the minute hand as accurately as possible over a minute gradation when the second hand is at 0. This reduces the risk of misreading the timepiece by a complete minute, which may easily happen if this point is neglected.

EXERCISE No. 9

(a) On 1975 Aug. 10th the error of the
chronometer was 3^m 42^s slow, and on Aug.
14th was 3^m 34^s slow. On Aug. 21st a sight
was taken when the chronometer read 16^h
43^m 18^s. What was the correct GMT?

(b) Near Vancouver BC a local time signal gave
the time as 1200 midday. Standard Time is
$Z + 8$. What was GMT?

(c) An evening twilight sight was taken on 1975
May 20th when in 50° N 128° W by DR. The deck
watch (after correction for DWE) showed
4^h 54^m 13^s. What was the GD and GMT to use for
the sight?

(d) A morning twilight sight was taken on 1975
Feb. 15th when in DR 22° S 100° E. The deck
watch, which was 1^m 32^s fast, showed 10^h 48^m
20^s. What is the date and time to use for the
sight?

10. Planet, star, and moon sights

Four planets, Venus, Mars, Jupiter and Saturn, are easily identified and, when visible, provide good sights for a position line. If used in conjunction with one or more stars observed simultaneously (within a few minutes of each other) an observed position is obtained. This should be more accurate than a position found by observing the sun only, since there must be a time interval of some hours between the necessary two sun observations, and the accuracy of a 'sun—run—sun' position (as described in chapter 8) must depend on the accuracy of both direction (course sailed) and the distance run (over the ground) between the two sights.

The Nautical Almanac gives, under 'Planet Notes' p. 8, details of the planets to aid identification, and states when each should be above the horizon and visible. A planet is most easily observed at morning or evening twilight, when the sky is dark enough for the planet to show up, but while the horizon is still clearly defined. It is sometimes possible to observe a planet in the sextant telescope by day, when it is invisible to the naked eye. To 'find' the planet by daylight it is necessary to work out in advance the approximate tabulated altitude, using the DR position, to convert this to a sextant altitude by applying the usual corrections (reversing the signs) and to set this angle on the sextant. The horizon is then swept on the planet's tabulated bearing and the planet should appear in the telescope.

To work up a sight the planet's GHA and Dec. are found for the exact time of the sight, a suitable CP selected and the tab. alt. and bearing taken from the same tables (AP 3270 Vol. 2 or 3) as were used for the sun. The tab. alt. is compared with the true alt. found by sextant, exactly as for a sun sight. The only differences are:

1. The planets' GHA and Dec. are given on each left-hand page of the Nautical Almanac (make sure the correct planet's column is used).

2. An additional increment to GHA is necessary. The factor to be used (v.) is given at the foot of the particular planet column used to find the GHA. The necessary correction is found in the 'v. or d. corrn.' panel used when finding the increments for minutes and seconds. The sign is always plus, except on the occasions when the v. factor is marked as minus, e.g.

1975 Feb. 15th Venus, v. −0·4

The d factor, given at the foot of the Dec. column, is used to find the 'd corrn.', exactly like the sun's, care being taken to see whether the Dec. is increasing (+) or reducing (−) each successive hour, e.g.

1975 Feb 15th Venus, d is −1·3 (reducing each hour).

3. Apparent alt. correction is found from the panel headed 'Stars—Planets' on inner front cover of the

ocean yacht navigator

Nautical Almanac.

Here is a fully-worked example:

EXAMPLE OF A PLANET SIGHT

On February 15 1975 when in 50°10'N 15°20'W by DR
an evening sight of VENUS is taken. The deck watch,
which had a DWE of 2m15s slow, read 6h50m09s.
The Sextant alt was 14°12'.6 and the error was 3'.0 on
the arc. Ht of eye 6ft.

1975 February 15	18-50-09 DWT		DR 50°10'N 15°20'W	
DWE	+ 2-15		IE -3.0, Ht of E 6ft	
	18-52-24 GMT			

GHA	18h 63°19'.2		Dec S 4°56'.6	
Increment	52-24 13 06 .0		d,-1.3 -1 .1	
v,-0.4	- 0 .4		S 4°55'.5	
GHA	76°24'.8			
CP long	W-15 24 .8			
LHA	61°			
CP lat	N 50°			
Dec	S 4°55'		Sext Alt VENUS 14°12'.6	
			IE -3.0	
Hc	14°55'		Dip-2.4 - 5 .4	
d,-49	- 45'			14°07 .2
Tab Alt	14°10'		Cor - 3 .8	
			Addn1 Cor + 0 .1	
	360°		TRUE ALT 14°03 .5	
	Z -116		TAB ALT 14°10 .0	
	Zn 244° Bearing		Intercept, AWAY 6'.5	

*Note the small additional correction for Venus (and Mars)
this year in Stars and Planets panel of NA Alt Correction
table A2.

Stars

Stars are extremely valuable for position-finding,
and particularly so when accuracy is important, as
when nearing dangers or prior to landfall. Stars
are not visible by day, but at dawn or dusk twilight
when the sky is clear, any number of stars can be
used for observations. Sometimes, when the
horizon is well-defined, star sights can be taken in
full darkness. The great virtue of star sights is that
a number of stars can be observed (almost)
simultaneously, which enables an observed
position to be established without the possible
inaccuracy caused by using a run between sights.
Star sights are so quick and easy to work up that
there is no reason why three or more stars should
not be observed at the same time. The proximity
of the resulting position lines to a point (or the
smallness of the 'cocked hat' formed) gives an
excellent guide as to the accuracy of each sight
and thus the reliability of the position found.

Many people are put off attempting star sights
because they feel it is difficult to identify the
individual stars. A little practice at home, or better
still during the night watches at sea, will quickly
enable a small number of brighter stars to be
identified, and one can add to one's stock of stars
gradually! First, identify the major
constellations, such as Ursa Major (the Plough),
Orion, Cassiopeia, square of Pegasus, and so on.
Note how the different constellations lie in relation
to each other, and how all wheel slowly round the
elevated pole (Polaris in N hemisphere; a point S
of the Southern Cross in S hemisphere) making
roughly a 180° turn from E to W between evening
and morning twilight. Then pick out prominent
stars in or near each constellation, noting how
they lie in relation to a constellation. Look these
up in a star chart (Nautical Almanac, pp. 266, 267
and other star charts).

The Nautical Almanac lists on every page, and

on the loose card, some 57 stars suitable for observation, though some of these are not very bright. The brightness of a star (which helps identification) is given by its 'Magnitude'. These are listed on the Nautical Almanac loose card under 'Mag.' The LOWER the Mag. number (or the larger the minus number) the BRIGHTER the star, e.g. Acamar, Mag. 3·1 is very dim, while Sirius, Mag. —1·6, is the brightest star in the heavens. Stars twinkle ; planets emit a steady light.

Star sights can be worked up by the same methods as are used for the sun or planets. We then need to find our star's LHA and declination, and this will be explained later. The quickest and easiest way is to use Sight Reduction Tables for Air Navigation, Vol. I Selected Stars, AP 3270 or HO 249. With this we only need to find LHA *Aries* at the moment we take our sight, and the longitude (to the nearest whole degree) of yacht's position by DR. This particular table (Vol. I) gives Hc (tab. alt.) and Zn (bearing) of seven selected stars. The tables are arranged to provide the best selection of seven stars which will be available at a particular position and time, anywhere in the world.

Aries (or strictly the 'First Point of Aries') is a point in the heavens which is used by astronomers as a datum point. One may imagine it as being an invisible star. To save us work, Vol. I (and ONLY Vol. I) tabulates Hc (Tab. Alt.) and Zn (Bearing) for each star selected, against LHA Aries. Like any other body. *GHA* Aries is listed in the Nautical Almanac for every hour of the day, on every daily page (extreme left-hand column). An example will show how extremely simple the work is :

On 1975 August 31st when in 49° 40′ N 7°20′ W by DR, at 19-53-50 GMT a sight of ARCTURUS is taken, sextant Alt. 36°07·2 IE —3·0. Ht of eye, 8 ft. Find the intercept and bearing.

GHA Aries 19^h	264°19·9	(Note use of Aries
Incr. 53–50^s	13°29·7	Col. incr.)
	277°49·6	
CP long. W	—7°49·6	
LHA Aries	270°	(Line on page)
Cp lat.	N 50°	(Page in Vol. I)
ARCTURUS Hc	36°06′	Tab. alt.
Zn	257° T	Bearing

Sextant alt.	36°07·2	
IE	—3·0	
Dip.	—2·7	
	—5·7	
	36°01·5	
Cor.	—1·3	(Star col.)
True alt.	36°00·2	
Tab. alt.	36°06·0	
Intercept, away,	5·8	

Bearing, 257° T.

The only drawback to using Vol. I is that we are only given seven named stars against each LHA Aries and CP lat. If we have observed one or more stars which do not happen to be among the particular seven given for our LHA Aries and our lat., we CANNOT use these tables. But we could still work up the sights by one of the alternative methods. It is therefore best to find out, well before star-observation time, which stars are listed for the actual time we expect to be taking our star sights. This is quite easily done as follows :

First, find the time it is expected the star sights will be taken. Normally this will be around civil twilight a.m. or p.m., found from the Nautical Almanac, which tabulates the time for the middle date on each page against the latitude of the position. The times given are GMT on the Greenwich meridian, which is also LMT on any other meridian. To get the GMT on the yacht's meridian (long.) we must apply long. in time, using the 'Conversion of Arc to Time' on the first buff page of the Almanac. Having found the GMT at twilight (either a.m. or p.m.) when the sight will be taken, we find GHA Aries at this time. Convert this to LHA by applying the yacht's long. by DR. Entering the page in Vol. I for the yacht's lat. by DR (to nearest whole degree) and line the LHA Aries, note which seven stars are listed. Note down the name, its Hc (alt.) and Zn (bearing) of each listed star. Those in capitals are bright stars. Those marked * are particularly well-placed in azimuth to give PLs with good angles of cut.

Our 'short-list' of stars can be used to look up our star chart in advance, or to help locate the stars by their altitudes and bearings. When the stars become visible (in the evening) if any doubt is felt, one can work out the approximate sextant alt. of a star by applying IE, dip. and corr. (reversing the signs) to the Hc noted earlier, and setting this on the sextant. Sweep the horizon on the star's approximate bearing (Zn) when it should appear somewhere in the telescope.

Example: It is proposed to take three star sights at evening twilight on 1975 August 30th (local date) when in 49°45 N 127°30 W. Which stars will be available then?

Check for GD and GMT:

Civil Twilight p.m. DR 50° N	30d	19 24	LMT
DR long. in time, 127°30 W =		+ 8 30	
Time at ship	31d	03 54	GD & GMT approx.

GHA Aries 31d 03h	23°40'·5	
Incr. 54m	13°32'·2	
	37°12'·7	

	360°	(Added to permit subtraction)
	397°12'·7	
CP long.	W−127°12'·7	
LHA Aries	270°	
CP lat.	N 50°	

Entering Vol. I with lat. N 50° and LHA Aries 270°, we see the following stars listed:

	Hc	Zn
*Mirfak	15°18'	025°
Alpheratz	20°42'	069°
*ALTAIR	42°56'	142°
Rasalhague	52°12'	190°
*ARCTURUS	36°06'	257°
Alkaid	50°18'	295°
Kochab	58°49'	337°

Those marked * are well-placed in azimuth. Altair and Arcturus, being printed in capitals, are bright stars (Mags. less than 1·0) while Mirfak is less bright (Mag. 1·9).

Here is a fully-worked example of three star sights taken almost simultaneously, which can be checked with the extracts of the NA and Vol. I AP 3270 in this book: Note that the exact time of each sight is necessary, and that this will produce three different CP long's. Also note that because the DR long: is well away from 0°, the GD is in this case different from the local date, which is the date shown in the log book.

Example: Star sights taken on the evening of August 30th 1975 when in 49°45' N 126°10' W. IE − 2·0, Ht of Eye, 8 ft.

Precession and nutation

Elsewhere it is stated that the stars are 'fixed in the heavens'. This is not strictly true. The earth spins on its axis daily like a top, and like a top the axis moves slightly, the projected axes describing a small circle. This is called Precession. The end of each axis also oscillates about this circular path. This is Nutation. This is caused by the varying attractions of the sun, moon and planets, and to

	Mirfak	ALTAIR	ARCTURUS
DWT	03-48-38	03-49-14	03-49-46
DWE	+3-32	+3-32	+3-32
GMT	03-52-10	03-52-46	03-53-18
Sext. alt.	15°42·2	43°18·8	35°34·1

Check for GD and GMT.

Civil twilight (p.m.) Aug. 30ᵈ 19 24 local date and time
Long. in time, W 126°   8 24

GD   Aug 31ᵈ 03 48 approx. GMT

	Mirfak		ALTAIR		ARCTURUS
GHA Aries 31ᵈ 03ʰ	23°40'·5		23°40'·5		23·40'·5
Incr: m & S 52–10	13°04'·6	52–46	13°13'·7	53–18	13°21'·7
GHA Aries	36°45'·1		36°54'·2		37°02'·2
	360		360		360
	396°45'·1		396°54'·2		397°02'·2
CP long. W	−125°45'·1		125°54'·2		126°02'·2
LHA Aries	271°		271°		271°
CP lat.	N 50°		N 50°		N 50°
Hc (tab. alt.)	15°35'		43°20'		35°29'
Zn (bearing)	026°		143°		257°
Sext. alt.	15°42'·2		43°18'·8		35°34'·1
IE −2·0					
Dip. −2·7					
	−4'·7		−4'·7		−4'·7
	15°37'·5		43°14'·1		35°29'·4
Cor.	−3'·4		−1'·0		−1'·4
TRUE ALT:	15°34'·1		43°13'·1		35°28'·0
TAB. ALT.	15°35'·0		43°20'·0		35°29'·0
INTERCEPT	AWAY 0'·9		AWAY 6'·9		AWAY 1'·0
BEARING	026°		143°		257°

Obs. pos. 50°05' N 126°02' W.
See plot on Fig. 66

the earth not being a perfect sphere.

We are not concerned with this problem when we are given the GHA or SHA and the declination of any body. Vols. 2 and 3 of AP 3270 and HO 249, and all volumes of NP 401 all give answers which require NO correction for precession and nutation. The slight change in SHA and Dec. of a star which takes place over the years due to this can be seen from the Nautical Almanac. For example, on 1975 February 16th star Achamar's SHA is 315°40'·2 and Dec. S 40°24'·5. By August 30th these have changed to SHA 315°39'·7 and Dec. S 40°23'·8.

However, Vol. I of AP 3270 and HO 249 tables have been computed to give stars' Hc and Zn on a particular date only. This date is called the Epoch. The edition of AP 3270 Vol. 1 published 1972 is for epoch 1975. (The previous edition which may still be in circulation is for epoch 1970.) Thus the answers Hc and Zn are therefore only strictly correct for 1974. However, if the date is not 1974 the small correction necessary for strict accuracy is readily found at the back of AP3270 Vol. 1 in 'Table 5—Correction for Precession and Nutation'.

Enter Table 5 with the year (month does not matter) and arguments LHA Aries and latitude of the CP. Extract the four figures given, e.g. :

Stars observed 1977 Aug, in DR 49°45 N 126° W.

Table 5. 1977, LHA Aries 270°, Lat. N 50° = 1' and 080°.

Plot the PLs as usual. Displace the OP which these give by 1 mile, in the direction 080°. If only a single PL is determined, displace or transfer the PL by this distance and direction. Interpolation is unnecessary.

As can be seen from Table 5, if precession and nutation is disregarded the error in the position is likely to be within the degree of accuracy to which sights can usually be taken from a yacht at sea, until 1978 or 1979 is reached.

If Vol. 1 of either AP 3270 or HO 249 is not available, or if it is wished to work up a sight of a star which is not one of the stars selected in Vol. I, then it can be done with either

Vol. 2 and 3 AP 3270 or HO 249, provided the star's declination is less than 30° N or S.

Vol. 2 covers DR lats.   0°–39° N or S

Vol. 3 covers DR lats. 40°–89° N or S

or NP 401 for stars of any declination. Each of the six volumes covers a band of lat. 15° wide.

Of the 57 selected stars listed in the Nautical Almanac, no less than 29 have declinations of less than 30° N or S and can therefore be worked up using AP 3270 or HO249 Vols. 2 and 3.

NP 401 enables stars of any declination to be dealt with, but four volumes are necessary to cover latitudes up to 60° N or S.

Using any of these tables the work is the same as that for a sight of the sun. The tables are entered with a CP lat., declination of the star and LHA star. We have first to consider how we find a star's declination, and also its GHA in order to get its LHA.

It would clearly be impractical to list in the Nautical Almanac the GHA of every star for every hour of every day throughout the year as is done for the four navigational planets. The stars are 'fixed in the heavens' and do not change their positions relative to each other. The GHA of Aries is therefore found and knowing the DIFFERENCE between the GHA of Aries and that of any required star, we can readily arrive at the GHA of the required star. (Fig. 67.)

The difference between the GHA of Aries and that of any star is called the particular star's SIDERIAL HOUR ANGLE (SHA). The angle is measured from Aries *to* the star, always in a westerly direction. The Nautical Almanac gives

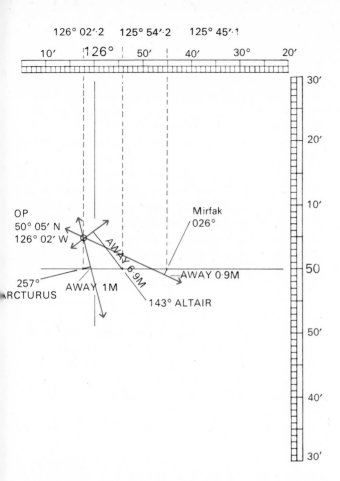

Fig. 66

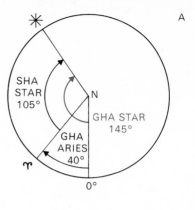

A

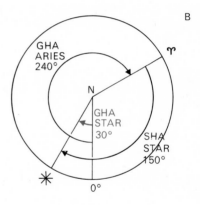

B

Fig. 67.   In upper diagram GHA of Aries is 40° and SHA of Star 105°. Therefore GHA of Star is 145°. In lower diagram GHA of Aries is 240°, SHA of Star is 150°, therefore GHA of Star is 30°.

EXAMPLE

1975 August 29, at 19-55-22 GMT
Required: GHA and Dec of Star ARCTURUS

SHA Arcturus		$146°21'.7$	Dec N $19°18'.7$
GHA Aries	19h	$262°21 .7$	
Increment	55-22s	$13°52 .8$	
		$422°36'.2$	
		-360	
GHA Arcturus		$62°36'.2$	

EXAMPLE

1975 August 30, in DR 50°10'N 128°45'W a sight of
RIGEL taken at 12-54-42 gave sext alt 24°13'.6
Index error, -2'.0 Ht of eye 6ft.

SHA Rigel		$281°39'.4$				
SHA Aries	12h	$158°03 .6$				
Increment 54-42s		$13°42 .7$				
GHA Rigel		$453°25 .7$				
CP long		W-$128°25 .7$				
LHA		$325°$				
CP lat	N	$50°$	Sext Alt Rigel	$24°13'.6$		
Dec	S	$8°14'$	IE	-2.0		
			Dip	-2.4	-	4 .4
Hc		$24°30'$				$24°09'.2$
d,-54		- 13	Cor		-	2 .2
Tab Alt		$24°17'$	TRUE ALT			$24°07'.0$
			TAB ALT			$24°17'.0$
	Z,$141°$ = Zn		Intercept AWAY			10'.0

Fig. 68.

the GHA of Aries for every hour, every day, as for the planets (see left-hand pages, left-hand column) and increments for minutes and seconds. It also lists the SHA of the 57 principal stars on every daily page. The Declinations of these stars are also given against their SHAs. As these hardly change throughout the year, *no* increments for hours or minutes are required for a star's Dec.

To find the GHA of any listed star, first find the SHA and Dec. of the required star on the N. Almanac daily page. Then find GHA of Aries for the particular time of the sight, adding increments for minutes and seconds, from the buff pages, using the column headed 'Aries'. Add GHA Aries to SHA star and we have GHA star.

From GHA star onwards to tab. alt. the work is exactly as for any other sight. Apply CP long. to get LHA star, and enter sight reduction tables with CP lat., Dec. star and LHA star. The true alt. of the star is also as usual, except remember to use the correction for STAR, in centre panel of Nautical Almanac cover. A full star sight is given on Fig. 68.

Moon

For long periods during any month the moon is visible in clear weather, and sufficiently above the horizon to provide excellent sights. There are times during the day when the moon can be 'shot' at the same time as the sun. At other times the moon may be up at dawn or dusk twilight and can be observed at the same time as one or more stars or a planet. In all such cases the 'simultaneous' sights will provide an immediate observed position without the delay (and inevitable slight inaccuracy) unavoidable when only one body (e.g. the sun) is used.

Sights of the moon are taken, and worked up,

in just the same way as those of the sun, but two points require particular treatment:

(a) The moon is relatively near the earth, and this distance is not constant. This produces parallax, which varies with the altitude observed, and with the moon's distance from the earth.

(b) The v. and d. corrections necessary alter so quickly that it is not sufficient to use only one figure for a whole three days (as for planets). The v. and d. factors to be used are therefore given in the Almanac against every hour. (See p. 148 et seq.)

As for the sun, we 'sight' either the lower limb (LL) or the upper limb (UL), but with the moon, which limb we use will depend on which edge is fully visible, see chapter 3.

Instead of a single 'Total correction' (as for the sun) to adjust the app. alt. for semi-diameter, refraction and parallax, the corrections for the moon are taken out in two figures. A clear explanation is given on the inside back cover of the Nautical Almanac (see extract, p. 158) and the examples given below will show the procedure:

Example: Find the true alt. of the moon on 1975 Feb. 17th at 13-54-20 GMT. Index error 2'·0 on the arc, Ht of eye, 6 ft.

Sextant alt. LL	27°40'·1	
IE	−2'·0	
Dip.	−2'·4	
	−4'·4	
App. alt.	27°35'·7	

Corr.	59'·9	Upper panel } }N. Alm.
HP 55'5*	2'·4	Lower panel } }Moon corr. Table
TRUE ALT.	28°38'·0	

(* Picked up when extracting GHA, v, Dec., d, and HP on daily page against date and hour.)

MOON SIGHT

Example:

On 1975 February 17 at 13-54-20 GMT, when in 50°10'N 25°15'W by DR, the sextant alt of the Moon's lower limb was 27°40'.1.   Index error, -2'.0   Ht of eye 6ft.

GHA	13h	307°27'.9	Dec	N 16°19'.3	HP 55.5
Increment	54-20	12°57 .9			
v, 12.2		11 .1	d,+7.9 +	7 .2	
		320°36 .9		N 16°26'.5	
CP long	W-	25°36 .9	SEXT ALT LL	27°40'.1	
LHA		295°	IE	-2.0	
CP lat	N	50°	Dip -2.4 -	4 .4	
Dec	N	16°26'		27°35'.7	
			Cor	+ 59 .9	
Hc		28°11'	HP 55.5 +	2 .4	
d,+45	+	20'	TRUE ALT	28°38'.0	
Tab Alt		28°31'	TAB ALT	28°31'.0	

Z 99° = Zn   Intercept, TOWARD 7'.0

Fig. 69.

Note how the lower correction table has two columns in each panel, headed respectively L and U. The correct column must be used according to which of the moon's limbs was observed, obviously L for lower, U for upper limb.
Remember to *subtract* 30' if *upper* limb is used. (See notes on Nautical Almanac p. xxxiv, lower right-hand corner and extracts p. 158.)

The Almanac shows in the moon panel, against every hour, FIVE figures:
GHA, v., Dec., d., HP. (Horizontal Parallax)

Make a habit of always extracting and writing on your sight form *all five* figures in one operation. This saves time and removes the risk of looking on the wrong line (or even on the wrong page) if you omit, say, the HP figure, and have to find it at a subsequent point in the calculation.

The v correction is always *plus*, but (like the sun), the d correction may be plus or minus, so always check, when writing down the d factor, whether the moon's Dec. is increasing (+) or reducing (−) each successive hour. As you can see from the almanac, the d correction is often quite a large figure (much bigger than the sun's) and it is therefore even more important that the sign, + or −, is correct or the intercept will be badly out. (Fig. 69.)

When deciding whether the correction for the given d factor is + or −, remember to check whether successive Dec. figures are increasing or reducing (NOT the d factors). This is a little trap for the unwary.

Latitude by meridian altitude of the moon

There are a number of days during the lunar month when a meridian altitude of the moon can be observed during daylight hours. This will provide the yacht's latitude, and if this is combined with a simultaneous sight of the sun, will fix the yacht's observed position.

First, we must find the GMT when the moon will be on the meridian of our DR long. The easiest way is explained in Naut: Alm: p. 258. Here are two examples:

(a) On 1975 Aug. 30th, when in DR 50°15′ N
27° W, find time of moon's Mer: Passage.
Naut: Alm: page for the day, box in lower right hand corner headed "MOON—Mer: Pass: Upper" gives GMT when moon is on Greenwich meridian, 0°.

Moon Mer: Pass: 30th 06^h 01^m at 0°
31st 06 55
change for 1 day (360°) $+54^m$, $\times \dfrac{27°}{360°} = 4^m$

Mer: Pass: 30th   06 01 GMT at 0°
Corr. for long. 27° W =   +4
06 05 LMT at 27° W
Long. in time, 27° W   +1 48 (Arc to Time, p. 155)

MER: PASS: 07 53 GMT at 27° W

(b) 1975 Feb. 15th in DR 48°15′ S 120° E.
Moon Mer: Pass: 15th 15 07
14th* 14 24
change for 1 day (360°) -43^m,
$\times \dfrac{120°}{360°} = -14^m$

Mer: Pass: 15th   15 07
Corr. for long. 120° E   −14
14 53 LMT at DR
Long. in time, 120° E −8 00
MER: PASS: 06 53 GMT at DR.

(* because E long. = earlier.)

These can be checked by finding the time when

moon's LHA will be 0°. It will be recalled that LHA is the angle between the meridian of the observer's position and the meridian through the body's GP, measured westward. When this is 0°, both observer and the body must be on the same meridian, and the body will be at it's highest altitude

$$\text{GHA} \begin{cases} +\text{E long.} \\ -\text{W long.} \end{cases} = \text{LHA},$$

$$\text{so LHA} \begin{cases} -\text{E long.} \\ +\text{W long.} \end{cases} = \text{GHA.}$$

(a) 1975 Aug. 30th in DR 50°15′ N 27° W, time of moon mer: pass:

LHA Moon	0°
DR long. W	+27°
Time reqd when GHA is	27°
GHA will be	14°14′·2 at 07ʰ (Per
remainder	12°45′·8 Naut. Alm.)
v.9.3 (in 52ᵐ incr)	8′·1
	12°37′·7 = Incr.
	52ᵐ 55ˢ

LHA is 0° at 07ʰ 52ᵐ 55ˢ GMT.

(b) 1975 Feb. 15th DR 48°15′ S 120° E

LHA Moon 0° or	360°
DR long. E	−120°
GHA reqd	240°
Per Naut. Alm.	227°18′·3 = 06ʰ
remainder	12°41′·7
v.15.1 is	13′·2 in 52ᵐ panel
	12°28′·9 = 52ᵐ 15ˢ

LHA is 0° at 06ʰ 52ᵐ 15ˢ GMT.

We should observe the moon at our calculated time of mer. pass. (or start a few minutes earlier and watch it climb till it dips, in case our DR long. is in error). We note whether upper or lower limb was observed, and correct sextant altitude to true altitude as already explained for moon sights. From here on the procedure is exactly the same as for a sun mer. alt. (see chapter 7).

Example: On 1975 Feb. 15th when in DR 48°15′ S 120°03′ E a mer. alt. of the moon gave a sextant alt. of 33°09·2 bearing N. Lower limb. IE −2·0, Ht. of eye 8 ft. Find the latitude.

Sext. alt. moon's LL		33°09′·2 N
IE	−2·0	
Dip.	−2·7	
		−4′·7
		33°04′·5
Corr.		57′·4
HP 54·4		1′·3
True alt.		34°03′·2 N
from		90°
TZD		55°56′·8 S
Dec.	7°43′·1 N	
d, + 10·5	+9′·2	
		7°52′·3 N
LATITUDE		48°04′·5 S

If a sun sight is taken at about this time, it's altitude will be about 42° and the bearing of the intercept 305°. This will provide a position line running 035°–215°, to cross the latitude PL obtained from the moon's mer. alt. above, and thus to give an observed position.

Latitude by meridian altitude of a planet

The same technique can be used for finding the time of mer. pass. of a planet or star. This is seldom required in practice because it is so simple to obtain multiple star sights from which a good observed position can be determined. However, as this problem might crop up in an examination it is included here.

The times of mer. pass. of planets is given in the Naut. Alm. on each daily page, left hand page, foot of r.h. column. This is the time for the middle date of the three dates on the page. The time for the first and last date can be interpolated by reference to the time on the preceding or succeeding page. If the exact time is required, the time when the planet's LHA will be 0° can be calculated, as was explained for the moon.

Example: Find the time of mer. passage of Mars on 1975 Aug. 30th when in DR 36° S 14° W.

Mer. Pass. Mars		05 59 per Naut : Alm :
DR long. in time 14° W		+56
		06 55 GMT at DR.

or

LHA	0°
DR long. W	14°
GHA	14°
Mars, per Naut. Alm.	0°12'·2 = 06^h
remainder	13°47'·8
v 1·0	0'·9 (from incr. panel for 55^m)
	13°46'·9 = 55^m 07^s

Time of mer. pass. is therefore 06^h 55^m 07^s GMT. at DR

And if the sextant alt. was 33°31', bearing N, and IE −1'·8 and Ht of eye 8 ft, find yacht's latitude.

Sext. alt. Mars			33°31'·0 brg. N
	IE	−1'·8	
	Dip.	−2'·7	
			−4'·5
			33°26'·5
	Corr.		−1'·5
	True alt.		33°25'·0 N
		from	90°
	TZD		56°35'·0 S
Dec. 06^h	20°45'·7 N		
d, + 0'·3 55^m	+0'·3		
			20°46'·0 N
LATITUDE			35°49'·0 S

Latitude by meridian altitude of a Star.

This can be found in the same way.

$$GHA* = SHA* + GHA \text{ Aries}$$

and $\quad LHA* = GHA* \begin{cases} +E \text{ long.} \\ -W \text{ long.} \end{cases}$

We want to find time when LHA* is 0° (or 360°).

$$LHA* = SHA* \begin{cases} +E \text{ long.} \\ -W \text{ long.} \end{cases} + GHA \text{ Aries.}$$

so $\quad GHA \text{ Aries} = LHA* - SHA* \begin{cases} -E \text{ long.} \\ +W \text{ long.} \end{cases}$

Example : On 1975 May 19th when in DR 50° N 13°40′ W find time of mer. pass. of star DENEBOLA.

LHA*	360°	
SHA*	−183°02′·6	(from daily page in N. Alm.)
= LHA Aries	176°57′·4	
long. W	+13°40′·0	
GHA Aries	190°37′·4	
GHA Aries	176°52′·0	= 20^h
remainder	13°45′·4	= 54^m 52^s

Time of star's mer. pass. is therefore 20-54-52 GMT.

If the sextant altitude of DENEBOLA at mer. pass. was 54°59′ bearing S on May 19th when in DR 50° N 13°40′ W, what was the yacht's latitude? IE −1′·6, Ht of eye, 8 ft.

Sextant alt. Star		54°59′·0	brg. S
IE	−1′·6		
Dip.	−2′·7	−4′·3	
		54°54′·7	
Corr.		−0′·7	
True alt.		54°54′·0 S	
	from	90°	
TZD		35°06′·0 N	
Dec. Star		14°42′·5 N	
LATITUDE		49°48′·5 N	

(a) On 1975 May 20th at 20-53-55 GMT in DR 49°40 N 3°40 W the sextant alt. of VENUS was 23°02′·4. IE −2·6. HE 6 ft. Find the CP, Intercept and bearing.

(b) On 1975 Feb. 15th 17-53-15 GMT in DR 49°50 N 130° W the sextant alt. of MARS was 17°12′·4. IE −2·1, HE 8 ft. Find the CP, Intercept and bearing.

(c) On 1975 May 19th when in DR 49°40 N 6°25 W dawn twilight sights of stars are planned. Select the three best placed stars and give their approx. alt. and bearings. If the following observations were made later, find the OP.
03-54-42 GMT ALTAIR 48°35·8 sext. alt.
03-55-10 GMT MIRFAK 21°07·3 sext. alt.
03-55-50 GMT ARCTURUS 24°20·8 sext. alt.
IE −2·6. H of E 6 ft.

(d) On 1975 Aug. 31st (GD) at 20-54-50 GMT when in DR 49°45 S 165° E sextant alt. of MOON'S LL was 18°28·6. IE −1·9, H of E 8 ft. Find CP, Intercept and bearing.

(e) On 1975 Feb. 16th when in DR 56° S 44°30′ W find the GMT of MOON's mer. pass. If the sextant alt. LL was 18°49′·4 bearing N, what was the observed latitude? IE −1·9, H of E 8 ft.

11. Position without a chart

How to use the sights

In chapter 6 we discussed plotting position lines on a chart. Plotting a number of simultaneous sights (say four stars) was explained in chapter 8. We have seen that a fresh EP (loosely called a DR) must be found before a fresh sight can be worked out, to provide the DR from which to work. If (as they should be) two or more sights are taken each day, it is clear that there will be a great many lines to be drawn on a chart. The chart we shall be using for a long off shore passage will probably be on a fairly small scale. In this case the lines are likely to be tightly packed, crossing and overlapping, and generally difficult to read. Some method of 'blowing up' the chart, or using a large-scale chart, is required so that our intercepts, PLs, courses run, transferred PLs and so on are clear and intelligible.

Large-scale charts of the middle of empty oceans are not produced—they would contain nothing but useless soundings of great depths. Even if they were, one would require dozens of them to cover all possible areas one might be in. The Hydrographic Office produce Plotting Sheets. These are sheets, blank in their main area, with lat. and long. scales printed on their margins (Fig. 70.) The long. scales only mark minutes of long., leaving the user to insert the degrees of long. for the area he is dealing with. The vertical borders show several alternatives lat. scales, each suitably expanded to match the long. scale spacings. The user reads only the scale covering his lat., disregarding the others. Three plotting sheets are available:

'Chart' No. 5331. Scales (5) for lats. 0°–30° (and any long.).
'Chart' No. 5332. Scales (3) for lats. 30°–48° (and any long.).
'Chart' No. 5333. Scales (2) for lats. 48°–60° (and any long.).

Another plotting sheet No. 5004, is also printed, suitable for any lat., but is more complicated to use. The plain plotting sheets are simple to use, but are full chart-size and the user must rule in his own meridians and parallels from the border gradations, which is far from easy on a yacht at sea.

A further set, having the same chart numbers but with the suffix 'A', have the meridians of longitude and one central parallel of latitude printed in, and show a compass rose. If these are available, they are much to be preferred to the plain ones without these rulings.

Having written in on the correct plotting sheet the longitudes appropriate for the yacht's position, and decided which lat. scale to use, plotting is done exactly as on a normal chart.

An easy way to make an 'expanded portion' of a chart is to use squared paper. A suitable paper is one ruled with 1 inch and 1/10th inch squares.

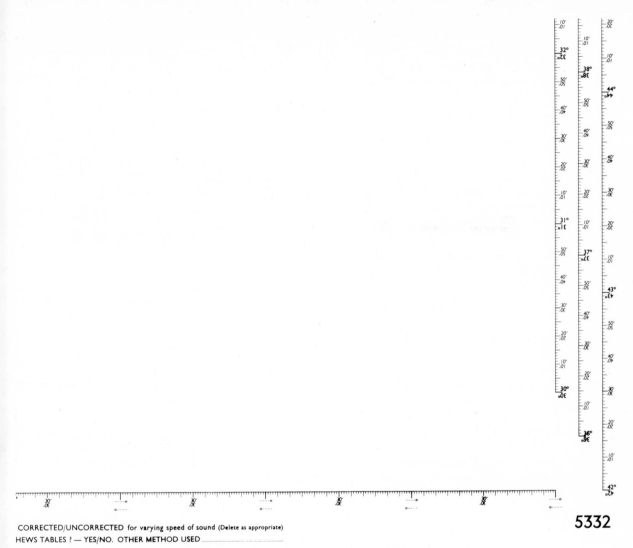

5332

CORRECTED/UNCORRECTED for varying speed of sound (Delete as appropriate)
HEWS TABLES ? — YES/NO. OTHER METHOD USED ....

Fig. 70.   Part of a plotting sheet.

Each 1/10th division can then represent a mile. When using squared paper remember that

A mile measured vertically represents 1′ of lat.

A mile measured horizontally represents 1 M of Departure (Dep.) and does NOT equal 1′ of long. (except only on the equator).

So we have to use the traverse tables to convert between *departure* and *longitude*. (Dep. and d. Lon.) (See Extract at end of book p. 174.)

Example. Our DR position is 50°10′ N 6°35′ W in the morning, when we take a sight of the sun which gives the following results:

CP 50° N 6°06′ W. Intercept. AWAY 20 M, bearing 096° T.

We have squared paper, ten small squares to one large one inch square. Mark the CP anywhere on the paper, preferably at an intersection of large squares. Against the mark write 'CP'. With protractor, lay off a line through the CP running 276° (the reciprocal of 096° as intercept is AWAY). From the CP along the intercept measure with dividers a distance 20 small squares (20 M intercept) to B. Through B draw a line at right angles to the intercept. This is the first position line. (PL 1.)

We then sail 041° T till local midday, when we take a meridian altitude of the sun which gives us our lat. as 50° 28′ N. We find (by log) we have sailed 24 miles since the first sight. From any point on the PL, say B, lay off the run, a line bearing 041° T, length 24 small squares = 24 M, to C. Through C draw a line parallel to PL 1, this is the 1st PL transferred. The original CP was 50° N. The second PL (lat.) will be a parallel through 50°28′ N (by obs.) and is therefore 28 small squares N of the CP. Count 28 lines up from the line through the CP and draw a line to cut the transferred PL. Where the second PL and the first PL transferred intersect is the Obs. Position at the time of the second sight, F. By counting

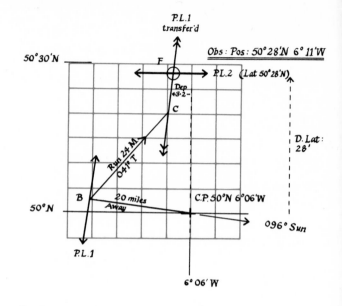

Fig. 71a.

the squares we can see that F is about 3·2 miles to W of the CP, i.e. Departure is 3·2 W.

The relationship between Dep. and minutes of long. depends on the *lat. of the position*. Our lat. is 50°, so we turn up the Traverse Tables, page headed 40° at top, 50° at bottom. Reading the italics captions 'D. Lon. and Dep.' at the bottom (because our lat. 50° appears at the bottom), we find our 3·2 Dep. and against it, 5·0 D. Lon. So in this lat., 3·2 M Dep. = 5'·0 long.

See Fig. 71a.

Write down the CP	6°06'·0 W
From CP to F, dep. is 3·2, in lat. 50° = d. Lon.	5'·0 W
So the long. of F is	6°11'·0 W

and we already know F's lat. is 50°28'·0 N.

Suppose we wish to plot two simultaneous sights of, say, the sun and moon (or it could be two stars). Each will have its own CP. Both will be on the same latitude, but their longitudes will certainly be different, as we must select 'chosen longs. which give each sight whole degrees of LHA.

Example: Our DR position is 40°20' N 18° W Our sights give:

Sun—CP 40° N 18° 28' W, Intercept 18 M, TO Bearing 113°.

Moon—40° N 18°53' W, Intercept 27 M, AWAY. Bearing 195°.

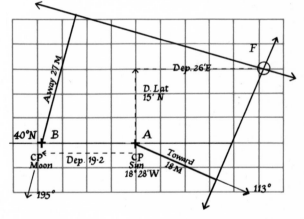

Fig. 71b.

At any point mark CP sun (A). This is 40° N	18°28' W	
CP of moon is 40° N	18°53' W	
So moon's CP is W of sun's CP by	25' W D. Lon.	

Entering Traverse Tables with lat. 40°, find what is the Dep. of a D. Lon. of 25'. This is Dep. 19·2 miles.

From A count 19·2 small squares to westward, to B. This is the moon's CP.

From each CP lay off the respective Intercepts, lengths the small squares equal to miles of intercept, and draw PLs at right angles. The intersection of these PLs is the Observed Position (F).

To find the lat. and long. of the Obs. Position F, we can use the sun's CP as a datum point. Count the squares vertically between A and F; this is the D. Lat., about 15' N. Count the squares horizontally between A and F. This is the Dep., about 26 miles E'ward. (Fig. 71b.)

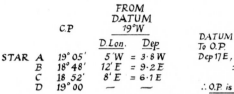

STAR	C.P	FROM DATUM 19°W	
		D.Lon.	Dep.
A	19°05'	5'W	= 3·8 W
B	18°48'	12'E	= 9·2 E
C	18 52'	8'E	= 6·1 E
D	19°00	—	—

DATUM   40°00'N 19°00W
To O.P.   D.Lat. 11'N
Dep 17 E, in M. Lat 40°
           = D. Lon.   22'E

∴ O.P. is   40°11'N 18°38'W

CP of sun was	40°00' N	18°28' W
From A to F is d. Lat.	15' N	
and Dep. 26 E, in Lat. 40° = d. Lon.		34' E
So F, the OBSERVED POSITION, is	40°15' N	17°54' W

If squared paper is not available, exactly the same technique can be used, with a set square (or Douglas protractor), and a ruler marked either in inches and tenths, or cm and mm.

It will be seen that in each of the examples given, the first CP has been used as a datum point from which to mark off the other CPs, or departure to the obs. pos. Where a number of CPs are involved, it may pay to work from one (main) vertical line designated an exact degree.

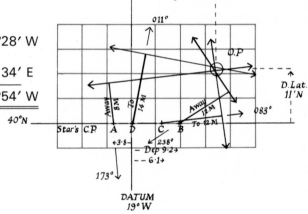

Fig. 72.

Example:

Star A	CP 40° N	19°05' W	Intercept	AWAY	8'	brg.	173°
B	,,	18°48' W	,,	AWAY	12'	,,	238°
C	,,	18°52' W	,,	TO	12'	,,	083°
D	,,	19°00' W	,,	TO	14'	,,	011°

In Fig. 72 the position of each CP is first compared with the 'datum' 19° to give each its D. Lon. This is converted into Dep. by traverse tables, and each CP marked off its Dep. from the datum 19° W.

Intercepts and PLs are plotted and the OP marked at the intersection of the PLs. The OP's D. Lat. and Dep. is counted from the datum, Dep. converted into D. Lon. The lat. and long. of the OP is arrived at as shown on the right of Fig. 73.

There is a rather more elegant, and possibly simpler way of plotting a sight by transferred position line, as when plotting a sun—run—sun sight. This is quite simple once the principles of a transferred PL are understood. This way can be used whether plotting direct on a chart, or when using a plotting sheet or on squared paper. The first CP is plotted, as before, but the intercept and

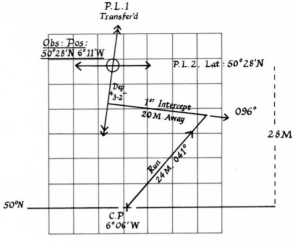

Fig. 74.

1ˢᵗ C.P.		6° 06'W
To O.P. Dep 3·2 W		
in Lat 50° = D. Lon		5'W
∴ O.P.'s Long. =		6° 11'W

PL are not laid off from this CP. Instead, the 'run' is first plotted forward from the CP (as usual, course and distance between sights). The first intercept and resultant PL is laid off from the *end* of the 'run'. The second CP is then plotted, and the second intercept and PL plotted as usual. Where the two PLs cross is the observed position. This method saves transferring the first PL forward, parallel, and eliminates one possible source of error, besides saving time.

Example : When in 50°10' S 171°30' E an afternoon sun sight gave CP 50° S 171°20'·5 E. Intercept, 8 M, AWAY, 255°.
Yacht then sailed 22 M, Co 035° T, when a sight of a star gave CP 50° S 171°46' E, Intercept, 14 M TO, 352°. (Fig. 73)

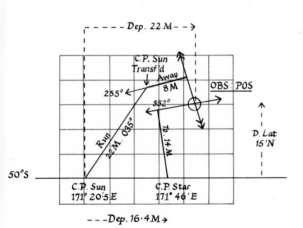

--- Dep. 16·4 M →

C.P. Sun		171° 20'·5 E
C.P. Star		171° 46'·0 E
D. Lon:		25'·5 E
in Lat : 50°, Dep =		16·4

C.P. Sun		50° 00'S 171° 20'·5 E
To O.P	D. Lat.	15' N
Dep .22 M.E		
in Lat . 50° =	D. Lon.	34·2 E
OBS : POS :		**49° 45'S 171° 54'·7 E**

Fig. 73.

The traverse tables can, of course, also be used for plotting a new DR required for a sight after a run from an OP (or DR) established earlier. Suppose the last OP was 36°05' N 25°14' W. Yacht then sailed 24 M, Co 210° T, and there was a current setting 146° T, drift 5 M during this period. In the example given, a 'datum' 25° W line and a 36° N parallel are drawn in. The Dep. of the OP is found, as shown, and the OP plotted. Distance sailed and current are plotted on and the resultant DR found. Its lat. is 'counted' direct from the paper, and the long. arrived at from the DR's Dep. from the datum line. (Fig. 75.)

Alternatively, a fresh position after a run can be determined, without plotting, by the use of traverse tables. For example, using the figures in the last exercise:

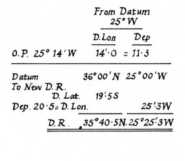

	From Datum 25° W	
	D. Lon	Dep
O.P. 25° 14' W	14'·0 = 11·3	

Datum	36°00' N	25°00' W
To New D.R.		
D. Lat.	19'·5 S	
Dep. 20·5 = D. Lon.		25'·3 W
D.R.	35°40·5 N.	25°25'·3 W

	Lat.	Long.
Last OP	36°05'·0 N	25°14'·0 W
Run, 210° = S 30° W, 24 M d. Lat.	20'·8 S	
Dep. 12'·0 W in lat. 36° = d. Lon.		14'·8 W
Current, 146° = S 34° E, 5 M d. Lat.	4'·1 S	
Dep. 2'·8 E in lat. 36° = d. Lon.		3'·5 E
New DR	35°40'·1 N	25°25'·3 W

If the yacht is beating to windward and is making repeated tacks, and/or is subject to several tidal streams or currents, a new EP is most readily got by 'tabulating' the various courses and distances sailed, and/or currents involved, as follows.

An OP is established in 49°41' N 17°24' W. Yacht then sails the following courses:

Co. 040° T	distance	19 M
310° T	,,	29 M
040° T	,,	18 M
320° T	,,	26 M

During this period the current is estimated at:

Setting 140° T at 1 kn for 8 hours

,,   130° T ,, ½ ,, 6 hours

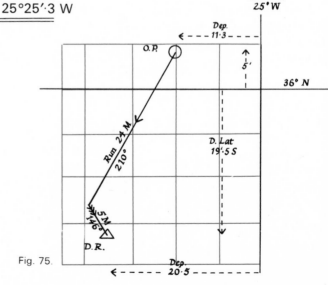

Fig. 75.

What is her new EP? The single-page extract from Norie's Traverse Tables given at the end of this book will enable the figures to be checked.

	D. lat.		Dep.	
	N	S	W	E
Co. 040° = N 40° E 19 M	14·6			12·2
310° N 50° W 29 M	18·6		22·2	
040° N 40° E 18 M	13·8			11·6
320° N 40° W 26 M	19·9		16·7	
Current				
140° = S 40° E 8ʰ 1 kn = 8 M		6·1		5·1
130° S 50° E 6ʰ ½ kn 3 M		1·9		2·3
	66·9	8·0	38·9	31·2
	8·0 ←		31·2 ←	
D. Lat.	58·9 N			
Dep.			7·7 W	

Old OP		49°41'·0 N	17·24'·0 W
Runs	d. Lat.	58'·9 N	
Dep. 7·7 W in mean lat. 50° = d. Lon.			12'·0 W
New EP		50°39'·9 N	17°36'·0 W

Note how the three-figure courses are converted into quadrantal notation, and how the 'name' of every d. Lat. (N or S) and every Dep. (E or W) is always the same as the quadrantal 'name'.

The EP found this way is likely to be more accurate than one found by plotting on the chart, and will in fact be as accurate as the record of courses steered and distances run.

Exercise No. 1

From the given DR, calculate the new DR after the RUN given:

	DR		*RUN*	
			Course	Distance
(a)	39°50 N	3°25 E	040°	25 M
(b)	40°10 N	6°24 W	140°	24 M

(c) 40°15 S   12°30 E   230°   21 M
(d) 50°10 S   18°20 W   130°   30 M
(e) 49°45 N   175°25 E   310°   67 M

(f) Approaching Vancouver Island, a morning sun
sight gave:

   CP 50° N 128°55'·6 W Intercept TO, 3'·7,
bearing 093°.
Yacht then sailed Co 120° for 18 M, when a
meridian altitude sight gave lat. 49°36' N. Find
the observed position then.

(g) Approaching South Island, New Zealand a
meridian altitude of the sun provided lat. 49°44' S.
   Yacht then sailed Co 080° T for 21 miles by log.
when an afternoon sun sight gave:

   CP 50° S 159°49' E, Intercept TO, 11' bearing
282°.
   Find her OP then.

(h) When in 50°15' N 38°20' W by DR, evening
sights gave:

   Moon CP 50° N 38°39'·9 W, Intercept AWAY
         8.3, Zn 182°.

   Venus CP 50° N 37°55'·5 W, Intercept TO
         23·5 Zn 280°.

   Spica CP 50° N 37°50'·6 W, Intercept AWAY
         15.5, Zn 161°.

   Arcturus CP 50° N 38°17'·5 W, Intercept AWAY
         11·5, Zn 132°.

   Find the OP.

12. The Navigator at work

Practical application of celestial sights

Good navigation starts with good records of all navigational matters. Written records are clearly necessary for a number of purposes. For navigation, accurate details of courses steered, times and mileages, bearings taken and so on, are needed. For historical record, broader details of passages, times of departure and arrival, names of crew and similar details are wanted. To attempt to incorporate all this in a single book would be cumbersome and confusing. It is better to have more than one record, each for a specific purpose.

The records recommended are:

1. A deck log, in which the helmsman or watch leader records all events as they occur.
2. A navigator's log, in which the navigator records all, and only, that information, extracted from the deck log and elsewhere, which is necessary to plot the yacht's position and progress.
3. A ship's log, in which probably the skipper records the 'story' of each passage, listing the crew, ports visited, times of arrival and departure, interesting occurrences and so on.
4. Note book(s) for recording all sights worked, calculations of heights of tides, radio time checks and the like.

The deck log

This will often be written up, and referred to, on deck, so a stout notebook (preferably of waterproof paper) is advisable. The ruling can be varied, but one recommended is given in Appendix 4 p. 140.

Time recorded

This will normally be time by 'ship's clock', if this differs from GMT, then the Zone should be noted at the head of every page. (See chapter 9.) At midnight each day draw a line right across the page and below it, insert the next day and date.

Course required

This should be entered by the navigator before the watch takes over. This should eliminate any risk of error or misunderstanding, which can easily occur if the course is passed on by word only. Some skippers hang a child's slate near the compass on which the course required is boldly chalked.

Course steered

The helmsman enters this with the compass course he has been steering. With a free wind, this should be the same as the 'Course Required', but when sailing to windward the helmsman must keep his eye on the compass and record his best estimate of the average or mean course he has been able to keep since the last entry. The inexperienced helmsman should be cautioned of the importance of this being as true as possible, and not over-optimistic.

Wind

An estimate of wind strength and direction can help in predicting the future weather and wind direction.

Barometer

Regular recording of the reading, preferably in millibars, will also help in forecasting likely weather changes. It is particularly important to keep regular track of the barometer when in the tropics. In latitudes below about 30°, in the summer, pressure falls off as little as 3 mb below the seasonal normal, or the ceasing of the regular diurnal variation, may herald the approach of a tropical revolving storm.

Frequency of entries

The deck log should be written up at regular, prescribed intervals, and at the time of any occurrence. Every entry must start with time and log reading (miles and tenths). The intervals prescribed will depend on circumstances. When ocean racing or on short passages, and when approaching any dangers, entries every half-hour are advisable. On a long passage, entries every one or perhaps two hours would suffice. Apart from their value for navigational purposes, regular entries give the man on watch an interest. He can check the speed, and if it falls off, check the trim of the sails. Patent logs often get fouled by weed and either stop or register slow. Frequent log reading ensures that this is detected, the log cleared and the recorded mileage corrected.

The navigator's log

It is unlikely that a printed log book will be found which has captions and rulings for all (and only), the information that should be recorded for navigational purposes. No two navigators will agree on the precise rulings required, so it is best to rule and head one up oneself. If one is typed, an ample supply can be run off on a duplicator (preferably the Rank Xerox type) and put on a binder. A ruling which has proved useful is given at Appendix 4, p. 141.

A fresh entry is necessary to record every alteration of course steered, significant alteration of tidal stream or current, or of leeway, and whenever a new EP is to be plotted or calculated. Positions obtained by fixes of landmarks or by celestial observations should be recorded. There is provision for recording variation (which may be changing quite often on a long passage), and for deviation (if any), and leeway, to provide the wake course (T°). Entries in the Tidal Stream section will vary with circumstances. Tidal streams do not always run exactly as predicted, and often there is no precise information on an ocean current and a broad estimate has to be made. It may therefore be possible to enter an average set and rate applying between two or more entries, and thus to enter the drift (rate times time elapsed) experienced over the period between two or more entries. If the stream is fast or changing direction, each hour's set since last wake course entry can be recorded.

Before starting to plot on the chart, or to calculate a fresh position by traverse tables, all entries in the navigator's log should be *checked*, from the deck log, from the tidal atlas or other evidence, and for arithmetical accuracy.

Note books

One note book should be reserved for recording and working up all celestial sights. A convenient book is one having squared paper one side and ruled paper opposite. The squared paper is useful for working up a sight without plotting the intercept on the chart, and for perhaps making a graph of a series of sights to get a good average (as described later).

Time checks (by radio) on the deck watch or chronometer should all be methodically recorded in a small notebook reserved for this purpose.

The navigator should enter up his log at regular intervals and, of course, whenever he decides to bring the chart position up to date and to plot a fresh EP. How often he does this will depend largely on the yacht's position. When in open ocean, miles from any danger, once a day will be sufficient. As land (or any danger) is approached he will probably plot his position more frequently. The EP will, of course, be required whenever he decides to take a celestial sight. Whenever a 'fix' (by landmarks) or an 'observed position' (by celestial sights) is obtained, the fix or OP should be compared with the EP. The EP is then abandoned and the fix or OP, if considered reliable, is then used to plot forward further EPs till a new fix or OP is available.

In earlier explanations of sights reference was made to the position by DR. This term is commonly used for a position arrived at by reference to 'best available evidence' other than a fix or OP, and is more correctly named an Estimated Position or EP. The strict definition of a position by DR or Dead Reckoning is one arrived at by reference only to the course steered and distance sailed. The EP is therefore the DR position corrected for leeway and tidal stream or current. The EP should of course always be determined and used for working up sights.

When an observed position or a fix is compared with the EP at that time, and an appreciable difference between the two is found it is advisable to investigate further and to seek to account for the difference. First, is the OP by sights correct?

If so, then perhaps the log is mis-reading (high or low), or the course or courses reported in the deck log were not correctly recorded. Possibly the tidal stream or current was wrongly assessed, or leeway suffered was different from that allowed for. Such checks give a backlog of experience on which to judge the reliability of the positions and to assess the validity of assumptions which have been made, e.g. on the leeway figure.

Frequency of sights

The frequency of celestial observations, and the routine and type of sight taken will depend on circumstances and location. A point to bear in mind is that the last sight you took may be the *last* sight you are able to take for perhaps several days. Suppose one is in mid-Atlantic, the weather is fair and no sights are taken for a week. Then foul weather sets in and sights cannot be taken for six days (storms, fog). One would then be nearly a fortnight without knowing one's position except by DR—and in this interval the DR could be a long way out.

When in open ocean, with no land within 100 miles, the daily routine should be a forenoon sun sight, a meridian altitude at (local) midday, and an afternoon sun sight. The forenoon and afternoon sights should be taken at about the time when the sun will be bearing as nearly as possible due E or due W, i.e. is on the 'prime vertical'. If it does bear exactly due 90° or 270°, then the sight will provide the longitude at the time. When this is crossed with a mer. alt. at local midday we have a perfect 'cut', at 90°. However, there are times and localities where the sun will not cross the prime vertical, or will only do so when it is too low for a good sight. The sun does not cross the prime vertical when the Lat. of the position and the sun's declination are of contrary names (N & S, or S & N). In such cases the best that can be done is to observe the sun as soon as its altitude has reached about 15° in the morning, or when it has fallen to about this altitude in the afternoon. The position line will then not provide our immediate longitude, but (provided the sun's bearing is within say 30°–40° of due E or W) will produce a PL which may be transferred to cross with the meridian latitude to give an acceptable 'cut'.

Multiple sights are worth taking occasionally, even when the exact position is not critical. Three or more sights of stars, planets, moon at twilight, will verify the accuracy of the sights being taken. If three or more (ideally six) sights are taken simultaneously, and all PLs cross nearly at a point, or form a small 'cocked hat', all must be good sights, correctly worked out and plotted. If only two sights are taken simultaneously, or if one is using only the sun and a transferred PL, then one could consistently be getting false PLs and thus a false observed position, without knowing it. This could occur if, for example, one regularly mis-placed the sun on the horizon, (e.g. a gap between sun and horizon, or the sun's limb overlapping the horizon) or were using a very wrong height of eye, or there were a mis-calculated index error, or if an error were being made such as a wrong total correction figure.

Before making a landfall or approaching any dangers multiple sights are very desirable, as one then needs all the confirmation possible. For the most accurate and up-to-the-minute position fixing the routine should be:

Morning Twilight—multiple stars, planet, moon (as available).

Forenoon—sun, when as near the prime vertical as possible.

Noon—sun, for lat. by meridian altitude.

Afternoon—sun, as for forenoon sight.

Evening Twilight—as for morning twilight.

If conditions are particularly favourable, night sights of stars, planet or moon may be taken also.

Compass check

On a long voyage it is prudent to make a compass check occasionally, to guard against some alteration in the deviation or a fresh deviation arising. There may be occasions, in areas where the variation is changing rapidly, when one wishes to check the variation. It could be that a compass which has been professionally adjusted is lost or stolen in port, and has to be replaced by another, unswung, compass. In any such case it may be necessary to check the compass error.

When no landmarks are visible, as in mid-ocean, the only way of checking the error of the compass is by the bearings of heavenly bodies. When in sight of landmarks the error of the compass is found by comparing landmarks' true bearings with bearings of the same landmarks taken with the steering compass, any difference being the 'total error' of the compass, which is a combination of variation and (if present) deviation on the yacht's heading at the time.

The skipper of a steel yacht should certainly check the error of his compass at intervals during a long voyage, as the yacht's own magnetism can alter appreciably over a few weeks.

The true bearing or azimuth of any heavenly body is, of course, found whenever a sextant observation is worked out; it is the Zn we use for plotting the intercept. However, if the sun is at an appreciable altitude it is almost impossible to ascertain its bearing by most yachts' steering compasses with any accuracy, unless a compass azimuth ring is fitted, and very few yachts can mount one. It is much easier, and far more accurate, to take the compass bearing of the sun when it is on the horizon, at sunrise or sunset. One can often 'take a bead' on the sun over the compass then. It is also extremely simple to calculate the sun's true bearing at this moment.

The true bearing of the sun at sunrise and sunset is given in Norie's or Burton's Tables under 'True Amplitudes', and in Reed's Almanac under 'Sun— True Bearing at Sunrise and Sunset'. There is a minor difference between the tables, but all require only two pieces of information:

1. Yacht's latitude at the time, approx. only to the nearest 1°, from the position by DR.

2. Sun's declination on the day, approx. only to nearest $\frac{1}{2}$°, from daily page in Nautical Almanac.

Entered with these as arguments, the tables give either sun's True Amplitude (Norie and Burton), or sun's True Bearing (given by Reed's). (Fig. 76) The only difference is that Amplitude is the number of degrees between due E (90°) on rising, or due W (270°) on setting, and the direction of the sun. It is measured towards N when the sun's decl. is N, or towards S when sun's decl. is S.

The bearing given in Reed's NA is the true bearing measured from N if sun's decl. is N, or from S if decl. is S, towards E on rising or towards W on setting.

Example 1. On 1975 Aug. 30th when in 43° N 18° W by DR the sun's bearing by steering compass at sunrise was 096° C. What was the total error of the compass? If variation locally was 12° W, what was the deviation on the yacht's heading at the time?

Using Norie's (or Burton's) Nautical Tables:
DR Lat. 43° (immaterial whether N or S, so omit).
Sun's Dec. N 9°.
Amplitude, per Table, 12°·4, say 12°.
Rising, so E 12°
Dec. N, so E 12° N

Fig. 76.

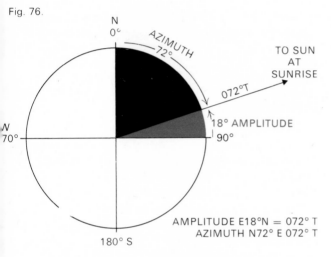

AMPLITUDE E18°N = 072° T
AZIMUTH N72° E 072° T

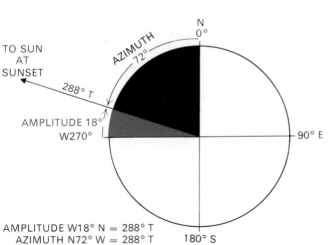

AMPLITUDE W18° N = 288° T
AZIMUTH N72° W = 288° T

E 12° N   = 078°·T
by compass,   096° C

Total error   18° W

Of which, Variation is 12° W so remainder is
        Deviation 6° W.
Using Reed's Nautical Almanac:
Sun's True Bearing, per Table, 77°·6, say 78°.
Sun's Dec. N, so N 78°
Rising, so   N 78° E = 078° T
bearing by compass,   096° C

Total Error   18° W

Example 2. On 1975 Feb. 17th when in 13° S
164° E by DR, the sun's bearing at sunset by
steering compass was 256°. Find the total error
of the compass, and if the local variation was
15° E, find the deviation on the yacht's heading at
the time.
Using Norie's or Burton's Tables:
DR Lat. 13°.
Sun's Dec. S 12°.
Amplitude, per tables, W 12° S = 258° T
by compass,   256° C

Total error   2° E

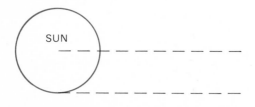

SUN

½ DIAM.

Fig. 77.

Var'n   15° E
∴ Dev'n   13° W

Using Reed's Table:
DR Lat. 13°.
Sun Dec. S 12°.
Sun's true bearing S77°·8 W = 257°·8,

say	258° T
by compass	256° C
Total error	2° E

Another way of getting the deviation from a
known total error and known variation which
may be found easier is:
Bearing by Amplitude or Azimuth,   258° T
Variation   15° E

                   243° Mag.
Bearing by steering compass   256° C

∴ Deviation   13° W

The sun's bearing should be observed when its
lower limb is about half the sun's diameter above
the horizon because, due to refraction, when the
sun is thus seen, its centre is in fact on the
horizon. (Fig. 77.)

If the steering compass is fixed where it is
difficult or impossible to 'take a bead' on the sun
at sunrise or sunset, here is a method which can
often be used. If the course is roughly E, then at
sunrise steer at the sun, lining up mast, pulpit etc.
accurately on the sun. Note the compass course
and compare this with the sun's true bearing as
worked out. If the course is roughly W, do the
same at sunset. The error of the compass and
hence the deviation found will, of course, only
be strictly valid when sailing on the course
steered when the observation was made, but
provided the course required is not too different
the deviation should not be far out. If the course

were roughly N or S, then it may be possible to line up on the sun a transverse bulkhead or any other objects on deck which are truly athwartships. When 90° is added to or subtracted from the course being steered when the bulkhead is lined up on the sun, the sun's bearing by steering compass is found.

Alternatively, the deviation of the steering compass (but not the total error or variation) can be found by taking a bearing of the yacht's head with a hand bearing compass held well aft, exactly amidships and well away from rigging or other metal. The hand bearing compass will give the magnetic (not true) heading for comparison with the heading by steering compass, the difference (if any) being deviation. Remember that this is the deviation for the particular course being steered at the time, and that it may well be very different when an appreciably different course is steered. This method is not recommended in a steel yacht, since the hand bearing compass may well also be subject to deviation.

If the true bearing of the sun (or any body) is required at times *other than* at rising or setting, the procedure is simply to work out the first part of a sight, i.e. find the body's LHA and Dec. at the moment observed. With these and the Lat. by DR the sight reduction tables are entered and Z, the body's azimuth, is extracted. (For this purpose we are not interested in its alt., Hc and d.) Again, this is the body's true bearing, from which the total error of the compass can be found.

Exercise No. 12

Compass check by Sun's Amplitude.

(These require use of Norie's, Burton's, Reed's N. A., or other naut. tables.)

Find the total error of the compass, and if the variation was as stated, find the deviation on ship's heading at the time.

(a) Sunrise on 1975 Feb. 17th in DR 18° N 48° W sun's bearing 114° C, variation 17° W.

(b) Sunset, 1975 May 21st, DR 50° N 128° W, sun's bearing 305° C, variation 25° E.

(c) Sunrise, 1975 Aug. 30th, DR 49° S 165° E, sun's bearing 050° C, variation 19° E.

13. Some useful tips

When visibility is good, sights should be taken from as high a position as can be conveniently arranged. The horizon seen then will be as far off as possible, and thus least affected by wave- or swell-tops on the horizon, which will be correspondingly small in appearance.

In poor visibility when the distant horizon is indistinct or invisible in mist, the position taken up should be as low as possible so that a close horizon is used. Remember to use the actual height of eye employed (to the nearest foot) for finding dip.

When using a sextant in a seaway it is advisable to wear life-harness, clipped on. When busy taking sights one is not in a position to spot in advance the odd rogue wave which may cause the yacht to pitch or roll suddenly. Except in calm seas it is not advisable to take sights standing : unless perhaps in the companionway where one can chock oneself off against the coachroof. Adopt any position where the lower part of the body is well anchored but the upper torso is free to sway with the motion of the yacht, so that one can maintain a (roughly) vertical position. Remember always to 'rock' the sextant to ensure that it is vertical. The body viewed should coincide with the horizon at its lowest point of 'rock'. To guard against the risk of dropping the sextant—easily done when making one's way up on deck or back—it is a good idea to have a lanyard on the sextant which can be slipped over the head.

Sight-taking is much easier if a second person is available to note the time and the sextant angle. This is particularly helpful when it is desired to take simultaneous sights of several stars, or to take a series of sun sights in rapid succession. If single-handed or no one is available, wear a wrist watch and sit on a corner of the sight book so that it is not blown away but you can enter each sight's time and altitude without shifting the sight book. The times by wrist watch must of course be checked against the deck watch (or chronometer), and this also corrected for DWE to give exact GMT, but this can all be done when back at the chart table.

Always use an index mirror shade before even 'finding' the sun. Picking up the sun is sometimes easier with a pale shade, but this should be replaced by a suitably dark one for final coincidence adjustment. If the horizon sparkles or is very bright (as when the sun is low) use a horizon mirror shade too. A sight of a bright moon at twilight may be improved by using a pale shade on the index mirror.

In rifle-shooting one is recommended not to spend too long in trying to get a perfect aim, but to fire quite quickly as soon as the sights are 'on'. The same applies to sextant 'shooting'. Try to establish coincidence quickly then take the time at once. Do not spend minutes striving for perfection—the result will not be so good as the sight taken carefully but smartly.

If the sea is rough and the yacht is pitching or rolling heavily, perfect sights are impossible. It then pays to take a series of sights over a short period (noting the time and alt. of each sight), and then either to take the mean or average, or better still, to plot the results on squared paper—to make a graph—plotting the alt. of each sight against its time along the bottom of the paper. It is then possible to see the odd sight which is clearly an 'outsider'. This is discarded and a straight line of best fit is drawn over the remainder. Any convenient point on the line can then be selected, and the corresponding angle and time used for working up the sight.

Alternatively, having discarded the obvious 'outsider', the remaining times and altitudes can be averaged by adding up and dividing the total by the number of sights, as shown in Fig. 78.

Easy way to plot intercept

A Douglas protractor is a quick way of plotting intercepts (and PL's) on chart or squared paper. Try this way:

First, set compasses to length of intercept, from Lat. scale.

Next, place centre of protractor over the CP, protractor lined up with meridians or parallels of Lat.

if intercept TOWARDS, protractor's N point upward

if intercept AWAY, protractor's N point downward

Then find body's bearing (Zn) on outer scale of protractor and stab chart at this point with compass point. Hold compass point there and swivel any straight edge of protractor round compass point, to align on the CP. Hold protractor there. Transfer compass point to CP and make small arc close to protractor edge. Still holding protractor firm, now draw line from CP to arc.

This method is quick, saves unnecessary movements, helps ensure intercept is correctly 'towards' or 'away' (and saves working out the reciprocal for 'away') and eliminates long and unnecessary lines which may confuse.

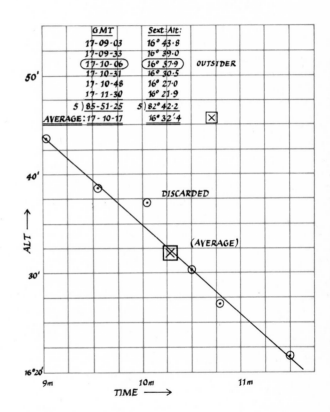

GMT	Sext Alt:
17-09-03	16° 43·8
17-09-33	16° 39·0
17-10-06	16° 37·9 OUTSIDER
17-10-31	16° 30·5
17-10-48	16° 27·0
17-11-30	16° 21·9
5)85-51-25	5)82° 42·2
AVERAGE: 17-10-17	16° 32·4

Fig. 78.

Spurious accuracy

It is seldom possible to take sextant sights to an accuracy of better than 1′ or 2′ from a yacht in a seaway. It may therefore be considered a waste of time to worry about decimals of a minute of arc in GHA or declination. It is recommended that, initially at least, all figures are worked out as accurately as the tables permit for two reasons:
(a) errors due to working only to whole numbers may happen to be all in the same direction as the inevitable error in the sight taken, thus making it even worse, and
(b) if one develops the habit of being meticulous with decimals one is more likely to be right with units—and tens—which *do* matter.

The thoroughly experienced navigator knows when he can afford to take 'short cuts', and whether the possible error is acceptable, but this practice is not recommended. v or d factors can often be interpolated by eye, but beware of the large ones arising with moon sights.

Sights for latitude in the tropics

When sailing in the tropics there may be occasions when the sun passes almost exactly overhead at midday, local time. This will occur when the yacht's latitude is almost the same as the sun's declination, and of the same name, N or S. The sun then rises almost exactly due E, remains almost due E till local midday, then suddenly becomes almost due W, finally setting in the west. It may then be difficult to obtain the sun's altitude when it is exactly on the meridian, as it will then be almost 90° (overhead).

If the latitude of the DR is within about 2° of the sun's declination, and same name (N or S), a special technique is called for.

The sun's declination represents the latitude of the sun's GP, so if this is very nearly the same as the yacht's latitude, the sun's GP will sweep very close to the yacht's position when the sun's GHA and the yacht's longitude are the same, at local midday. The LHA will then be 0°.

The technique is to take three observations of the sun, the first a few minutes before its expected time of meridian passage, the second at about mer. pass., and the third a few minutes after. The sun's GP when each sight was taken can be plotted, and the observations will provide the respective Zenith Distances. A circle round each GP of radius the sun's true ZD can be drawn, and the intersection of the three circles of position will be the yacht's position.

If, as is likely to be the case on an ocean passage, only a small-scale chart is available, the plotting may be done on squared paper, or on plain paper, the d. long. being changed into departure by traverse tables. Alternatively a blank plotting sheet can be used. (Fig. 79.)

Procedure:
1. Calculate the time of mer. passage at the DR.
2. Take the first sight between 4 and 10 minutes before the approximate time of mer. pass.

Take the second sight at mer. pass. time.

Take the third sight approximately the same time after mer. pass. as the first sight was taken before mer. pass.

Note exact GMT of each sight.
3. For each sight, turn sext. alt. into TZD, and find GHA.
4. Plot sun's GP when each sight was taken, Lat. = sun's Dec. long. = sun's GHA (in E long. subtract GHA from 360°).
5. With each GP as centre and each respective ZD expressed in minutes of arc as radius, describe three arcs. These should intersect at a point. This is the obs. position.

To plot on squared paper

Any horizontal line will represent the latitude of

SIGHTS FOR LATITUDE IN THE TROPICS

Worked Example:

On passage to Barbados, the latitude is required on 1975 May 20. The DR is 21°N 59°30'W Index error -2'.0 Height of eye, 6ft

Mer pass	11 56	
DR long	59°30W	+ 3 58
	15 54	GMT at ship

Sights taken: 1st at 15-52-10 GMT
2nd at 15-55-40
3rd at 15-58-35

First Sight		Second Sight		Third Sight	
15-52-10		15-55-40		15-58-35	
GHA 15h	45°53'.1	45°53'.1	N19°56'.0	45°53'.1	
Increment	13°02.5	13°55'.0	d+0.5 + .5	14°38.8	
Long of GP	58°55'.6W	59°48'.1W	N19°56'.5	60°31.9W	
2nd sight		59°48.1		59°48.1	
d.long	52'.5E			43'.8W	
in lat 20°,				Dep 41'.2	
Dep =		49'.3			
Sext Alt	LL88°43'.5	88°56'.5		88°36'.5	
IF and Dip	- 4 .4	- 4 .4		- 4 .4	
	88°39'.1	88°52.1		88°32.1	
Cor	+ 15 .9	+ 15 .9		+ 15 .9	
True Alt	88°55'.0	89°08'.0		88°48'.0	
from	90°	90°		90°	
TZD	1°05'	52'		1°12'	
=	65 M	52 M		72 M	

Fig. 79a.

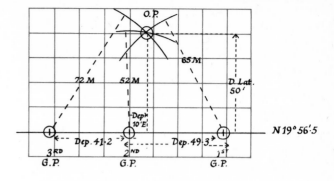

2ND G.P.	19°56'.5 N	59°48'.1 W
To O.P. D.Lat.	50' N	
Dep. 10 E		
in Lat : 20°= D.Lon.		10'.7 E
∴ O.P.	20°46'.5 N	59°37'.4 W

Fig. 79b.

the sun's GP (lat. = Decl.). The GHA of each sight will represent the longitude of the sun's GP at the time of each sight.

GHA less than 180°, GHA = long. W
GHA more than 180°, 360°–GHA = long. E

On the horizontal line, mark a middle point to represent the sun's GP at the SECOND sight, mark it with the long. Compare the first and third sight's GP with that of the second. The difference will give the d. Lon. of each from the second GP. Convert these d. Long. into Dep. by traverse tables.

Measure off the Dep. of 1st GP from 2nd GP, to RIGHT.

Measure off the dep. of 3rd GP from 2nd GP, to LEFT

(Remember the sun's GP always travels from E to W.) The GPs of the three sights have now been plotted. With centre each sight's GP and radius the ZD of each sight (expressed in minutes =

miles), describe arcs of circles. If at second sight the sun bore N, describe arcs on S side of line, and vice versa. The three arcs should intersect. This is the obs. position. Measure the distance of the OP from the second sight's GP in terms of d. Lat. and Dep., and apply these to the position of the second GP, as shown in the examples.

If the distance travelled between the times of the first and last sight is considerable, the first and second circles of position should be transferred forward to the time of the last sight by shifting the first and second GP by the course and distance made good in the two intervals. In practice, this will be unnecessary unless the vessel was travelling at about 20 knots or more.

If the three arcs do not intersect at a point, or nearly so, the sights should be disregarded. In clear weather it should be possible to observe a star, planet (or moon occasionally) which is on or near the meridian at twilight, thus providing a position line of latitude, or to take multiple star sights at twilight.

Observations by mixed methods

Keep in mind that a single position line obtained by one method may be crossed with a PL by another method. For example, approaching the Azores from the SW, the tip of Mt Pico is seen in the afternoon. It's bearing, taken by compass, is 235° T. A sun sight is taken and the intercept bears 246° T, which provides a PL running 156°–336°. This cuts the first PL well and will give us an observed position.

Or a single RDF bearing might be available, say by Consol. The single PL provided may be crossed with a single sextant observation. Whenever one can only get a single PL from one type of observation, consider whether any other type may be available, e.g.

Sun observation

Compass bearing of an identifiable landmark
R.D.F. bearing
Line of soundings.

Altitude and accuracy

The importance of rocking the sextant to ensure it is vertical has been stressed. If a sight is taken when the sextant is not plumb vertical the altitude measured will always be greater than the real altitude. The amount of this error depends on
(a) the angle the sextant is out of the perpendicular, and
(b) the altitude of the body being observed.
The larger the altitude the greater the error. On the other hand, refraction is greater the lower the body viewed, and any abnormal refraction (due to temperature or pressure) is greatest at very low altitudes. To give an idea of the errors which can arise, here are some figures:

Sextant tilted by	Altitude of Body			
	10°	25°	50°	89°
2°	0'·4	0'·9	1'·8	3'·2
5°	2'·3	5'·7	11'·4	20'·2
10°	9'·2	23'·1	46'·2	82'·2

Looking at the Nautical Almanac 'Additional Correction Table for non-standard conditions' (p. A4), note how these vary from maxima of

App. alt.	2°30',	between	−2'·5 and	+2'·5
„	5°	„	−1'·5 „	+1'·5
„	10°	„	−0'·8 „	+0'·8
„	20°	„	−0'·4 „	+0'·4
„	50°	„	−0'·1 „	+0'·1

Experience has shown that the most reliable sights are taken when the body is not less than about 15° and not more than 45° alt. When there is any option, the bodies selected and times of sights should be chosen with this in mind. The meridian altitude of the sun, particularly when in the tropics, will often be far greater than the 45°

mentioned and special care regarding perpendicularity of the sextant is then essential.` Alternatively, sights of any star, planet or the moon may be taken when one of these bodies is on or close to due N or S, and at suitable lower altitude, to provide the yacht's latitude.

Sights in heavy weather
If sights are essential at a time when seas are rough, special care of both the sextant and the observer is essential. Wear life-harness, clipped on and with a short scope. Wrap a dry towel loosely round the sextant while carrying from chart table to deck, and back, to protect it from knocks en route. Stuff some dry paper tissues in pocket, to wipe the mirrors or lens should they get covered with salt spray. If possible, take a series of sights, calling them to a writer below. Average, or better still, graph the results to weed out the bad sights. Clean the sextant, if possible with fresh water, paying particular attention to the mirrors, before putting away.

14. Planning an ocean voyage

The speed—and the comfort—of an ocean passage will largely depend on the winds encountered and the currents prevailing. So a choice of the best route is of considerable importance. Many ocean areas are subject to hurricanes or typhoons at certain periods of the year. The name varies according to the area, but all are classified as Tropical Revolving Storms, and can be called hurricanes. It goes without saying that these are to be avoided at all costs. Yachts have survived them, but even large liners take great pains to avoid them, and the operative word for any small vessel is survival, bearing in mind that winds may exceed 120 knots.

Clearly, a route on which mainly favourable winds of average strength not above force 6 can be expected is far preferable to one where mainly head winds, or winds from forward of abeam, or gales, prevail. Ocean currents too may have a significant effect on the length of the passage. A modest current of only half a knot in the wrong direction means that the yacht has to sail twelve miles each day before she has made any progress towards her destination. This soon mounts up on, say, a 2,500 mile passage.

Planning the route should begin with a careful study of the routing charts of the ocean involved, for the month(s) when it is proposed to be on passage. For each ocean twelve routing charts are published, one for each month in the year. These are:

Chart No. 5124 Routing Chart for N. Atlantic Oc.
       5125   ,,   ,,   S. Atlantic Oc.
       5126   ,,   ,,   Indian Oc.
       5127   ,,   ,,   N. Pacific Oc.
       5128   ,,   ,,   S. Pacific Oc.

These contain a mass of information of vital interest to the mariner, and particularly to the yacht navigator, who is more dependent on the wind than his commercial counterpart. In particular, routing charts show:

(a) Winds
(b) Currents.
(c) Ice and fog limits.
(d) Air- and sea-temperatures, dew points.
(e) Tracks of tropical revolving storms (if any) in recent years.
(f) Steamer tracks (semi-great circle tracks) between many ports.

Winds are indicated by wind 'roses', placed all over the chart. Each shows the percentage of winds from various directions, and their strengths, predicted at the position of each wind rose. The general direction and average rates of ocean currents are shown by green arrows. Ice and fog areas and limits are marked, and small chartlets show temperature contours of both sea and air, and contours of mean barometric pressure in millibars. Paths of tropical storms which have occurred in recent years are also given.

The first consideration in planning an ocean passage is to seek to avoid periods when hurricanes may be expected. These are:

		Named
N. Atlantic, western side	June to Nov.	Hurricanes
S. Indian Ocean	Dec. to Apr.	Cyclones
Arabian Sea and Bay of Bengal	June and Nov.	Cyclones
N. Pacific, east side	June to Nov.	Hurricanes
west side	All year, but most frequently June to Nov.	Typhoons
S. Pacific west side	Dec. to April	Hurricanes

Route choices

Having settled on the months when there is least likelihood of tropical storms, the next step is to decide on the best route. This may be influenced by the relative importance of speed or of pleasure and comfort, and on the windward ability of the yacht. The shortest distance between two places is a straight line, but quite often this will not be the best route, even if there is clear water and no dangers along this route. For example, a direct route from UK to the West Indies passes through large areas of contrary, or light, winds, while a more southerly route will lead through the belt of the NE Trade Winds where for days on end a good stiff sailing wind from well abaft the beam can almost be guaranteed.

Where the routing charts show that there is nothing to be gained by taking a more roundabout route, then a straight line may be best. On a sphere—and on the earth's surface—a straight line, and therefore the shortest distance, is a portion of a great circle passing through departure and destination. A piece of string stretched taut between two points on a globe is part of a great circle. Except when stretched exactly N and S (forming a meridian), or along the equator (the only parallel which is a great circle) the string will cross each meridian at a different angle—the bearing of the string changes all along its length. This is why a great circle track on a mercator projection chart appears as a curve, bowed away from the equator. A straight line on a mercator chart (such as a routing chart) is called a rhumb line and crosses each meridian at the same angle—its bearing remains constant. Thus a rhumb line is always longer than part of a great circle drawn between two places (except only when the places are both on the same meridian (same long.), or both are on the equator).

However, the difference in the length of a rhumb line and that of a great circle between two places is insignificant if the distance is only a few hundred miles and the latitudes are below about 60° N or S. On ocean crossings of several thousand miles a great circle route can be appreciably shorter than a rhumb line, in certain cases. This is why commercial vessels tend to follow great circle tracks. The case is different for yachts, whether sail or power. A sailing yacht usually shapes a course which will take her through areas where winds and currents are most likely to be favourable, avoiding areas where bad weather can be expected. The moderate sized power yacht also is more interested in hospitable seas and winds, and both types will normally reach their destination more quickly, and certainly more comfortably, by selecting courses based on the expectations of wind, weather, tides and sunshine, as indicated by routing charts and pilot books.

Some ideas of the difference in distance between a rhumb line and a great circle course may be seen from the following examples:

	Rhumb line	Gr. Circle	Saving
1. Off Orkney Is. to off Stavanger	92·7 M	91·5 M	Negl.
2. Lizard (UK) to Azores	1,128	1,123	5 M
3. J. de Fuca Str. (Vancouver Is.) to Honolulu	2,201	2,186	15
4. Yokohama to San Francisco	4,708	4,456	252
5. Durban to Melbourne	5,710	5,296	414
6. Yokohama to J. de Fuca Str.	4,345	4,080	265

In the last example, however, a great circle course would take the yacht up north of the Aleutian Isles, a quite impossible route. This is a case where the shortest practical route would be a great circle up to the highest desirable latitude, say 50° N, the second 'leg' sailing due E along the 50°th parallel, and a third 'leg' another great circle to destination.

The maximum saving of a great circle against a mercator or rhumbline track occurs when the course is mainly in a E–W or W–E direction (major change in long.) and when the course is in a high latitude (N or S) (e.g. Nos. 4 and 5 above). There is little advantage when the course is mainly N–S (e.g. Nos. 2 and 3 above).

The great circle route between two places is found very simply by using an Admiralty Great Circle Diagram, chart No. 5029 (HMSO). The diagram contains instructions for using it. Briefly, this is as follows:

The diagram shows a series of lines representing meridians of longitude. These are all parallel and run due N and S on the sheet, but are not equally spaced. The parallels of latitude are printed as hyperbolic curves (see reproduced portion), Fig. 80.

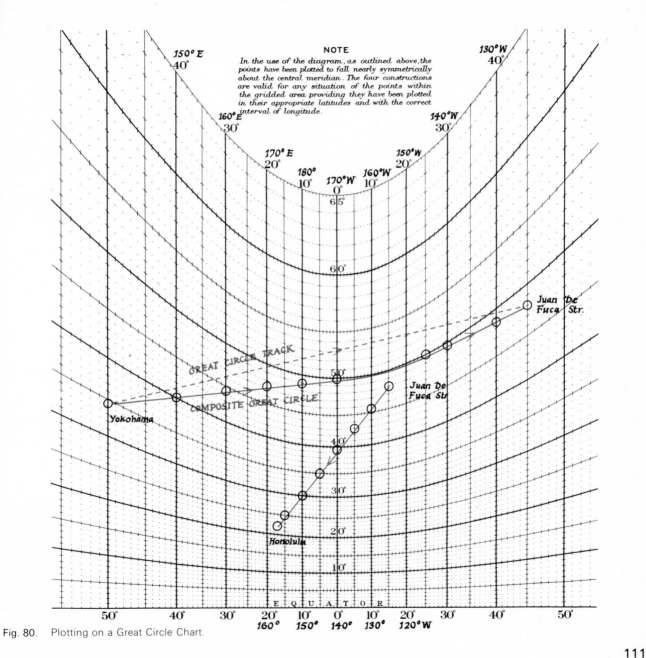

NOTE

In the use of the diagram, as outlined above, the
points have been plotted to fall nearly symmetrically
about the central meridian. The four constructions
are valid for any situation of the points within
the gridded area providing they have been plotted
in their appropriate latitudes and with the correct
interval of longitude.

Fig. 80. Plotting on a Great Circle Chart.

111

ocean yacht navigator

Assume the great circle track is required from Victoria BC to Honolulu. First find the mid-longitude between the two places, to the nearest 10°, viz:

Juan de Fuca Str. 48° N	125° W
Honolulu	22° N	157° W
d. Long.		32°
half =		16°
add to		125°
mid-lat.		141°, say 140°

Pencil in, under the printed 0° long. meridian on the diagram the mid-long., 140°, and pencil in under the adjacent meridians the corresponding figures, 130°, 120° and 150°, 160°.

Using the pencilled longs. and the printed lats., plot the starting and finishing positions' lats. and longs., and connect with a straight line. This represents the great circle track required.

Pick off the Lats. of points along this line at 5° or 10° intervals of longitude, and write down, e.g.

long.	
130° W.	45°30′ N
135°	43° N
140°	39°30′ N
145°	35° N
150°	30° N
155°	25° N

Plot these positions on a mercator projection chart (e.g. the routing chart) and connect each position to the next with a straight line. Course is then shaped to each successive point, course being altered at each to fetch the next.

In the case of a Yokohama to Juan de Fuca Strait passage, when the great circle track is marked on the diagram it will be seen that the track would run up to over 53° N, north of the Aleutian Islands. Inspection of the routing chart shows that the northerly limit should be, say,

50° N. A composite great circle track is therefore required. Pencil in on the diagram the mid-long., say 170° E, and pencil in each 10° long. Plot on the diagram the positions of starting and finishing points. From the Yokohama point draw a tangent to the curved 50° parallel. This touches the 50° parallel at 170° W. Draw another tangent from Juan de Fuca Str. to the 50° curve. This touches at about 145° W. The composite track should then be

(a) A great circle track from 34°40′ N 140° E to 50° N 170° W.
(b) A parallel sailing track from 50° N 170° W to 50°N 145° W.
(c) A great circle track from 50° N 145° W to 48° N 125° W.

Intermediate points where alterations to course should be made would be

First to	40° N	150° E
Then to	44°30′ N	160° E
	47°15′ N	170° E
	49° N	180°
	50° N	165° W

Thence due E (remaining on 50° N) till 50° N 145° W, when the second great circle track is reached, then shaping courses to

	49°50′ N	140° W
	48°50′ N	130° W
and	48° N	125° W entrance to Juan de Fuca Str.

This composite great circle course is 4,110 M, which is only 30 M more than the (impossible) great circle of 4,080 M, compared with the rhumb line of 4,345 M—an appreciable saving of 235 M, with winds mostly abaft the beam throughout.

Measuring distances

Neither a rhumb line nor a great circle distance can be measured on a small-scale mercator projection chart, such as a routing chart, except very roughly and over short distances.

To find the rhumb line distance between two places over, say, 500 miles apart with any accuracy, the tables of meridional parts and of trigonometrical functions must be used. It is not necessary to go into the theory involved, and a little practice will enable the simple formula to be used to find the distance. In fact, two formulae are required to find the rhumb line distance between, say, points A and B. These are:

(a) $\dfrac{\text{d. Lon.}}{\text{DMP}} = \tan \text{course}$

(b) Distance = d. Lat. × sec. course.

D. lon. is simply the difference in longitude between A and B. DMP is the difference between the meridional parts of the respective latitudes of A and B, extracted straight from the Meridional Parts table in Norie's or Burton's Tables.

Example. Find the rhumb line distance between points 48° N 125° W and 22° N 157° W.

1. Find mer. parts of the two lats.

Lat.	Mer. parts	Norie's	Burton's
48° N =	3274·13	p. 144	p. 96
22° N	1344·92	p. 142	p. 94
DMP	1929·21		

2. Long.   125° W
            157° W

d. Lon. =   32°   (× 60) = 1920′

To save division, turn up the log of each figure and subtract (1) from (2).

		Norie	Burton
d. Lon. 1920′	= log 3·28330	p. 160	p. 123
−DMP 1929·21	= log 3·28538	p. 160	p. 123

Tan. co. 9·99792

If we wish to know the rhumb line course between A and B we have only to find what angle has tan. 9·99792 in Logs of Trig functions table,

ocean yacht navigator

which is 44°52′. See Norie p. 237, Burton p. 151. But on the same page we can see what is the log. sec. of an angle whose log. tan is 9·99792. By interpolation we see this is 10·14948, ready for the next little formula.

3. Lat. A = 48° N
   B = 22° N

				Norie	Burton
d. lat. 26° (× 60) = 1560′ = log.		3·19313		p. 159	p. 122
log. tan. 9·99792 = log. sec.		10·14948		p. 237	p. 151
log		3·34261			
=		2,201 miles		p. 161	p. 124

This is rather more compactly laid out below the next example.

The distance between two points on a great circle is calculated in exactly the same way as we find the calculated zenith distance of a heavenly body's GP from a chosen position using AP 3270 or HO 249 but substituting the terms, as follows:

For the CZD of a heavenly body	For a Great Circle Distance
LHA of body	d. Lon. between the 2 points
Lat. of CP or DR	Lat. of starting point
Decl. of body	Lat. of finishing point

The Juan de Fuca Straits to Honolulu great circle distance is worked out:

Juan de Fuca Straits 48° N	125° W	
Honolulu	22° N	157° W
d. Lon.	32° = LHA	
Lat. J. de Fuca Str	N 48° = Lat.	
Lat. Honolulu	N 22° = Dec.	
Hc = 53°34′		
from 90°		
CZD 36°26′ = 2186′ = miles		

If the smaller lat. exceeds 29° N or S, AP 3270 or HO 249 cannot be used, but NP 401 or HO 229 can. Alternatively, the Haversine/Cosine formula can always be applied, thus:

d. Lon.	32°	log. hav.	8·88068
Lat. J de F.	N 48°	log. Cos.	9·82551
Lat. Honolulu.	N 22°	log. Cos.	9·96717
		log. hav.	8·67336
	=	nat. hav.	04714
Lat. ~ Lat.	26°	nat. hav.	05060
		nat. hav.	09774
	= 'CZD'		36°26′·2 (° × 60)
	=		2,186′·2 = miles

The length of a rhumb line between these places is calculated:

				Meridional Parts
J. de Fuca	48° N	125° W		3,274·13
Honolulu	22° N	157° W		1,344·92
d. Lat.	26°		DMP	1,929·21
= 1,560′				
d. Lon.	32°			
= 1,920′				

$$\frac{\text{d. Lon.}}{\text{DMP}} = \tan \text{Co.} \quad \frac{1{,}920}{1{,}929 \cdot 21} = \begin{matrix} \log\ 3 \cdot 28330 \\ - \log.\ 3 \cdot 28538 \end{matrix}$$

$$\log.\ \tan\ 9 \cdot 99792 = \text{C.}\ 44°52'$$

Distance = d. Lat. sec. Course

d. Lat. 1,560 = log. $3 \cdot 19313$

log tan $9 \cdot 99792$ = log. sec. $10 \cdot 14948$

log $3 \cdot 34261$

Distance = 2,201 M.

Rhumb line exceeds great circle by $14 \cdot 8$ M only.

Sailing directions

The Admiralty publish no less than 73 books of Sailing Directions (commonly referred to as 'Pilots) which together cover the world. When stocking up charts for a long voyage it is simplest to consult the Admiralty Catalogue of Charts & Publications (available for purchase or inspection, at all appointed chart agents). This contains a map of the world on which the borders of the area covered by each Sailing Direction book are lined in. Although much of the contents of these 'pilots' is primarily for commercial vessels, there is much information of practical value to yacht navigation and pilotage. For example, the following types of information are given:

General description of islands and archipelagos
Lighthouses, lights (if any), landmarks
Leading lines, offlying dangers, shoals, rocks
Tidal streams
Anchorages
Port facilities, pilot stations, etc.

Charts

The number of charts bought for a long voyage is likely to be limited by considerations of space, if not also of cost. Nevertheless, it is imperative that all areas likely to be visited are covered. It is preferable to have medium-scale charts covering all areas rather than the same number of large-scale charts covering fewer places. The appropriate 'pilot' book usually contains details for safe pilotage into a port for which a large-scale chart is not aboard.

A voyage may need fifty or more charts. These should be arranged in the sequence in which they are likely to be needed, and divided up into batches of 6–12 each. Each such batch should be kept (flat) in a separate envelope or 'folio'. The most convenient is a clear plastic envelope measuring about 32 × 22 in. (say 82 × 56 cm) and preferably with the opening along the *long* side. Each batch should be placed in its folio with all the titles (which are printed on one of the lengthwise edges when folded) the same way up. This way, one can riffle through the edges to find the chart required, without withdrawing them all. A card should be stuck inside each envelope or folio, which can be read through the plastic, listing the number and title of each chart it contains.

It is probably unnecessary to remind you to make sure all charts have been 'corrected' by an official chart agent immediately prior to departure, to ensure they are up-to-date.

Ocean passages for the world

This HMSO publication is well worth studying by those planning an extensive trans-ocean voyage.

Exercise No. 13

1. On May 20th 1975, when in 49°40′ N
128°45′ W by DR a morning sun sight taken when
the chronometer (which was correct) showed
3ʰ 52ᵐ 10ˢ gave a sextant reading LL 27°49′.
Index error was 2·4 on the arc, ht of eye 10 ft.
   Yacht then sailed Co 120° T a distance 18 M,
when the sun's meridian alt. was, sextant LL
60°12′9 bearing S. Find the time of mer. pass.
GMT, and the OP then.

2. On February 17th 1975 when in 49°50′ S
159° E by DR a sun meridian alt. was taken. Find
the time by GMT of mer. pass., and the latitude if
sextant alt. LL was 52°19·8 bearing N. IE 2·0 on
the arc, H of E 8 ft.
   Yacht then sailed Co 080° T, 21 M by log, when
an afternoon sun sight was taken when the time
by (correct) chronometer was 05-54-50 GMT.
Sextant alt. LL 25°18·5. IE and dip same as before

3. On May 20th 1975 when in DR 50°15′ N
38°20′ W the following sights were taken at
evening twilight, sextant alts.

Moon, LL	33°35·1	at	22-54-12	GMT
Venus	25°58·1	at	22-54-45	GMT
Spica	27°03·1	at	22-55-25	GMT
Arcturus	51°03·0	at	22-55-51	GMT

Index error, 3·0 on the arc. H of E 8 ft. Find the
OP.

4. On May 20th 1975 when in DR 49°45′ N
18°15′ W morning twilight star sights are
planned. Using AP 3270 Vol. I 'Selected Stars',
choose the three stars best placed in azimuth. If
their sextant altitudes at the times given were as
follows, find the yacht's OP.
   At 04-52-35 GMT, sextant alt. 22°57·9

| 04-53-10 | ,, | 48°48·0 |
| 04-53-42 | ,, | 21°43·0 |

Index error, −3′·0, H of E 10 ft.

15. Radio and electronic aids

There are so many radio and electronic aids to navigation that several books would be required to cover the subject fully. Factors which have to be considered in deciding what equipment to carry include the space and the power available, distances involved and crew carried, and above all, the depth of one's pocket. It may simplify matters if we divide the subject over the principal uses to which such equipment can be put.

Communication and distress
The least expensive and simplest communication system is that provided by an 'emergency and survival' beacon. A number are available which will transmit and receive ONLY on the distress frequency 2182 kHz. These contain their own batteries, may be hand-held (some operate even when floating), and some will transmit a continuous two-tone signal to operate automatic alarm decoders in ships and coast stations within range. These cost around £80–150. Their range is very limited—probably 20 M to a maximum of 40 M. If no other radio telephone is carried, they are useful on coastal and short sea passages. With such a set one might have some chance of being heard in mid-ocean when on a shipping route— provided a ship happened to be in the vicinity.

VHF radio telephones (R/T) are carried by many yachts wishing to be able to contact other ships, port operations and for distress calls, but not GPO telephone subscribers. Rather more expensive VHF sets have 'twin-headed' receivers which can be used for GPO phone connections in addition to the foregoing. Again, their range is restricted to about 40 M. Prices range between about £300 and £600.

For R/T communication at ranges from 40 to about 400 M a radio telephone operating on the MF (2 MHz) shipping band is necessary. All fitted after 1 January 1973 must be SSB (single-sideband) sets, which cost appreciably more than the original DSB sets. These, and the VHF sets already mentioned, can be operated off a yacht's normal 12 or 24 volt supply, but as power to transmit may be up to 70–80 watts there must be provision for keeping batteries charged, either from the yacht's engine or by a separate generator. Prices vary between about £500 and upwards of £1,500.

For really long-range communication one has to have a R/T set which works on the HF bands 4–22 MHz, and costing £1,500 upwards. With such a set it is possible to communicate up to perhaps 3,000 M, but due to their relatively low power compared with the transmitters of ocean-going ships, difficulty may arise in establishing contact with shore stations. This is best dealt with by arranging, in advance, a schedule of calling-up dates and times with the GPO or other national body.

ocean yacht navigator

A compact radio telephone of VHF type. The Seavoice 25 watt 12 channel.

All R/T sets require a good aerial and earth. The backstay or triatic stay fitted with compression-insulators normally makes a good aerial. The best earth in a non-steel hull yacht is a copper plate (unpainted) of several square feet on hull exterior. As this is extremely inconvenient the 'Dynaplate' earth, made in USA, can be recommended. This is a small slab of sintered bronze pellets and is equivalent in action to a copper sheet of far greater area. All R/T equipment really must be installed by a competent marine radio expert—there are many pitfalls and unqualified installation is definitely not recommended.

Time signals

Probably the most valuable use of radio on long-distance passages is for getting time signals. If for any reason exact GMT is 'lost', celestial observations by sextant can only provide the ship's latitude. The determination of longitude depends on knowing GMT to an accuracy of about 5 seconds. A reliable radio receiver is

therefore essential. Any transistor radio capable of picking up the long wave band (200–400 kHz) used for broadcasting can be used, provided it is coupled to a good aerial, but its range may be restricted to under 1,000 M. Time signals are also available on many medium wave broadcasting services. Better sets, preferably those designed for marine use (such as the Zenith, B & G Ltd 'Homer', Sailor and many others) are recommended, at prices from about £100 upwards. Details of stations giving time signals are

One type of radio direction finder, the Autofix, which when tuned to the station finds its bearing automatically.

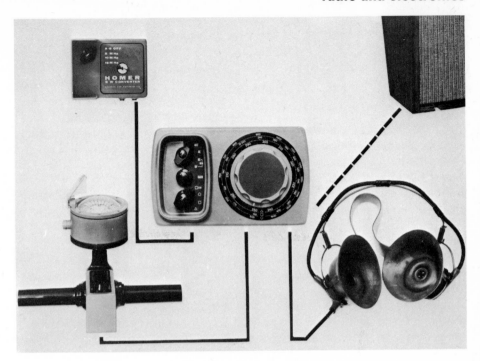

A reliable radio receiver and direction finder. The Brookes and Gatehouse Homer/Heron with a short wave converter which is very valuable for time signals at long ranges in the ocean.

given in ALRS Vol. V, Reed's nautical almanac and other books.

For very long-range work, a set capable of receiving the HF bands (4–22 MHz) is required. Even with the best of sets there are areas where time signals may not be heard. Recourse can sometimes be made to commercial and other stations broadcasting news and entertainment, when the announcer gives the time, accurate to perhaps a quarter of a minute, at programme changes. This is better than nothing. This underlines the necessity of maintaining good records of all proper time signals received so that the current deck watch error can be calculated from the record of the daily rate of change of the DWE. Even if a quartz crystal chronometer is carried, periodic time checks are still advisable.

This is referred to later under Clocks.

Good stations for time signals are BBC Radio 2 on 200 kHz (1,500 m), and the Overseas Service on a number of frequencies between 3·2 and 26·1 MHz. The powerful US station WWV on a number of frequencies between 2·5 and 25 MHz transmits continuous time signals by 'pips', the time (GMT) being stated by speech every five minutes. See ALRS Vol. V.

A point worth bearing in mind. An alarm clock is invaluable for avoiding missing a time check or a weather report.

Direction finding

Direction finding by radio (RDF) is available by a variety of systems and equipment. In general, the more expensive the equipment carried the

119

greater the range and accuracy.

Marine radiobeacons. Along coasts with a high density of shipping there are numerous radiobeacons. Their range is deliberately restricted to between 20 and 200 M to avoid interference with each other. They provide good position-finding when well within their listed range. At distances approaching their listed range one is unlikely to achieve an accuracy of bearing better than 3°–10°. Used in conjunction with a depth meter or leadline they can be of value, particularly in fog, on coastal and inshore passages. They should not be relied on for making a landfall unless the position is known to a fair degree of accuracy by other means.

Full details of all radiobeacons worldwide are given in ALRS Vol. II, together with method of using, frequencies, call signs and ranges. The book of diagrams issued with this book (NP 275,2a) charts all the radiobeacons. Study of this will show that there are vast lengths of coast where marine radiobeacons are hundreds of miles apart (Carribean, Africa, Australia and elsewhere), or non-existent (W. seaboard of S. America).

Aero radiobeacons. These can also be used for marine navigation, and there are now far more aero- than marine-radiobeacons. These are also listed in ALRS Vol. II and in the accompanying book of diagrams. Those in red are aero ; those in black are marine. Most aero beacons have quite limited range, but some have ranges of 200–500 M, making them of some use in long-distance passages. However, at distances approaching the listed range one is unlikely to achieve accuracy of bearing of better than 5°–10°. At 500 M range this could give a position line error of 40–80 M, i.e. a 'lane' up to 160 M wide. Compare this with a position line from a celestial sight, which even under poor conditions should be within say 10 M.

Sets capable of using marine or aero radiobeacons include :

(a) Self-contained hand-held sets incorporating a compass, enabling the compass bearing of a beacon within range to be read directly. Tune in to the beacon's frequency, turn the set to the direction of silence—the 'null' position, and read the bearing (C°). This may require correcting for the factors mentioned later. It is usually necessary to swing the set through a small arc horizontally so that the signal is just audible on each side of the 'null' position, reducing the swing till judged to be in the middle. Care should be taken to maintain the instrument level (not heeled). Cost in the bracket £30–£50. Batteries self-contained.

(b) Receiver incorporating a rotatable ferrite rod aerial (without compass). This will provide a relative bearing which must be related to the compass bearing of ship's head at the moment of taking the bearing. Some are provided with an azimuth ring which can be set to ship's head by steering compass, the compass bearing then being read direct. These will only give reliable results when the yacht's head can be relied on to be held steady while the bearing is being taken. Self-contained batteries, cost from about £30 to £120.

(c) As (b) above, but connected to a rotatable loop aerial either mounted on the set, or on coachroof or wheelhouse roof externally. Suitable for larger yachts or ones of steel construction. Can be used in conjunction with some R/T sets. Price bracket is £50 to £200.

(d) Receiver connected by co-axial cable to a hand-held ferrite rod aerial which incorporates a compass, enabling compass bearings to be read direct. The aerial/compass can be used with many R/T sets. Very suitable for most (non-steel) yachts. Cost of aerial/compass only, £100 upwards.

(e) Automatic direction finding set (ADF). When

tuned to the frequency of a beacon, or chain of beacons, the instrument locks-on to the transmitting station and automatically indicates its relative bearing. There are two main types of ADF set. With one type the relative bearing is indicated by means of a pointer and azimuth scale. In the other, a cathode ray tube is employed, on the screen of which a bright radial line is displayed in a direction corresponding to the relative bearing. An azimuth ring is fitted round the periphery of the CRT. Again, these are only suitable on a yacht which will hold a steady course while the bearing is being taken. Self-contained batteries. Prices are about £300 upwards.

(f) Fixed crossed-loop aerial with a Gonio DF tuner, coupled with a separate receiver or the receiver of a R/T set. This is best for the larger yacht which is relatively steady. An advantage is that the fixed loop aerial can be mounted, possibly at masthead, where it will be clear of structures or rigging which might otherwise induce radio distortion by re-radiation. Properly installed, this is probably the most accurate. Cost of aerial and tuner, but excluding receiver, is about £200.

Caution. All the foregoing DF sets may give erroneous bearings if the following points are overlooked:

(a) The direction of signals received may be distorted by Quadrantal Error (QE). (Fig. 81.) This may occur whenever the signal comes in from a direction over either fore- or aft-quarter, i.e. from around 45° from ahead or astern. The direction of the signal is distorted by re-radiation from mast or rigging. This can be minimized by insulating life-lines, wire rigging etc, so as to break any electrical 'loop' so formed. The amount and direction of the error must be determined, rather as one does for checking deviation, by sailing within sight of a radiobeacon. (Some radiobeacons transmit continuously at stated times for

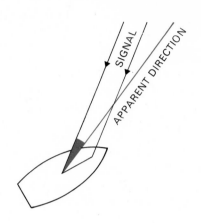

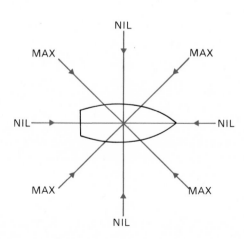

Fig. 81. Possibilities of error in an RDF signal. Quadrantal error depends on the direction of the signal in relation to the yacht and may be nil in fore and aft and athwartships directions.

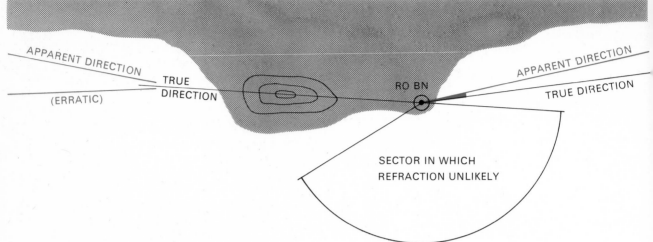

APPARENT DIRECTION

TRUE
DIRECTION

(ERRATIC)

RO BN

APPARENT DIRECTION

TRUE DIRECTION

SECTOR IN WHICH
REFRACTION UNLIKELY

Fig. 82.   Coastal refraction.

calibration purposes.) The relative bearing of the beacon taken visually is compared with that shown by the RDF aerial, while sailing on each of eight equidistant headings, from 'station ahead' round in a complete circle. A QE card can then be prepared, showing the amount and direction of the error for various relative bearings.

(b) If the RDF set incorporates an in-built compass (Seafix, B & G Heron, and others) the compass must be checked for deviation (when in its working position), as is required for a steering compass, and if any deviations exceeding 1°–2° are found on any ship's heading, a deviation card should be prepared—and USED.

(c) Coastal Refraction may cause RDF bearings to be distorted if the signal's path runs parallel to, or at a small angle from, the coast, or over high ground. Select beacons which are located where this will not arise. (Fig. 82.)

(d) Night Effect. At night, and particularly between an hour each side of sunrise and sunset, bearings taken of beacons more than about 20 M may be seriously distorted due to sky-wave effects. This is unlikely under 20 M.

Consol. Consol signals can be received on any radio capable of picking up the long wave band (200–400 kHz). No directional aerial is needed. All sets suitable for radiobeacons can be used. The set should have a BFO (beat frequency oscillator), on some sets marked 'navigate'. Consol is a long- to medium-range system for use between 25 M (minimum) and about 1,000 M from the Consol station. Unfortunately, the only areas covered are around UK and west of the Bay of Biscay. Its principal value is when entering (or leaving) the Western Approaches and in the North Sea. Consol stations are sited at Bushmills (N. Ireland), Stavanger (Norway), Ploneis

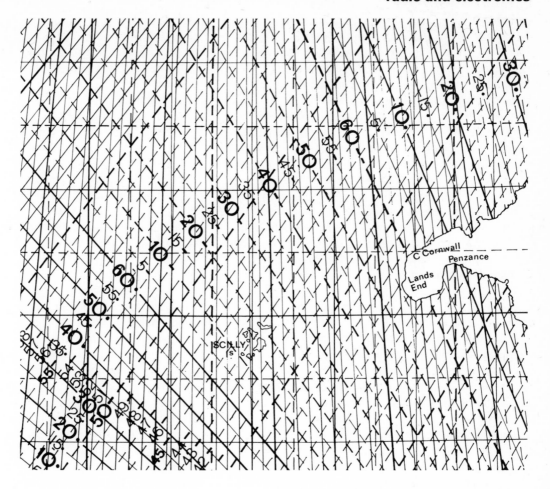

Fig. 83.   Part of a Consol chart

(Brittany), Lugo and Seville (Spain). There are other stations in the Arctic circle near Russia, but these are unlikely to be of interest to yachtsmen. Each station transmits continuously a signal consisting of its call sign for identification, in slow morse code, followed by a series of dots and dashes. From these it is quite easy to determine on which of a series of hyperbolic curves, radiating from each station, is the yacht's position. Beyond about 25 M (the minimum distance usable) these lines are great circle lines. The intersection of position lines from each of two, or preferably three, Consol stations gives the position. The position lines can most easily be found by using the Consol lattice chart for the area, which shows numbered lines radiating from the stations, each Consol's lines being printed in a different colour keyed to the appropriate station. If a Consol chart is not available, the true bearings of each 'count of dots and dashes' heard are tabulated for each station in ALRS Vol. 5. As these are great circles bearings they require converting to Mercator bearings by applying half-convergency, if the difference in longitude between ship and Consol station exceeds about 3°. (Below this it can be disregarded.)

The pattern of signals is repeated over sectors about 15° wide (depending on position) radiating from each station. It is therefore necessary to know the yacht's position to within (say) about 40 M to know in which sector she is. This is usually known, but if the DR position is seriously in doubt, a DF bearing, using a directional aerial on the Consol station should be quite accurate enough to resolve any ambiguity, the full 'count' giving the line within the sector on which is the position.

Accuracy to within 10 M is likely when within 500 M of the western seaboard of UK and N. France, and within 5 M when within 100 M.

These figures apply during daylight. At night, accuracy falls off steeply. The 'count' of each station should be repeated to check for consistency. This system should NOT be used for making a final landfall, for coastal navigation, nor when nearing dangers as it's accuracy is insufficient. Full details of the Consol stations, method of use, accuracy and warnings on use are given in ALRS Vol. V, Reed's Nautical Almanac and other publications.

Decca. This system is used by most merchant vessels, and by offshore fishermen and coastal shipping. In coastal waters its accuracy can be measured in yards rather than miles, and up to about 300 M from a Decca station accuracy of 2 M by day and 8 M at dusk (the worst time) is achieved. Special equipment, available only on hire from the Decca Navigation Co Ltd, is required. A chain of Decca transmitting stations, each having a master and two slave transmitters, send patterns of signals along hyperbolic lines radiating from each station. The Decca receiver displays on each of three dials coloured red, green and purple, corresponding to three Decca stations, the number of the line on which the ship is. The Admiralty publishes charts overprinted with the Decca lattices in the same three colours. A fourth dial is fitted for positive lane (segment) identification.

Busy shipping areas are covered, and certain major ports, but the system does not cover infrequented areas and is not suitable for ocean position-finding. Decca is relatively easy to use, but due to cost and size is seldom seen on yachts.

Loran-A and -C. Originally designed for aircraft, Loran can be used by vessels equipped with the necessary Loran equipment. This costs upwards of £1,000 and needs a fair degree of skill to operate. Loran-A is medium-range (500 M by day), and operates on the low-frequency band

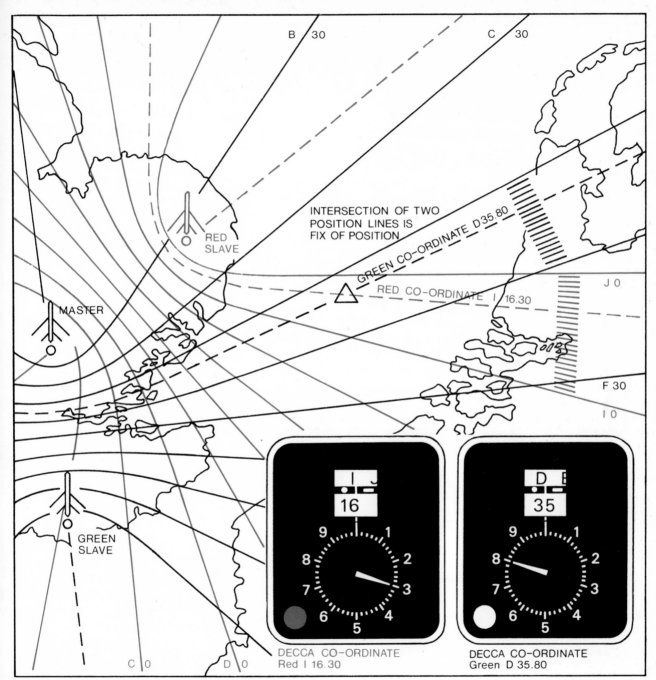

B 30 C 30

INTERSECTION OF TWO
POSITION LINES IS
FIX OF POSITION

GREEN CO-ORDINATE D 35.80

RED CO-ORDINATE I 16.30

J 0

F 30

I 0

RED
SLAVE

MASTER

GREEN
SLAVE

C 0 D 0

DECCA CO-ORDINATE
Red I 16.30

DECCA CO-ORDINATE
Green D 35.80

Fig. 84 Decca plotting chart.

ocean yacht navigator

Decca Navigator set, giving readings from which a plot can be made by reference to a chart with special overlay.

Decca Track Plotter. This maintains a plot of the ship's course, obtaining its information from a Decca Navigator.

1850–1950 kHz, while Loran-C is long-range (1,000 M) on low frequency band (90–110 kHz). The systems are not worldwide but cover the N. Atlantic, Mediterranean, North Sea, N. Pacific. Accuracy is high with Loran-C, moderate with Loran-A. Further details are given in ALRS Vol. V.

Omega. This system provides hyperbolic position-line data, as do both Consol and Loran, but over much greater ranges. At all points on a particular curve the phase difference between two Omega stations' signals is the same. To provide a position, two pairs of Omega stations' signals are received. The designation or number of each of two position lines is given on a digital readout. Reference to the Omega chart, overprinted with numbered position lines and segments provides the position. At present, Omega charts are only available covering N. Atlantic, the Mediterranean and western seaboard of N. America, but by 1975 worldwide cover should be available. Accuracy to 2 M is claimed, but some skill is required to lock-on to the transmitting stations to ensure correct segment identification, and to make the necessary corrections for diurnal shifts due to the sky waves.

The equipment has to be set up when at a known position (say in harbour) by establishing from the Omega lattice chart the segment numbers of the two lines of position (LOP) on which the yacht lies, and setting the instrument's counters to correspond. Provided the instrument is kept operating the counters will continue altering as the yacht's position changes. If the instrument stops working at sea the correct lane count will be lost. A very reliable power supply, and standby batteries are essential. Consumption is up to 40 watts. Cost is something over £1,500.

Satnav. Navigation by satellite is already in use by some HM ships, important ships like QE2, and special survey vessels. Accuracy is said to be

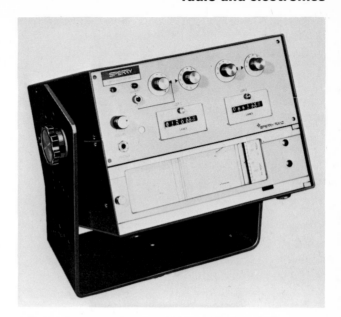

A Sperry Omega receiver set which provides hyperbolic position line data . . .

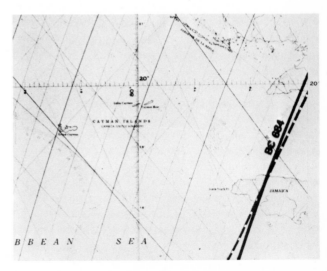

. . . which is read off from the Omega Lattice Chart.

to within a mile, but the cost may run to over £100,000. An equipment of slightly lower performance is said to be available at around £20,000, and with the speed of advance in miniaturization it is possible that the cost may fall dramatically in time. However, at present it has little application for the average yacht and will not be further discussed.

In conclusion, it is important to carry the best radio equipment you can afford which is suitable for your yacht and its electrical supply. But all such equipment is best regarded as only an extra AID to orthodox navigation, not as a substitute. Consider it as another 'shot in the locker', to be used to confirm or support other evidence, or to use when visual methods are not available. Even then, confirm by SOUNDINGS if in shoal water.

Other electronic navigational aids

A master magnetic compass directing one or more repeater heads or compass faces has some advantages. The master compass can be located anywhere in the yacht, perhaps in the position where it is subject to the least yaw and pitch movement and away from ferrous material. More reliable and steadier readings can then be expected under rough conditions. The repeater heads can be sited wherever they will be most visible and useful. Some have grid-steering facilities which remove much of the strain of keeping a lubberline to a particular compass reading, it only needing one line or pointer to be maintained over another. A possible disadvantage is that all require a constant and reliable electrical supply, albeit of only about 100 milliamps. If such a compass is to be the principal steering compass it is essential that a normal magnetic compass is also carried, with suitable provision for fixing it, in case of breakdown.

This type of compass is also available with an 'off-course alarm', invaluable when a yacht may be on self-steering by windvane or by auto pilot, for obvious reasons. A further refinement is available in the Brookes and Galehouse 'Hadrian 2' Course Indicator and Distance-off-course computer. In addition to an off-course alarm, this instrument, when coupled to a 'Harrier' log, will give on a dial up-to-date information of the distance in miles (to two decimal places) which the yacht has wandered off course, to port or starboard, from a required, pre-set course. It cannot of course make allowance for drift by set of tide, or for leeway, which must be applied on the chart. Subject to this, it shows the amount and direction of helm correction needed to bring the yacht back on to the required track line. A second simple pointer dial also shows the helmsman the amount and direction of helm correction required to bring the yacht back on course, i.e. a very simple 'grid' arrangement.

Log. Probably the second most important instrument, after the compass, is the log, necessary for recording the distance sailed through the water. The traditional and well-proven method is with the so-called 'patent log', by Walkers and other makers. It comprises a rotating impeller towed on a long line connected to a deck-mounted head or recorder. These are also available with a speed indicator. There are a number of electronic logs which are driven by quite a small rotating impeller protruding only an inch or two from the hull, which have the advantage of being less susceptible to fouling by weed, and to being bitten off by sharks, which can happen to a towed log. Some models have impellers which can be retracted from inside the hull for clearance.

The latest logs have no external moving parts and work on the Doppler principle. A high-frequency signal is beamed ahead from a small transducer on the underwater hull. A small

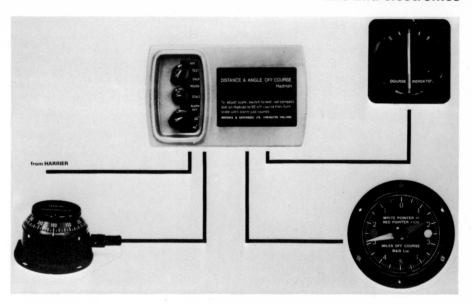

The Hadrian device which shows how far the helmsman has strayed off the ordered course. The course indicator at top right can be mounted in the cockpit, the course selected on the compass (bottom left), and the helmsman keeps the needle lined up.

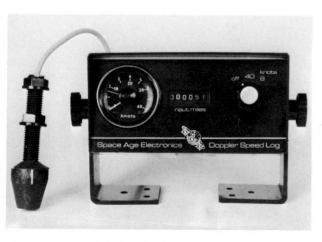

A Doppler type speedometer and log.

An electro-magnetic log set for the navigator.

A walker display for log and speed.

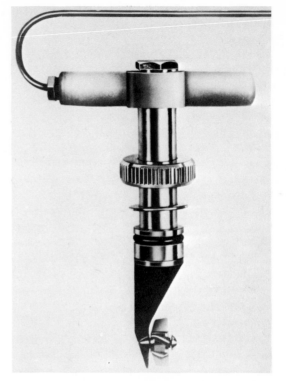

The Walker impeller unit for log and speed.

part of the signal is reflected back from the boundary layer between water and hull. The difference between the frequency of the outgoing and incoming impulses is translated into speed. The instrument relates this speed to time and thus computes distance, which is displayed in digits. Accuracy of 1% for distance and 3% for speed is claimed.

Another distance and speed meter which has no external moving parts is the Walker Electromagnetic log. A virtually flush-fitting transducer on the hull skin creates a magnetic field in the water. The field is changed by the speed of passage of

water, and the instrument computes from this both speed and distance run, which are displayed on the instrument which can be located wherever most convenient.

Depth meters. Most yachts now have an echo sounder. The less expensive ones (below about £100) are usually calibrated only to 60 fathoms, and some of these will not in fact register depths beyond about half this depth. Excellent for inshore work, their value for offshore sailing is somewhat limited. For example, on a passage to the Channel Islands it can be useful to know when the yacht crosses the Hurd Deep—well over 50 fathoms.

It is also useful to be able to take soundings when approaching or over the Continental shelf. For these purposes a depth meter which will register to 100 fathoms or more can be of great help to the ocean navigator. These are available at not unreasonable cost, but unlike the 'shallow' ones which will work off internal dry cells, they need a yacht's supply of electricity.

Clocks. Reference has already been made to the necessity for accurate GMT (to within 2–5 secs.) to be available for taking celestial sights. A number of quartz crystal chronometers are now on the market at prices considerably below those of spring-driven chronometers. Powered by internal batteries with a life of over a year, their daily rate may be no more than 0·1 sec per day. Even with these, periodic radio time checks are advisable to confirm the current error and to check the daily rate. As the best of electric equipment CAN go wrong, an orthodox (spring-driven) deck watch, or other reliable timepiece should be carried as a reserve—AND be duly checked for DWE regularly. Remember, you CANNOT find longitude by sextant without accurate time.

Alarm Clock. All prudent inshore yachtsmen listen in to shipping and coastal waters weather reports, and few have not at some time missed an important one by switching on a minute or two late. If time signals, and possibly weather and other messages are to be regularly received, some form of alarm, set to go off a few minutes before the required time, is invaluable. Even a cheap bedside alarm clock is better than nothing. There are a few ship's clocks with this facility.

Tape recorder. Apart from its more obvious uses, a tape recorder which can be plugged in or can 'listen in' to the radio can be useful for recording a complete weather report in speech. This enables it to be transcribed later on to a proper weather report pad, from which one may construct one's own synoptic chart. From this fair predictions of weather can be made. Many shore stations, and weather ships, transmit weather reports ('Synop' or 'Ship') by W/T (morse code). Few yachtsmen who are not qualified signallers can read this morse at the speed used. However, if recorded, it is by no means impossible to tape the message and subsequently to listen to 'bits' at a time, to transcribe and, with the aid of the meteorological codes given in ALRS Vol. III to de-code and thus to form a picture of the weather pattern.

Barometer and barograph. Changes in

Modern quartz chronometer.

barometric pressure are vital indications of weather, and a regular record should be maintained. An aneroid barometer (the type most usually carried) should be read, and recorded, in the log book at least at two-hourly intervals. When in the tropics or other areas where tropical revolving storms may occur, regular recording of pressure is most important. Hourly barometric pressure can be plotted on graph paper, or more readily on paper designed for use on a barograph. If space and the pocket permit, a barograph is preferable as it gives a continuous trace of pressure, from which the steepness of the line shows the rate of change at a glance.

There are some further instruments that help navigation, such as wind direction indicators (apparent wind; 360° and close-hauled), wind speed indicators and v.m.g. computers, but these are principally of value to the racing yacht. Radar sets are of value when navigating within about 20 M of land, and for collision avoidance in fog. (Details are given in *Practical Yacht Navigator*.) Some can be fitted with an alarm triggered off by 'targets' within a pre-set distance. These have their use in coastal and inshore waters, and some for racing yachts, but would seem to be of very limited value for an ocean passage.

Appendix 1
Alternative Sight Reduction Tables

Several different Sight Reduction Tables are available. All are designed to give the true altitude of a heavenly body as at a chosen position, and the bearing of its GP, at any required time, and thus to work up a sight.

The principal ones are:

(a) Sight Reduction Tables for Air Navigation AP 3270 (UK) or HO 249 (US).

Vol. 1 gives the Tabulated Alt. & Bearing (not Azimuth) of 7 selected *stars*, against LHA Aries and lat. of chosen position.

Various stars are tabulated, those selected being the 7 most favourably placed for particular lats. and LHA Aries.

Advantages: Alt. & Bearing are shown against LHA Aries (not LHA Star), thus saving one calculation. The stars listed are situated at suitable altitudes and bearings relative to each other to give good angles of cut of the position lines. Certainly the quickest way of working up multiple star sights.

Disadvantages: Covers stars only: cannot be used for planets, moon or sun.

Vol. 2 gives tab. alt. (Hc) and Azimuth (Z) for observations of ANY heavenly body having a Declination between 0° and 29° N or S, and where the CP is between 0° and 45° N or S. Table entered with lat. of CP, Dec. of body, LHA of body observed.

Vol. 3 as Vol. 2 but for lats. of CP between 45° and 89° N or S.

Thus, Vols. 2 and 3 will cover sights taken anywhere in the world of sun, moon, planets and of 29 of the 57 stars listed in the Nautical Almanac. Stars with Dec. exceeding 30° N or S cannot be used.

Accuracy, within 1', often within 0'·2.

(b) Tables of Computed Altitude & Azimuth. NP 401 (UK) or HO 229 (US).

Published in six volumes, each covering a band of latitudes 15° wide (N or S), and decl. from 0° to 89° N or S. Tabulated for every $\frac{1}{2}$° of Dec., and every 1° of Lat. If required, corrections for minutes of Lat. can be made.

Advantages: Each volume deals with *all* bodies of any declination, within bands of lats. covered by the volume, so will deal with *all* stars. Fractionally more accurate than AP 3270, but this has no practical advantage for yacht navigation.

Disadvantages: Four quite large volumes are required to cover the world up to 60° N or S. Weight, space and cost.

Appendix 2
The P Z X Triangle

The altitude which a heavenly body would be, if observed from a chosen position (or a DR) of known lat. and long. can be found by calculation, instead of sight reduction tables. Calculation requires the solution of a spherical triangle, commonly referred to as the PZX triangle, where P is the Pole, Z is the chosen position and X the body's GP. (Fig. 85.)

In spherical trigonometry, the sides of a spherical triangle are measured in arc (degrees & minutes). The arc Z–X is the angular distance, measured at the centre of the earth, between Z and X. It is part of a great circle, and is the zenith distance of the body as observed at Z. The compliment of the ZD is the altitude. If we can calculate the angle Z–X we can determine the 'calculated alt.' at Z (the CP or DR). We can then compare this with the true alt. (as found by sextant) and thus find the distance of our true circle of position from the CP or DR, which gives us the Intercept.

If we know two sides of a spherical triangle and the included angle, we can find the third side, and either of the two other angles. In the illustration Fig. 85, we know

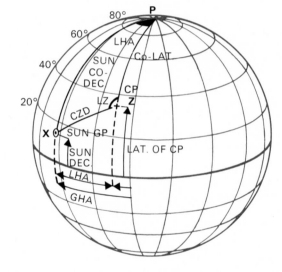

Fig. 85.

Lat. of CP, so the Co-lat. (90°-lat.) = PZ
Dec. of body, so the Co-dec. (90°-dec.) = PX
LHA is same as angle at the pole, between PZ and PX = the angle P

The formula for finding the side ZX (the CZD) is:
Hav. ZX = (Hav. P × sin. PZ × sin. PX) + Hav. (PZ ~ PX)

We can substitute our terms:
Hav. CZD = (Hav. LHA × cos. Lat. × cos. Dec.) + Hav. (Lat. ~ Dec.)

As logs. are being used, multiplication is not required, and we can re-write:

```
   log. Hav. LHA          . . . . . .
 +log. Cos. Lat.          . . . . . .
 +log. Cos. Dec.          . . . . . .
                          _____
              = log Hav.  . . . . . .
              = Nat. Hav. . . . . . .
Nat. Hav. (lat. ~ dec.)   + . . . . . .
                          _____
              Nat. Hav.   . . . . . .
              = CZD       . . ° . .'
              from        90° . .
                          _____
         CALC. ALT   . . ° . .'
```

(Lat. ~ dec.— same names, subtract smaller from larger; contrary names, add together.)

We also need the bearing of the body's GP from the CP (or DR if we are using it). This is the angle PZX, and is the Z found when using AP 3270. If sight reduction tables are not being used, this too can be calculated, but there is little point in doing so as it can be much more easily found by using the ABC tables (explained in Appendix 3).

The term Polar Distance is used by some authorities instead of co-dec.

Appendix 3
Marcq St Hilaire Haversine Method

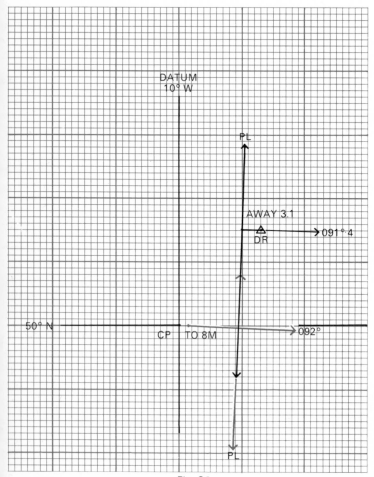

Fig. 86

This method is of value

(a) If no sight reduction tables are available, or those available do not cover the yacht's lat. or the dec. of a required star.

(b) If it is desired to purchase or carry the minimum number of books. (Only a nautical almanac and Norie's, Burton's or other table book having Haversine table and logs. of trig. functions are required—two books in all.)

(c) For checking sights taken from a known position, for practice. No plotting is then necessary. The known position can be used instead of a chosen position to get the calculated altitude (instead of tab. alt.) for comparison with the true alt. from sextant. A perfect sight would give an intercept of nil. the difference between calc. alt. and true alt. will at once give the error of the sight.

The Marcq St Hilaire method requires the same data as is called for when using any sight reduction tables, namely:

> LHA of body sighted
> Lat. of DR (or CP)
> Dec. of body sighted.

This data should be laid out in precisely the same order as that recommended earlier for all sights. Instead of getting a Tabulated Alt. (from sight reduction tables) the equivalent figure is calculated, and called the Calc. Alt. This is arrived at in the following way, the sequence of working recommended being shown on the left, and the method stated below:

Example:

						Page in
	GHA^h	46°08'				
Sequence	Incr.	8°14'				
of		54°22'				Page in
working	DR long. W	−10°22'			Norie	Burton

						Norie	Burton
4.	LHA	44°00	log. Hav.	9·14715		441	181
2.	DR lat.	N 50°	log. Cos.	9·80807		243	151
3.	Dec.	S 16°57'	log. Cos.	9·98071		209	142
5.			log. Hav.	8·93593			
6.		= nat. Hav.		08628		431	178
1, 7.	Lat. ~ dec.	66°57' → nat. Hav.		30423		463	189
8.		nat. Hav.		39051			
9.		= Calc. ZD	77°21'·1			474	192
10.		from	90°				
		CALC. ALT.	12°38'·9				

Sequence of work:

1. Lat. ~ dec.
   if **S**AME NAMES (N or S), **S**UBTRACT
   if **C**ONTRARY NAMES,   ADD (**c**ombine)
2 & 3. Under table of 'Logs of Trig. Functions, find angle in column 'Cosine' (Burtons 'Cos.' col.). (We have now finished with this table.)
4. In Haversine table, column headed 'Log'.
5. Add up, discarding tens unit (e.g. 28·93593 above).
6. In Haversine table, find the log. Hav. just determined. Read the equivalent Nat. Hav. printed alongside it.
7. In same table, find the Nat. Hav. of lat. ~ dec.
8. Add up the two Nat. Hav.s (6 & 7).
9. In same table, find the Nat. Hav. just determined (8). Read equivalent angle from table. This is the Calc. ZD.
10. Subtract the answer from 90°. This is the Calc. Alt.

Then compare Calc. Alt. with True Alt. exactly as before. Result using AP3270 tables. If the same data (LHA, lat. & dec. are used, AP 3270 gives tab. alt. 12°39′, and bearing 223°.

To find the bearing of the body, use A B C Tables

LHA 44° ⎫ Lat. 50° ⎬	Value 'A' = S 1·23		Norie p. 516	Burton p. 264
LHA 44° ⎫ Dec. 16°57 ⎬	'B' = S ·44		517	265
	'C'	S 1·67 & lat. 50°		
	= S 43° W		540	279
Bearing	= 223° T			

The A B C Tables are used as follows:
(a) Using Norie's Tables, pp. 504–552.

Enter Table A with LHA at the top, and lat. down the side. Extract the value 'A', interpolating if necessary. Enter Table B (which will always face the page of Table A just used) with LHA again at top and now Dec. down the side. Extract the 'B' value. Give both 'A' and 'B' values the name as indicated in margin of each page.

Sum up 'A' and 'B'. (Same names, add; contrary names, subtract smaller from larger and name as the larger.)

The result is the value 'C'.

Enter Table 'C' with the 'C' value found, at top and with lat. down the side. The figure found is the Azimuth, which should be named as given at the foot of the C table page.
(b) Using Burton's Tables, pp. 246–285.

A & B tables as Norie's but using signs instead of N or S. Follow precept at top of page. Burton's Table 'C' is laid out differently. This lists LHA across the top of each page, and lat. down the side.

To use, first find the lat. down the side of a page. Having found the correct horizontal line, follow this along, if necessary from one page to the next, till the 'C' factor (found from A and B combined), is reached. Travel up this column to top, where the Azimuth is read. Name the azimuth according to the precepts given at the top. Interpolate as necessary.

Example of a full Sight worked out by Marcq St Hilaire Haversine method.

1975 May 19th at 07-52-15 GMT, DR 50°15′ N 9°40′ W. IE −2′0. H of E, 6 ft.

GHA^h 07	285°54·1	Dec.	N 19°38·9
Incr. 52 – 15ˢ	13°03·8	d + 0·5	+0·4
	298°57·9		N 19°39·3
DR long. W	−9°40·0		
LHA	289°17·9	log. Hav.	9·52473
DR lat.	N 50°15·0	log. Cos.	9·80580
Dec.	N 19°39·3	log. Cos.	9·97393

log. Hav.	9·30446
= Nat. Hav.	20158
Lat. ∼ Dec. 30°35·7 → Nat. Hav.	06960
Nat. Hav.	27118
= CZD	62°45·9
from	90°
Calc. Alt.	27°14·1

Sext. alt. LL	27°01·3
IE −2·0	
Dip. −2·4	
	−4·4
	26°56·9
Cor.	+14·1
True Alt.	27°11·0
Calc. Alt.	27°14·1

INTERCEPT AWAY 3·1

Bearing of Intercept:

Using Norie's A B C Tables:

LHA 289°17·9 ⎫
Lat.   50°15·0 ⎭ A = 0·42 S

LHA 289°17·9 ⎫
Dec.   19°39·3 ⎭ B = 0·38 N

C   0·04 S = S 88°·6 E = 091°·4, say 091°

or using Burton's Tables:

Same data as above   A = +·421

B = −·377

C   ·044 = S 88°·6 E = 091°·4, say 091°

If this sight (using the DR position) and the sight on Fig. 93, p. 144 (using a CP) are compared, the lengths of the intercepts will be seen to differ —because each starts from a different point (DR and CP). But when both are plotted the respective position lines correspond to within the thickness of a pencil line. (Fig. 86, p. 136.)

Appendix 4
Log book examples

Deck log book

DATE	TIME Z + 1	LOG READING	COURSE REQ'D	COURSE STEERED	WIND	BARO.	REMARKS
Aug 28	1200	648	065°	065°	SW 4	1004	Mer. Alt. Sight
	1400	659	"	"	WSW5	1006	
	1600	671	"	"	W6	1008	Reefed Main, No 2 jib
	1800	682	"	"	W5	1010	
	2000	694	"	"	NW4	1006	Unreefed, No 2 genoa
	2200	704	"	"	W4	1004	
	2400	715	"	"	W3	1004	Set No 1 genoa
Aug 29			Similar entries				
Aug 30	0400	863	065°	065°	SW4	996	
	0600	875	"	"	"	994	
	0655	888	"	"	"	994	a.m. Sight A
	1000	906	"	"	WSW3	998	
	1145	916	"	"	SW4	1000	Mer. Alt. Sight B
	1400	923	"	"	"	1004	Saw tanker. 5M to S
	1800	945	"	"	"	1004	
	2400	977	"	"	W5	1008	
Aug 31	0400	999	065°	065°	NW4	1008	
	0600	016	"	"	NW3	1002	
	0750	023	"	"	W4	1002	DR worked up for a.m. sight C

Fig. 87.

140

Navigators log book

DATE Z+1 TIME 1975	LOG		COURSE						STREAM			POSITION
	READ'G	MILES SINCE LAST PLOT	Co. C°	DEV.	VAR.	T°	LEE WAY	WAKE Co. T°	DIR.	RATE	DRIFT	
Aug 28 1200	648											O.P. 47°50'N 17°30'W
30 0655	888	240	065°	E +4	W -12	057°	+5	062°	090°	½ k	21·5	D.R. 49°43'N 11°41'W [A] a.m. sight
1145	916	28	065°	+4	-12	057°	+5	062°	090°	½ k	2·5	Mer. Alt [B] O.P. 49°53'N 10°48'W
31 0750	23	107	065°	+4	-12	057°	+5	062°	090°	½	10	D.R. 51°02'N 8°25'W [C]

Fig. 88.

SIGHT BOOK [A]

1975 Aug 30   0655 Z+1   Dr 49°43'N   11°41'W
                     07-49-11 DWT   IE -2'.2
          DWE +   4-04
                     07-53-15 GMT

GHA   07h   284°47°.7   N 9°12'.1
      53-15   13 18 .8   d-0.9   -0 .8
                298°06 .5   N 9°11 .3
CP long   W - 11 06 .5
   LHA   287°
CP lat   N   50°   SEXT ALT LL   17°33'.9
   Dec   N   9°11   IE   -2.2
                              Dip   -2.7   -   4 .9
   Hc   17°47'   17°29 .0
   d,+46   +   8   Cor   +   13 .0
   Tab Alt   17°55   TRUE ALT   17°42
                            TAB ALT   17°55
   Z,97° = Zn   INTERCEPT (away)   13'

Fig. 89.

ocean yacht navigator

NAVIGATOR'S CALCULATIONS   1975 Aug 30   DR 49°55'N 10°47'W   IE -2'.2   Ht of E 8ft

1975   OP   47°50'.0N 17°30'W

Aug 28   Z+1   1200
                  to
Aug 30   Z+1   0655
                 Co.062°T=N62°E 240M
                 D.Lat 112'.7   =   1°52'.7N
                          Dep   211.9E
                 Current 090' at ½kn
                 43 hrs= N90°E 21.5M
                 D.Lat   nil
                          Dep   21.5E
                 Total Dep   233.4
                 In mean lat48° =
                 D.Lon 349'E   =   5°49'E
                 DR for am sight   49°42'.7N 11°41'W

Aug 30   Z+1   1145   OP B   49.53'.0N 10°48'W
                  to
Aug 31   Z+1   0750
                 Co.062°T=N62E 107M
                 D.Lat   68.8N   =   1°08'.8N
                          Dep   82.0E
                 Current 090°at ½kn
                 20 hrs= N90°E 10M
                 D.Lat   nil
                          Dep   10.0E
                 Total Dep   92.0E
                 In mean lat50° =
                 D.Lon 143'E   2°23'E
                 DR for am sight C   51°02'.0N   8°25'W

Fig. 90.

Mer Pass   1201 LMT
Long 10°47'W = + 43
                  1244 GMT

SEXTANT ALT LL 49°03'.8 Brg S
IE   -2.2
Dip   -2.7   -   4 .9
                  48°58'.9
Cor   +   15 .2
TRUE ALT   49°14'.1 S
       from   90°
TZD   40°45'.9 N
Dec 12h 9°07'.7N
d,-.9 44m - .6   9°07 .1 N
LATITUDE   49°53'.0 N

Fig. 91

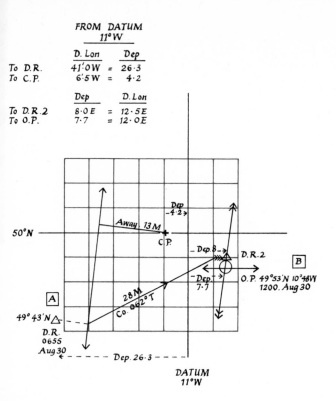

Fig. 92.

Appendix 5
Sight forms

EXAMPLE OF A SUN SIGHT

1975 May 19	07-52-05 DWT	DR 50°15N 9°40'W
DWE	+ 10	IE -2.0 H of E 6ft
	07-52-15 GMT	

GHA	07h 285°54'.1	Dec N 19°38'.9	
Inc 52m15s	13°03 .8	d,+0.5 + 0 .4	
	298°57'.9	N 19°39'.3	
CP long	W- 9°57'.9		
LHA	289°	Sext Alt L.L.27°01'.3	
CP lat	N 50°	IE -2.0	
Dec	N 19°39	Dip -2.4 - 4'.4	
			26°56'.9
Hc	26°34'	Cor + 14'.1	
d,+44	+ 29'	TRUE ALT 27°11'.0	
Tab Alt	27°03'	TAB ALT 27°03'.0	
	Z, 92° = Zn	Intercept TO ____ ____ 8'.0	

Fig. 93.

SIGHT FORM   SUN

Date ____ 19 __ h __ m __ s		DWT in DR _____	Ht of E _____	
		DWE		
	____ GMT			
GHA m	h ___ ° ___ ' s	Dec ___ ° ___ '		
Incr	_____	d,+ _____		
GHA				
CP long (E+ W-)	_____	SEXTANT ALT: L ___ ° ___ '		
LHA	_____	IE		
CP lat		Dip _____ _____		
Dec		(App Alt)		
		Cor _____		
Hc	___ ° ___ '	TRUE ALT		
d,+	_____	TAB ALT		
TAB ALT	_____			
		INTERCEPT (towards) _____		
Z Zn	_____	(away) _____		

True Alt: GREATER than Tab: TOWARDS
True Alt: LESS than Tab: AWAY

Fig. 94.

SIGHT FORM   SUN - MERID ALT

Date _____ 19   Position by DR _____ Ht of E _____

Mer Pass _____ h ___ m on G.Merid
DR long in time (W+ / E- _____
Time of transit _____ GMT at DR

SEXTANT ALT: L _____ ° _____
  IE
  Dip _____   _____

  Cor   _____
True Alt
  from   90° _____
  TZD
Dec _____ ° _____
d,± _____   _____
LATITUDE _____

Fig. 95.

SIGHT FORM   MOON

Date _____ ___h ___m ___s DWT DR _____ Ht of E _____

                DWE _____
                GMT _____

GHA ___h ___ ° _____ Dec _____
V, + _____   d,± _____

CPlong (E+ / W- _____   SEXTANT ALT LL/UL* _____ ° _____
  LHA   IE
CPlat   Dip _____   _____
  Dec
                                  Cor
Hc _____ ° _____   HP   _____
d,± _____   * (if UL, -30')
Tab Alt _____   TRUE ALT
                                  TAB ALT   _____
Z _____ ° Z _____ °   INTERCEPT (Towards)
     = Zn _____   (Away) _____

Fig. 96.

145

ocean yacht navigator

SIGHT FORM   STAR
(Using Vols 2 and 3 only of AP3270 or HO249 or NP401)

Date _____ h m s DWT   DR _____ Ht of E _____
             DWE _____
                   _____ GMT

SHA Star   ° '   Dec   ° '
GHA Aries h
        m s
             _____

GHA Star
CP long ($_{W-}^{E+}$) _____   SEXTANT ALT
  LHA Star   IE
CP lat   Dip   _____ _____
  Dec Star
                                        Cor   _____
HC   ° '   TRUE ALT
d,+   TAB ALT   _____
TAB ALT   INTERCEPT (towards)
          Z   °   (away)   _____

        = Zn   °

Fig. 98.

SIGHT FORM   POLARIS

Date _____ h m s DWT   DR _____ Ht of E _____
             DWE _____
                   _____ GMT

GHA Aries h   SEXTANT ALT   °
        m s   ° '   IE
             _____   Dip   _____

DR long ($_{W-}^{E+}$) _____   Cor   _____
LHA Aries   _____

                                Polaris A$_o$
                                        A$_1$
                                        A$_2$
                                                       -1°
                                LATITUDE   _____

Appendix 6
Nautical Almanac, extracts from 1975

A2 ALTITUDE CORRECTION TABLES 10°-90°—SUN, STARS, PLANETS

SUN — OCT.—MAR.

App. Alt.	Lower Limb	Upper Limb
9 34	+10.8	−21.5
9 45	+10.9	−21.4
9 56	+11.0	−21.3
10 08	+11.1	−21.2
10 21	+11.2	−21.1
10 34	+11.3	−21.0
10 47	+11.4	−20.9
11 01	+11.5	−20.8
11 15	+11.6	−20.7
11 30	+11.7	−20.6
11 46	+11.8	−20.5
12 02	+11.9	−20.4
12 19	+12.0	−20.3
12 37	+12.1	−20.2
12 55	+12.2	−20.1
13 14	+12.3	−20.0
13 35	+12.4	−19.9
13 56	+12.5	−19.8
14 18	+12.6	−19.7
14 42	+12.7	−19.6
15 06	+12.8	−19.5
15 32	+12.9	−19.4
15 59	+13.0	−19.3
16 28	+13.1	−19.2
16 59	+13.2	−19.1
17 32	+13.3	−19.0
18 06	+13.4	−18.9
18 42	+13.5	−18.8
19 21	+13.6	−18.7
20 03	+13.7	−18.6
20 48	+13.8	−18.5
21 35	+13.9	−18.4
22 26	+14.0	−18.3
23 22	+14.1	−18.2
24 21	+14.2	−18.1
25 26	+14.3	−18.0
26 36	+14.4	−17.9
27 52	+14.5	−17.8
29 15	+14.6	−17.7
30 46	+14.7	−17.6
32 26	+14.8	−17.5
34 17	+14.9	−17.4
36 20	+15.0	−17.3
38 36	+15.1	−17.2
41 08	+15.2	−17.1
43 59	+15.3	−17.0
47 10	+15.4	−16.9
50 46	+15.5	−16.8
54 49	+15.6	−16.7
59 23	+15.7	−16.6
64 30	+15.8	−16.5
70 12	+15.9	−16.4
76 26	+16.0	−16.3
83 05	+16.1	−16.2
90 00		

SUN — APR.—SEPT.

App. Alt.	Lower Limb	Upper Limb
9 39	+10.6	−21.2
9 51	+10.7	−21.1
10 03	+10.8	−21.0
10 15	+10.9	−20.9
10 27	+11.0	−20.8
10 40	+11.1	−20.7
10 54	+11.2	−20.6
11 08	+11.3	−20.5
11 23	+11.4	−20.4
11 38	+11.5	−20.3
11 54	+11.6	−20.2
12 10	+11.7	−20.1
12 28	+11.8	−20.0
12 46	+11.9	−19.9
13 05	+12.0	−19.8
13 24	+12.1	−19.7
13 45	+12.2	−19.6
14 07	+12.3	−19.5
14 30	+12.4	−19.4
14 54	+12.5	−19.3
15 19	+12.6	−19.2
15 46	+12.7	−19.1
16 14	+12.8	−19.0
16 44	+12.9	−18.9
17 15	+13.0	−18.8
17 48	+13.1	−18.7
18 24	+13.2	−18.6
19 01	+13.3	−18.5
19 42	+13.4	−18.4
20 25	+13.5	−18.3
21 11	+13.6	−18.2
22 00	+13.7	−18.1
22 54	+13.8	−18.0
23 51	+13.9	−17.9
24 53	+14.0	−17.8
26 00	+14.1	−17.7
27 13	+14.2	−17.6
28 33	+14.3	−17.5
30 00	+14.4	−17.4
31 35	+14.5	−17.3
33 20	+14.6	−17.2
35 17	+14.7	−17.1
37 26	+14.8	−17.0
39 50	+14.9	−16.9
42 31	+15.0	−16.8
45 31	+15.1	−16.7
48 55	+15.2	−16.6
52 44	+15.3	−16.5
57 02	+15.4	−16.4
61 51	+15.5	−16.3
67 17	+15.6	−16.2
73 16	+15.7	−16.1
79 43	+15.8	−16.0
86 32	+15.9	−15.9
90 00		

STARS AND PLANETS

App. Alt.	Corrn
9 56	−5.3
10 08	−5.2
10 20	−5.1
10 33	−5.0
10 46	−4.9
11 00	−4.8
11 14	−4.7
11 29	−4.6
11 45	−4.5
12 01	−4.4
12 18	−4.3
12 35	−4.2
12 54	−4.1
13 13	−4.0
13 33	−3.9
13 54	−3.8
14 16	−3.7
14 40	−3.6
15 04	−3.5
15 30	−3.4
15 57	−3.3
16 26	−3.2
16 56	−3.1
17 28	−3.0
18 02	−2.9
18 38	−2.8
19 17	−2.7
19 58	−2.6
20 42	−2.5
21 28	−2.4
22 19	−2.3
23 13	−2.2
24 11	−2.1
25 14	−2.0
26 22	−1.9
27 36	−1.8
28 56	−1.7
30 24	−1.6
32 00	−1.5
33 45	−1.4
35 40	−1.3
37 48	−1.2
40 08	−1.1
42 44	−1.0
45 36	−0.9
48 47	−0.8
52 18	−0.7
56 11	−0.6
60 28	−0.5
65 08	−0.4
70 11	−0.3
75 34	−0.2
81 13	−0.1
87 03	0.0
90 00	

STARS AND PLANETS — Additional Corrn

1975

VENUS

Jan. 1 – June 7
App. Alt.	Additional Corrn
0° – 42°	+0.1

June 8 – July 21
App. Alt.	Additional Corrn
0° – 46°	+0.3

July 22 – Aug. 6
App. Alt.	Additional Corrn
0° – 11°	+0.4
11° – 41°	+0.5

Aug. 7 – Aug. 15
App. Alt.	Additional Corrn
0° – 6°	+0.6
6° – 20°	+0.7
20° – 31°	

Aug. 16 – Sept. 10
App. Alt.	Additional Corrn
0° – 4°	+0.6
4° – 12°	+0.7
12° – 22°	+0.8

Sept. 11 – Sept. 19
App. Alt.	Additional Corrn
0° – 6°	+0.5
6° – 20°	+0.6
20° – 31°	+0.7

Sept. 20 – Oct. 5
App. Alt.	Additional Corrn
0° – 11°	+0.4
11° – 41°	+0.5

Oct. 6 – Nov. 22
App. Alt.	Additional Corrn
0° – 46°	+0.3

Nov. 23 – Dec. 31
App. Alt.	Additional Corrn
0° – 42°	+0.1

MARS

Jan. 1 – Sept. 8
App. Alt.	Additional Corrn
0° – 60°	+0.1

Sept. 9 – Nov. 22
App. Alt.	Additional Corrn
0° – 41°	+0.2
41° – 75°	+0.1

Nov. 23 – Dec. 31
App. Alt.	Additional Corrn
0° – 34°	+0.3
34° – 60°	+0.2
60° – 80°	+0.1

DIP

Ht. of Eye (m)	Corrn	Ht. of Eye (ft)
2.4	−2.8	8.0
2.6	−2.9	8.6
2.8	−3.0	9.2
3.0	−3.1	9.8
3.2	−3.1	10.5
3.4	−3.2	11.2
3.6	−3.3	11.9
3.8	−3.4	12.6
4.0	−3.5	13.3
4.3	−3.6	14.1
4.5	−3.7	14.9
4.7	−3.8	15.7
5.0	−3.9	16.5
5.2	−4.0	17.4
5.5	−4.1	18.3
5.8	−4.2	19.1
6.1	−4.3	20.1
6.3	−4.4	21.0
6.6	−4.5	22.0
6.9	−4.6	22.9
7.2	−4.7	23.9
7.5	−4.8	24.9
7.9	−4.9	26.0
8.2	−5.0	27.1
8.5	−5.1	28.1
8.8	−5.2	29.2
9.2	−5.3	30.4
9.5	−5.4	31.5
9.9	−5.5	32.7
10.3	−5.6	33.9
10.6	−5.7	35.1
11.0	−5.8	36.3
11.4	−5.9	37.6
11.8	−6.0	38.9
12.2	−6.1	40.1
12.6	−6.2	41.5
13.0	−6.3	42.8
13.4	−6.4	44.2
13.8	−6.5	45.5
14.2	−6.6	46.9
14.7	−6.7	48.4
15.1	−6.8	49.8
15.5	−6.9	51.3
16.0	−7.0	52.8
16.5	−7.1	54.3
16.9	−7.2	55.8
17.4	−7.3	57.4
17.9	−7.4	58.9
18.4	−7.5	60.5
18.8	−7.6	62.1
19.3	−7.7	63.8
19.8	−7.8	65.4
20.4	−7.9	67.1
20.9	−8.0	68.8
21.4	−8.1	70.5

See table (lower heights)

Ht. of Eye (m)	Corrn		Ht. of Eye (ft)	Corrn
1.0	−1.8		2	−1.4
1.5	−2.2		4	−1.9
2.0	−2.5		6	−2.4
2.5	−2.8		8	−2.7
3.0	−3.0		10	−3.1

See table (higher heights)

Ht. of Eye (m)	Corrn		Ht. of Eye (ft)	Corrn
20	−7.9		70	−8.1
22	−8.3		75	−8.4
24	−8.6		80	−8.7
26	−9.0		85	−8.9
28	−9.3		90	−9.2
30	−9.6		95	−9.5
32	−10.0		100	−9.7
34	−10.3		105	−9.9
36	−10.6		110	−10.2
38	−10.8		115	−10.4
40	−11.1		120	−10.6
42	−11.4		125	−10.8
44	−11.7		130	−11.1
46	−11.9		135	−11.3
48	−12.2		140	−11.5
			145	−11.7
			150	−11.9
			155	−12.1

App. Alt. = Apparent altitude = Sextant altitude corrected for index error and dip.
For daylight observations of Venus, see page 260.

ocean yacht navigator

1975 FEBRUARY 15, 16, 17 (SAT., SUN., MON.)

G.M.T.	ARIES G.H.A.	VENUS −3.4 G.H.A.	Dec.	MARS +1.5 G.H.A.	Dec.	JUPITER −1.6 G.H.A.	Dec.	SATURN 0.0 G.H.A.	Dec.	STARS Name	S.H.A.	Dec.
15 00	144 22.8	153 25.9 S 5	19.6	214 55.7 S22	57.8	150 52.2 S 3	59.3	40 41.6 N22	32.0	Acamar	315 40.2	S40 24.5
01	159 25.3	168 25.5	18.3	229 56.1	57.6	165 54.1	59.0	55 44.2	32.0	Achernar	335 48.3	S57 22.0
02	174 27.7	183 25.1	17.0	244 56.6	57.4	180 56.1	58.8	70 46.8	32.0	Acrux	173 41.0	S62 57.7
03	189 30.2	198 24.8 ··	15.8	259 57.0 ··	57.1	195 58.0 ··	58.6	85 49.4 ··	32.0	Adhara	255 34.8	S28 56.5
04	204 32.7	213 24.4	14.5	274 57.5	56.9	211 00.0	58.4	100 52.0	32.1	Aldebaran	291 22.3	N16 27.6
05	219 35.1	228 24.0	13.2	289 57.9	56.7	226 01.9	58.1	115 54.6	32.1			
06	234 37.6	243 23.6 S 5	11.9	304 58.4 S22	56.5	241 03.8 S 3	57.9	130 57.1 N22	32.1	Alioth	166 45.4	N56 05.3
07	249 40.0	258 23.3	10.7	319 58.9	56.3	256 05.8	57.7	145 59.7	32.1	Alkaid	153 21.2	N49 25.9
S 08	264 42.5	273 22.9	09.4	334 59.3	56.0	271 07.7	57.4	161 02.3	32.1	Al Na'ir	28 20.1	S47 04.9
A 09	279 45.0	288 22.5 ··	08.1	349 59.8 ··	55.8	286 09.6 ··	57.2	176 04.9 ··	32.1	Alnilam	276 15.3	S 1 13.2
T 10	294 47.4	303 22.1	06.8	5 00.2	55.6	301 11.6	57.0	191 07.5	32.2	Alphard	218 24.0	S 8 33.2
U 11	309 49.9	318 21.8	05.6	20 00.7	55.4	316 13.5	56.8	206 10.1	32.2			
R 12	324 52.4	333 21.4 S 5	04.3	35 01.1 S22	55.2	331 15.4 S 3	56.5	221 12.7 N22	32.2	Alphecca	126 35.3	N26 47.6
D 13	339 54.8	348 21.0	03.0	50 01.6	54.9	346 17.4	56.3	236 15.3	32.2	Alpheratz	358 13.5	N28 57.3
A 14	354 57.3	3 20.7	01.7	65 02.1	54.7	1 19.3	56.1	251 17.9	32.2	Altair	62 36.5	N 8 48.1
Y 15	9 59.8	18 20.3 5	00.5	80 02.5 ··	54.5	16 21.3 ··	55.8	266 20.5 ··	32.2	Ankaa	353 44.3	S42 26.6
16	25 02.2	33 19.9 4	59.2	95 03.0	54.3	31 23.2	55.6	281 23.1	32.3	Antares	113 01.6	S26 22.6
17	40 04.7	48 19.6	57.9	110 03.4	54.0	46 25.1	55.4	296 25.7	32.3			
18	55 07.2	63 19.2 S 4	56.6	125 03.9 S22	53.8	61 27.1 S 3	55.1	311 28.3 N22	32.3	Arcturus	146 21.8	N19 18.4
19	70 09.6	78 18.8	55.3	140 04.4	53.6	76 29.0	54.9	326 30.8	32.3	Atria	108 29.4	S68 58.8
20	85 12.1	93 18.4	54.1	155 04.8	53.3	91 30.9	54.7	341 33.4	32.3	Avior	234 29.2	S59 26.0
21	100 14.5	108 18.1 ··	52.8	170 05.3 ··	53.1	106 32.9 ··	54.5	356 36.0 ··	32.3	Bellatrix	279 02.7	N 6 19.6
22	115 17.0	123 17.7	51.5	185 05.7	52.9	121 34.8	54.2	11 38.6	32.4	Betelgeuse	271 32.2	N 7 24.1
23	130 19.5	138 17.3	50.2	200 06.2	52.7	136 36.7	54.0	26 41.2	32.4			
16 00	145 21.9	153 17.0 S 4	49.0	215 06.6 S22	52.5	151 38.7 S 3	53.8	41 43.8 N22	32.4	Canopus	264 08.5	S52 41.2
01	160 24.4	168 16.6	47.7	230 07.1	52.2	166 40.6	53.5	56 46.4	32.4	Capella	281 16.7	N45 58.6
02	175 26.9	183 16.2	46.4	245 07.6	52.0	181 42.5	53.3	71 49.0	32.4	Deneb	49 51.5	N45 11.4
03	190 29.3	198 15.9 ··	45.1	260 08.0 ··	51.8	196 44.5 ··	53.1	86 51.6 ··	32.4	Denebola	183 02.6	N14 42.4
04	205 31.8	213 15.5	43.8	275 08.5	51.6	211 46.4	52.9	101 54.2	32.5	Diphda	349 24.9	S18 07.5
05	220 34.3	228 15.1	42.6	290 08.9	51.3	226 48.3	52.6	116 56.7	32.5			
06	235 36.7	243 14.8 S 4	41.3	305 09.4 S22	51.1	241 50.3 S 3	52.4	131 59.3 N22	32.5	Dubhe	194 26.1	N61 52.9
07	250 39.2	258 14.4	40.0	320 09.9	50.9	256 52.2	52.2	147 01.9	32.5	Elnath	278 48.8	N28 35.3
08	265 41.6	273 14.0	38.7	335 10.3	50.6	271 54.1	51.9	162 04.5	32.5	Eltanin	90 59.8	N51 29.3
S 09	280 44.1	288 13.6 ··	37.4	350 10.8 ··	50.4	286 56.1 ··	51.7	177 07.1 ··	32.5	Enif	34 15.6	N 9 45.6
U 10	295 46.6	303 13.3	36.2	5 11.2	50.2	301 58.0	51.5	192 09.7	32.6	Fomalhaut	15 55.9	S29 45.3
N 11	310 49.0	318 12.9	34.9	20 11.7	49.9	317 00.0	51.2	207 12.3	32.6			
D 12	325 51.5	333 12.6 S 4	33.6	35 12.1 S22	49.7	332 01.9 S 3	51.0	222 14.9 N22	32.6	Gacrux	172 32.6	S56 58.4
A 13	340 54.0	348 12.2	32.3	50 12.6	49.5	347 03.8	50.8	237 17.4	32.6	Gienah	176 21.6	S17 24.4
Y 14	355 56.4	3 11.8	31.0	65 13.1	49.2	2 05.8	50.6	252 20.0	32.6	Hadar	149 28.5	S60 15.1
15	10 58.9	18 11.5 ··	29.8	80 13.5 ··	49.0	17 07.7 ··	50.3	267 22.6 ··	32.6	Hamal	328 33.3	N23 20.8
16	26 01.4	33 11.1	28.5	95 14.0	48.8	32 09.6	50.1	282 25.2	32.7	Kaus Aust.	84 22.1	S34 23.8
17	41 03.8	48 10.7	27.2	110 14.4	48.5	47 11.6	49.9	297 27.8	32.7			
18	56 06.3	63 10.4 S 4	25.9	125 14.9 S22	48.3	62 13.5 S 3	49.6	312 30.4 N22	32.7	Kochab	137 18.5	N74 15.1
19	71 08.8	78 10.0	24.6	140 15.4	48.1	77 15.4	49.4	327 33.0	32.7	Markab	14 07.2	N15 04.3
20	86 11.2	93 09.6	23.3	155 15.8	47.8	92 17.4	49.2	342 35.6	32.7	Menkar	314 45.1	N 3 59.5
21	101 13.7	108 09.3 ··	22.1	170 16.3 ··	47.6	107 19.3 ··	48.9	357 38.1 ··	32.7	Menkent	148 41.3	S36 14.9
22	116 16.1	123 08.9	20.8	185 16.7	47.4	122 21.2	48.7	12 40.7	32.7	Miaplacidus	221 44.9	S69 37.1
23	131 18.6	138 08.5	19.5	200 17.2	47.1	137 23.2	48.5	27 43.3	32.8			
17 00	146 21.1	153 08.2 S 4	18.2	215 17.7 S22	46.9	152 25.1 S 3	48.2	42 45.9 N22	32.8	Mirfak	309 21.6	N49 46.6
01	161 23.5	168 07.8	16.9	230 18.1	46.7	167 27.0	48.0	57 48.5	32.8	Nunki	76 34.1	S26 19.7
02	176 26.0	183 07.5	15.6	245 18.6	46.4	182 29.0	47.8	72 51.1	32.8	Peacock	54 04.9	S56 48.8
03	191 28.5	198 07.1 ··	14.4	260 19.0 ··	46.2	197 30.9 ··	47.6	87 53.7 ··	32.8	Pollux	244 02.5	N28 05.1
04	206 30.9	213 06.7	13.1	275 19.5	45.9	212 32.8	47.3	102 56.2	32.8	Procyon	245 29.5	N 5 17.2
05	221 33.4	228 06.4	11.8	290 20.0	45.7	227 34.8	47.1	117 58.8	32.9			
06	236 35.9	243 06.0 S 4	10.5	305 20.4 S22	45.5	242 36.7 S 3	46.9	133 01.4 N22	32.9	Rasalhague	96 33.3	N12 34.5
07	251 38.3	258 05.6	09.2	320 20.9	45.2	257 38.6	46.6	148 04.0	32.9	Regulus	208 13.7	N12 05.1
08	266 40.8	273 05.3	07.9	335 21.3	45.0	272 40.6	46.4	163 06.6	32.9	Rigel	281 39.5	S 8 13.9
M 09	281 43.3	288 04.9 ··	06.7	350 21.8 ··	44.7	287 42.5 ··	46.2	178 09.2 ··	32.9	Rigil Kent.	140 30.8	S60 43.8
O 10	296 45.7	303 04.6	05.4	5 22.3	44.5	302 44.4	45.9	193 11.7	32.9	Sabik	102 45.6	S15 41.7
N 11	311 48.2	318 04.2	04.1	20 22.7	44.3	317 46.4	45.7	208 14.3	33.0			
D 12	326 50.6	333 03.8 S 4	02.8	35 23.2 S22	44.0	332 48.3 S 3	45.5	223 16.9 N22	33.0	Schedar	350 13.8	N56 24.3
A 13	341 53.1	348 03.5	01.5	50 23.6	43.8	347 50.2	45.2	238 19.5	33.0	Shaula	97 01.1	S37 05.1
Y 14	356 55.6	3 03.1 4	00.2	65 24.1	43.5	2 52.2	45.0	253 22.1	33.0	Sirius	258 58.8	S16 41.1
15	11 58.0	18 02.8 3	58.9	80 24.6 ··	43.3	17 54.1 ··	44.8	268 24.7 ··	33.0	Spica	159 01.3	S11 02.1
16	27 00.5	33 02.4	57.7	95 25.0	43.0	32 56.0	44.6	283 27.2	33.0	Suhail	223 13.1	S43 20.1
17	42 03.0	48 02.0	56.4	110 25.5	42.8	47 58.0	44.3	298 29.8	33.0			
18	57 05.4	63 01.7 S 3	55.1	125 25.9 S22	42.6	62 59.9 S 3	44.1	313 32.4 N22	33.1	Vega	80 58.7	N38 45.4
19	72 07.9	78 01.3	53.8	140 26.4	42.3	78 01.8	43.9	328 35.0	33.1	Zuben'ubi	137 37.2	S15 56.4
20	87 10.4	93 01.0	52.5	155 26.9	42.1	93 03.8	43.6	343 37.6	33.1		S.H.A.	Mer. Pass.
21	102 12.8	108 00.6 ··	51.2	170 27.3 ··	41.8	108 05.7 ··	43.4	358 40.2 ··	33.1	Venus	7 55.0	13 47
22	117 15.3	123 00.3	49.9	185 27.8	41.6	123 07.6	43.2	13 42.7	33.1	Mars	69 44.7	9 39
23	132 17.7	137 59.9	48.6	200 28.3	41.3	138 09.5	42.9	28 45.3	33.1	Jupiter	6 16.7	13 52
Mer. Pass. 14 16.2		v −0.4	d 1.3	v 0.5	d 0.2	v 1.9	d 0.2	v 2.6	d 0.0	Saturn	256 21.9	21 09

1975 FEBRUARY 15, 16, 17 (SAT., SUN., MON.) 41

G.M.T.	SUN G.H.A.	SUN Dec.	MOON G.H.A.	v	Dec.	d	H.P.
15 00	176 26.7	S12 57.8	139 52.5	15.4	N 6 39.7	10.6	54.3
01	191 26.7	56.9	154 26.9	15.3	6 50.3	10.6	54.3
02	206 26.8	56.1	169 01.2	15.3	7 00.9	10.6	54.3
03	221 26.8 ··	55.2	183 35.5	15.3	7 11.5	10.6	54.4
04	236 26.8	54.4	198 09.8	15.2	7 22.1	10.5	54.4
05	251 26.8	53.5	212 44.0	15.3	7 32.6	10.5	54.4
06	266 26.9	S12 52.7	227 18.3	15.1	N 7 43.1	10.5	54.3
07	281 26.9	51.8	241 52.4	15.2	7 53.6	10.4	54.4
S 08	296 26.9	51.0	256 26.6	15.1	8 04.0	10.5	54.4
A 09	311 27.0 ··	50.1	271 00.7	15.1	8 14.5	10.4	54.4
T 10	326 27.0	49.3	285 34.8	15.0	8 24.9	10.3	54.4
U 11	341 27.0	48.4	300 08.8	15.0	8 35.2	10.4	54.5
R 12	356 27.0	S12 47.5	314 42.8	15.0	N 8 45.6	10.3	54.5
D 13	11 27.1	46.7	329 16.8	14.9	8 55.9	10.3	54.5
A 14	26 27.1	45.8	343 50.7	14.8	9 06.2	10.2	54.5
Y 15	41 27.1 ··	44.9	358 24.5	14.9	9 16.4	10.2	54.5
16	56 27.1	44.1	12 58.4	14.8	9 26.6	10.2	54.5
17	71 27.2	43.3	27 32.2	14.7	9 36.8	10.1	54.6
18	86 27.2	S12 42.4	42 05.9	14.7	N 9 46.9	10.1	54.6
19	101 27.2	41.5	56 39.6	14.7	9 57.0	10.1	54.6
20	116 27.3	40.7	71 13.3	14.6	10 07.1	10.0	54.6
21	131 27.3 ··	39.8	85 46.9	14.6	10 17.1	10.0	54.6
22	146 27.3	39.0	100 20.5	14.5	10 27.1	10.0	54.6
23	161 27.4	38.1	114 54.0	14.5	10 37.1	9.9	54.7
16 00	176 27.4	S12 37.2	129 27.5	14.4	N10 47.0	9.9	54.7
01	191 27.4	36.4	144 00.9	14.4	10 56.9	9.8	54.7
02	206 27.4	35.5	158 34.3	14.3	11 06.7	9.8	54.7
03	221 27.5 ··	34.7	173 07.6	14.3	11 16.5	9.7	54.7
04	236 27.5	33.8	187 40.9	14.2	11 26.2	9.7	54.7
05	251 27.5	32.9	202 14.1	14.2	11 35.9	9.7	54.8
06	266 27.6	S12 32.1	216 47.3	14.1	N11 45.6	9.6	54.8
07	281 27.6	31.2	231 20.4	14.1	11 55.2	9.6	54.8
08	296 27.6	30.4	245 53.5	14.0	12 04.8	9.5	54.8
S 09	311 27.7 ··	29.5	260 26.5	14.0	12 14.3	9.5	54.8
U 10	326 27.7	28.6	274 59.5	13.9	12 23.8	9.4	54.9
N 11	341 27.7	27.8	289 32.4	13.8	12 33.2	9.4	54.9
D 12	356 27.8	S12 26.9	304 05.2	13.8	N12 42.6	9.4	54.9
A 13	11 27.8	26.0	318 38.0	13.8	12 52.0	9.3	54.9
Y 14	26 27.9	25.2	333 10.8	13.7	13 01.3	9.2	54.9
15	41 27.9 ··	24.3	347 43.5	13.6	13 10.5	9.2	55.0
16	56 27.9	23.4	2 16.1	13.6	13 19.7	9.1	55.0
17	71 28.0	22.6	16 48.7	13.5	13 28.8	9.1	55.0
18	86 28.0	S12 21.7	31 21.2	13.4	N13 37.9	9.0	55.0
19	101 28.0	20.8	45 53.6	13.4	13 46.9	9.0	55.0
20	116 28.1	20.0	60 26.0	13.4	13 55.9	8.9	55.1
21	131 28.1 ··	19.1	74 58.4	13.2	14 04.8	8.9	55.1
22	146 28.1	18.2	89 30.6	13.2	14 13.7	8.8	55.1
23	161 28.2	17.4	104 02.8	13.2	14 22.5	8.7	55.1
17 00	176 28.2	S12 16.5	118 35.0	13.1	N14 31.2	8.7	55.2
01	191 28.3	15.6	133 07.1	13.0	14 39.9	8.7	55.2
02	206 28.3	14.8	147 39.1	12.9	14 48.6	8.5	55.2
03	221 28.3 ··	13.9	162 11.0	12.9	14 57.1	8.5	55.2
04	236 28.4	13.0	176 42.9	12.8	15 05.6	8.5	55.2
05	251 28.4	12.2	191 14.7	12.8	15 14.1	8.4	55.3
06	266 28.5	S12 11.3	205 46.5	12.7	N15 22.5	8.3	55.3
07	281 28.5	10.4	220 18.2	12.6	15 30.8	8.2	55.3
08	296 28.5	09.5	234 49.8	12.6	15 39.0	8.2	55.3
M 09	311 28.6 ··	08.7	249 21.4	12.5	15 47.2	8.2	55.4
O 10	326 28.6	07.8	263 52.9	12.4	15 55.4	8.0	55.4
N 11	341 28.7	06.9	278 24.3	12.3	16 03.4	8.0	55.4
D 12	356 28.7	S12 06.0	292 55.6	12.3	N16 11.4	7.9	55.4
A 13	11 28.8	05.2	307 26.9	12.2	16 19.3	7.9	55.5
Y 14	26 28.8	04.3	321 58.1	12.2	16 27.2	7.8	55.5
15	41 28.8 ··	03.4	336 29.3	12.1	16 35.0	7.7	55.5
16	56 28.9	02.6	351 00.4	12.0	16 42.7	7.6	55.6
17	71 28.9	01.7	5 31.4	11.9	16 50.3	7.6	55.6
18	86 29.0	S12 00.8	20 02.3	11.9	N16 57.9	7.5	55.6
19	101 29.0	11 59.9	34 33.2	11.7	17 05.4	7.4	55.6
20	116 29.1	59.1	49 03.9	11.8	17 12.8	7.3	55.7
21	131 29.1 ··	58.2	63 34.7	11.6	17 20.1	7.3	55.7
22	146 29.2	57.3	78 05.3	11.6	17 27.4	7.1	55.7
23	161 29.2	56.4	92 35.9	11.5	17 34.5	7.2	55.7
	S.D. 16.2	d 0.9	S.D. 14.8		15.0		15.1

Lat.	Twilight Naut.	Civil	Sunrise	Moonrise 15	16	17	18
N 72	06 13	07 33	08 52	07 13	06 54	06 28	☐
N 70	06 12	07 24	08 32	07 24	07 14	07 02	06 42
68	06 10	07 16	08 17	07 33	07 30	07 27	07 24
66	06 09	07 09	08 05	07 41	07 43	07 46	07 53
64	06 08	07 03	07 54	07 47	07 53	08 02	08 15
62	06 06	06 58	07 45	07 53	08 02	08 15	08 32
60	06 05	06 54	07 37	07 58	08 10	08 26	08 47
N 58	06 04	06 50	07 31	08 03	08 17	08 36	08 59
56	06 03	06 46	07 25	08 06	08 23	08 44	09 10
54	06 01	06 43	07 19	08 10	08 29	08 52	09 20
52	06 00	06 40	07 15	08 13	08 34	08 58	09 28
50	05 59	06 37	07 10	08 16	08 39	09 05	09 ·36
45	05 56	06 30	07 01	08 23	08 48	09 18	09 52
N 40	05 53	06 25	06 53	08 28	08 57	09 29	10 06
35	05 50	06 20	06 46	08 33	09 04	09 38	10 17
30	05 47	06 15	06 40	08 37	09 10	09 47	10 28
20	05 41	06 07	06 29	08 44	09 21	10 01	10 45
N 10	05 33	05 58	06 20	08 50	09 31	10 14	11 00
0	05 25	05 50	06 11	08 56	09 40	10 26	11 16
S 10	05 15	05 40	06 02	09 02	09 49	10 38	11 29
20	05 02	05 29	05 52	09 09	09 59	10 51	11 44
30	04 46	05 16	05 41	09 16	10 10	11 05	12 02
35	04 36	05 08	05 34	09 20	10 17	11 14	12 12
40	04 23	04 58	05 26	09 25	10 24	11 24	12 24
45	04 08	04 46	05 18	09 31	10 33	11 35	12 39
S 50	03 47	04 32	05 07	09 38	10 43	11 50	12 56
52	03 37	04 25	05 02	09 41	10 48	11 56	13 04
54	03 26	04 17	04 57	09 45	10 54	12 03	13 13
56	03 12	04 08	04 50	09 49	11 00	12 12	13 23
58	02 56	03 58	04 43	09 53	11 06	12 21	13 35
S 60	02 36	03 46	04 36	09 58	11 14	12 32	13 49

Lat.	Sunset	Twilight Civil	Naut.	Moonset 15	16	17	18
N 72	15 38	16 57	18 17	23 43	25 43	01 43	☐
N 70	15 58	17 06	18 18	23 25	25 10	01 10	03 09
68	16 13	17 14	18 20	23 10	24 47	00 47	02 28
66	16 25	17 21	18 21	22 59	24 28	00 28	02 00
64	16 35	17 26	18 22	22 49	24 14	00 14	01 39
62	16 44	17 31	18 23	22 41	24 01	00 01	01 22
60	16 52	17 36	18 25	22 34	23 51	25 08	01 08
N 58	16 59	17 40	18 26	22 28	23 42	24 56	00 56
56	17 04	17 43	18 27	22 22	23 34	24 46	00 46
54	17 10	17 46	18 28	22 18	23 27	24 37	00 37
52	17 15	17 49	18 29	22 13	23 21	24 28	00 28
50	17 19	17 52	18 30	22 09	23 15	24 21	00 21
45	17 28	17 59	18 33	22 01	23 03	24 06	00 06
N 40	17 36	18 04	18 36	21 53	22 53	23 53	24 53
35	17 43	18 09	18 38	21 47	22 44	23 42	24 41
30	17 49	18 13	18 42	21 42	22 36	23 32	24 30
20	17 59	18 22	18 48	21 33	22 24	23 16	24 11
N 10	18 09	18 30	18 55	21 25	22 12	23 02	23 54
0	18 18	18 39	19 03	21 17	22 02	22 49	23 39
S 10	18 27	18 48	19 13	21 09	21 51	22 36	23 24
20	18 36	18 59	19 25	21 01	21 40	22 22	23 07
30	18 47	19 12	19 42	20 52	21 27	22 05	22 49
35	18 54	19 20	19 52	20 47	21 20	21 56	22 38
40	19 01	19 30	20 04	20 41	21 11	21 45	22 25
45	19 10	19 41	20 19	20 34	21 01	21 33	22 11
S 50	19 20	19 55	20 39	20 26	20 50	21 18	21 53
52	19 25	20 02	20 49	20 22	20 44	21 11	21 44
54	19 30	20 10	21 00	20 18	20 38	21 03	21 35
56	19 37	20 18	21 13	20 13	20 32	20 54	21 24
58	19 43	20 28	21 29	20 08	20 24	20 45	21 12
S 60	19 51	20 40	21 48	20 02	20 16	20 33	20 58

Day	SUN Eqn. of Time 00ʰ	12ʰ	Mer. Pass.	MOON Mer. Pass. Upper	Lower	Age	Phase
15	14 13	14 12	12 14	15 07	02 45	04	
16	14 11	14 09	12 14	15 51	03 28	05	◐
17	14 07	14 05	12 14	16 37	04 14	06	

1975 MAY 19, 20, 21 (MON., TUES., WED.)

G.M.T.	ARIES G.H.A.	VENUS −3.7 G.H.A.	Dec.	MARS +1.0 G.H.A.	Dec.	JUPITER −1.7 G.H.A.	Dec.	SATURN +0.4 G.H.A.	Dec.	STARS Name	S.H.A.	Dec.
19 00	236 02.7	134 41.2 N25	35.2	237 01.4 S 2	10.4	222 33.8 N 4	31.9	129 09.4 N22	24.4	Acamar	315 40.4	S40 24.1
01	251 05.1	149 40.6	35.1	252 02.1	09.6	237 35.8	32.1	144 11.6	24.4	Achernar	335 48.4	S57 21.5
02	266 07.6	164 40.0	34.9	267 02.8	08.9	252 37.8	32.3	159 13.8	24.3	Acrux	173 40.9	S62 58.1
03	281 10.1	179 39.4 ··	34.7	282 03.6 ··	08.2	267 39.8 ··	32.5	174 16.0 ··	24.3	Adhara	255 35.2	S28 56.5
04	296 12.5	194 38.8	34.5	297 04.3	07.4	282 41.8	32.7	189 18.2	24.3	Aldebaran	291 22.5	N16 27.6
05	311 15.0	209 38.2	34.3	312 05.0	06.7	297 43.8	32.9	204 20.4	24.3			
06	326 17.5	224 37.6 N25	34.1	327 05.8 S 2	06.0	312 45.7 N 4	33.1	219 22.6 N22	24.2	Alioth	166 45.3	N56 05.7
07	341 19.9	239 37.1	33.9	342 06.5	05.2	327 47.7	33.3	234 24.7	24.2	Alkaid	153 20.9	N49 26.2
08	356 22.4	254 36.5	33.7	357 07.2	04.5	342 49.7	33.5	249 26.9	24.2	Al Na'ir	28 19.5	S47 04.5
M 09	11 24.8	269 35.9 ··	33.5	12 08.0 ··	03.7	357 51.7 ··	33.7	264 29.1 ··	24.2	Alnilam	276 15.7	S 1 13.1
O 10	26 27.3	284 35.3	33.3	27 08.7	03.0	12 53.7	33.8	279 31.3	24.1	Alphard	218 24.2	S 8 33.3
N 11	41 29.8	299 34.7	33.1	42 09.4	02.3	27 55.7	34.0	294 33.5	24.1			
D 12	56 32.2	314 34.1 N25	32.9	57 10.2 S 2	01.5	42 57.6 N 4	34.2	309 35.7 N22	24.1	Alphecca	126 34.8	N26 47.8
A 13	71 34.7	329 33.6	32.7	72 10.9	00.8	57 59.6	34.4	324 37.9	24.1	Alpheratz	358 13.3	N28 57.2
Y 14	86 37.2	344 33.0	32.5	87 11.6 2	00.1	73 01.6	34.6	339 40.1	24.0	Altair	62 35.9	N 8 48.1
15	101 39.6	359 32.4 ··	32.3	102 12.4 1	59.3	88 03.6 ··	34.8	354 42.3 ··	24.0	Ankaa	353 44.1	S42 26.2
16	116 42.1	14 31.8	32.1	117 13.1	58.6	103 05.6	35.0	9 44.5	24.0	Antares	113 00.9	S26 22.7
17	131 44.6	29 31.2	31.9	132 13.8	57.8	118 07.6	35.2	24 46.7	24.0			
18	146 47.0	44 30.7 N25	31.7	147 14.6 S 1	57.1	133 09.6 N 4	35.4	39 48.9 N22	23.9	Arcturus	146 21.5	N19 18.5
19	161 49.5	59 30.1	31.5	162 15.3	56.4	148 11.5	35.6	54 51.0	23.9	Atria	108 27.9	S68 59.0
20	176 52.0	74 29.5	31.3	177 16.0	55.6	163 13.5	35.8	69 53.2	23.9	Avior	234 30.0	S59 26.2
21	191 54.4	89 28.9 ··	31.1	192 16.8 ··	54.9	178 15.5 ··	36.0	84 55.4 ··	23.9	Bellatrix	279 03.0	N 6 19.6
22	206 56.9	104 28.3	30.9	207 17.5	54.2	193 17.5	36.2	99 57.6	23.8	Betelgeuse	271 32.5	N 7 24.1
23	221 59.3	119 27.8	30.7	222 18.2	53.4	208 19.5	36.4	114 59.8	23.8			
20 00	237 01.8	134 27.2 N25	30.5	237 19.0 S 1	52.7	223 21.5 N 4	36.6	130 02.0 N22	23.8	Canopus	264 09.3	S52 41.2
01	252 04.3	149 26.6	30.3	252 19.7	51.9	238 23.5	36.8	145 04.2	23.8	Capella	281 17.1	N45 58.4
02	267 06.7	164 26.0	30.0	267 20.4	51.2	253 25.4	36.9	160 06.4	23.7	Deneb	49 50.8	N45 11.4
03	282 09.2	179 25.5 ··	29.8	282 21.2 ··	50.5	268 27.4 ··	37.1	175 08.6 ··	23.7	Denebola	183 02.6	N14 42.5
04	297 11.7	194 24.9	29.6	297 21.9	49.7	283 29.4	37.3	190 10.8	23.7	Diphda	349 24.7	S18 07.2
05	312 14.1	209 24.3	29.4	312 22.6	49.0	298 31.4	37.5	205 12.9	23.7			
06	327 16.6	224 23.7 N25	29.2	327 23.4 S 1	48.3	313 33.4 N 4	37.7	220 15.1 N22	23.6	Dubhe	194 26.4	N61 53.2
07	342 19.1	239 23.2	29.0	342 24.1	47.5	328 35.4	37.9	235 17.3	23.6	Elnath	278 49.1	N28 35.2
08	357 21.5	254 22.6	28.7	357 24.8	46.8	343 37.4	38.1	250 19.5	23.6	Eltanin	90 58.9	N51 29.4
T 09	12 24.0	269 22.0 ··	28.5	12 25.6 ··	46.0	358 39.4 ··	38.3	265 21.7 ··	23.6	Enif	34 15.1	N 9 45.7
U 10	27 26.4	284 21.5	28.3	27 26.3	45.3	13 41.3	38.5	280 23.9	23.5	Fomalhaut	15 55.5	S29 45.0
E 11	42 28.9	299 20.9	28.1	42 27.0	44.6	28 43.3	38.7	295 26.1	23.5			
S 12	57 31.4	314 20.3 N25	27.8	57 27.8 S 1	43.8	43 45.3 N 4	38.9	310 28.3 N22	23.5	Gacrux	172 32.4	S56 58.9
D 13	72 33.8	329 19.8	27.6	72 28.5	43.1	58 47.3	39.1	325 30.5	23.4	Gienah	176 21.5	S17 24.6
A 14	87 36.3	344 19.2	27.4	87 29.2	42.4	73 49.3	39.3	340 32.6	23.4	Hadar	149 27.9	S60 15.5
Y 15	102 38.8	359 18.6 ··	27.2	102 30.0 ··	41.6	88 51.3 ··	39.5	355 34.8 ··	23.4	Hamal	328 33.3	N23 20.7
16	117 41.2	14 18.1	26.9	117 30.7	40.9	103 53.3	39.6	10 37.0	23.4	Kaus Aust.	84 21.3	S34 23.7
17	132 43.7	29 17.5	26.7	132 31.4	40.1	118 55.3	39.8	25 39.2	23.3			
18	147 46.2	44 16.9 N25	26.5	147 32.2 S 1	39.4	133 57.2 N 4	40.0	40 41.4 N22	23.3	Kochab	137 17.6	N74 15.4
19	162 48.6	59 16.4	26.2	162 32.9	38.7	148 59.2	40.2	55 43.6	23.3	Markab	14 06.9	N15 04.3
20	177 51.1	74 15.8	26.0	177 33.7	37.9	164 01.2	40.4	70 45.8	23.3	Menkar	314 45.2	N 3 59.6
21	192 53.6	89 15.2 ··	25.8	192 34.4 ··	37.2	179 03.2 ··	40.6	85 48.0 ··	23.2	Menkent	148 40.9	S36 15.2
22	207 56.0	104 14.7	25.5	207 35.1	36.5	194 05.2	40.8	100 50.2	23.2	Miaplacidus	221 45.9	S69 37.4
23	222 58.5	119 14.1	25.3	222 35.9	35.7	209 07.2	41.0	115 52.3	23.2			
21 00	238 00.9	134 13.5 N25	25.1	237 36.6 S 1	35.0	224 09.2 N 4	41.2	130 54.5 N22	23.2	Mirfak	309 21.8	N49 46.4
01	253 03.4	149 13.0	24.8	252 37.3	34.2	239 11.2	41.4	145 56.7	23.1	Nunki	76 33.4	S26 19.6
02	268 05.9	164 12.4	24.6	267 38.1	33.5	254 13.2	41.6	160 58.9	23.1	Peacock	54 03.8	S56 48.6
03	283 08.3	179 11.9 ··	24.3	282 38.8 ··	32.8	269 15.1 ··	41.8	176 01.1 ··	23.1	Pollux	244 02.8	N28 05.2
04	298 10.8	194 11.3	24.1	297 39.5	32.0	284 17.1	42.0	191 03.3	23.1	Procyon	245 29.8	N 5 17.2
05	313 13.3	209 10.7	23.8	312 40.3	31.3	299 19.1	42.1	206 05.5	23.0			
06	328 15.7	224 10.2 N25	23.6	327 41.0 S 1	30.6	314 21.1 N 4	42.3	221 07.7 N22	23.0	Rasalhague	96 32.6	N12 34.6
07	343 18.2	239 09.6	23.4	342 41.7	29.8	329 23.1	42.5	236 09.8	23.0	Regulus	208 13.9	N12 05.2
W 08	358 20.7	254 09.1	23.1	357 42.5	29.1	344 25.1	42.7	251 12.0	23.0	Rigel	281 39.8	S 8 13.9
E 09	13 23.1	269 08.5 ··	22.9	12 43.2 ··	28.3	359 27.1 ··	42.9	266 14.2 ··	22.9	Rigil Kent.	140 30.1	S60 44.2
D 10	28 25.6	284 08.0	22.6	27 44.0	27.6	14 29.1	43.1	281 16.4	22.9	Sabik	102 45.0	S15 41.7
N 11	43 28.0	299 07.4	22.4	42 44.7	26.9	29 31.1	43.3	296 18.6	22.9			
E 12	58 30.5	314 06.9 N25	22.1	57 45.4 S 1	26.1	44 33.1 N 4	43.5	311 20.8 N22	22.8	Schedar	350 13.5	N56 24.0
S 13	73 33.0	329 06.3	21.9	72 46.2	25.4	59 35.0	43.7	326 23.0	22.8	Shaula	97 00.3	S37 05.2
D 14	88 35.4	344 05.7	21.6	87 46.9	24.7	74 37.0	43.9	341 25.1	22.8	Sirius	258 59.2	S16 41.1
A 15	103 37.9	359 05.1 ··	21.4	102 47.6 ··	23.9	89 39.0 ··	44.1	356 27.3 ··	22.8	Spica	159 01.1	S11 02.2
Y 16	118 40.4	14 04.6	21.1	117 48.4	23.2	104 41.0	44.2	11 29.5	22.7	Suhail	223 13.6	S43 20.3
17	133 42.8	29 04.1	20.8	132 49.1	22.4	119 43.0	44.4	26 31.7	22.7			
18	148 45.3	44 03.5 N25	20.6	147 49.8 S 1	21.7	134 45.0 N 4	44.6	41 33.9 N22	22.7	Vega	80 58.0	N38 45.5
19	163 47.8	59 03.0	20.3	162 50.6	21.0	149 47.0	44.8	56 36.1	22.7	Zuben'ubi	137 36.7	S15 56.5
20	178 50.2	74 02.4	20.1	177 51.3	20.2	164 49.0	45.0	71 38.3	22.6			
21	193 52.7	89 01.9 ··	19.8	192 52.1 ··	19.5	179 51.0 ··	45.2	86 40.4 ··	22.6		S.H.A.	Mer. Pass.
22	208 55.2	104 01.3	19.5	207 52.8	18.8	194 53.0	45.4	101 42.6	22.6	Venus	257 25.4	15 03
23	223 57.6	119 00.8	19.3	222 53.5	18.0	209 55.0	45.6	116 44.8	22.6	Mars	0 17.2	8 10
										Jupiter	346 19.7	9 05
Mer. Pass.	h m 8 10.5	v −0.6	d 0.2	v 0.7	d 0.7	v 2.0	d 0.2	v 2.2	d 0.0	Saturn	253 00.2	15 18

1975 MAY 19, 20, 21 (MON., TUES., WED.)

G.M.T.	SUN G.H.A.	Dec.	MOON G.H.A.	v	Dec.	d	H.P.
d h	° ′	° ′	° ′	′	° ′	′	′
19 00	180 54.3	N19 35.1	81 14.3	10.2	N 4 48.5	12.6	59.4
01	195 54.2	35.6	95 43.5	10.2	4 35.9	12.7	59.4
02	210 54.2	36.2	110 12.7	10.2	4 23.2	12.7	59.4
03	225 54.2 ··	36.7	124 41.9	10.2	4 10.5	12.7	59.4
04	240 54.2	37.3	139 11.1	10.2	3 57.8	12.8	59.4
05	255 54.1	37.8	153 40.3	10.2	3 45.0	12.8	59.4
06	270 54.1	N19 38.4	168 09.5	10.2	N 3 32.2	12.8	59.4
M 07	285 54.1	38.9	182 38.7	10.2	3 19.4	12.8	59.4
O 08	300 54.1	39.4	197 07.9	10.2	3 06.6	12.8	59.4
N 09	315 54.0 ··	40.0	211 37.1	10.3	2 53.8	12.9	59.4
D 10	330 54.0	40.5	226 06.4	10.2	2 40.9	12.8	59.4
A 11	345 54.0	41.1	240 35.6	10.2	2 28.1	12.9	59.4
Y 12	0 53.9	N19 41.6	255 04.8	10.3	N 2 15.2	12.9	59.4
13	15 53.9	42.1	269 34.1	10.2	2 02.3	13.0	59.4
14	30 53.9	42.7	284 03.3	10.3	1 49.3	13.0	59.4
15	45 53.9 ··	43.2	298 32.6	10.2	1 36.4	13.0	59.5
16	60 53.8	43.8	313 01.8	10.2	1 23.4	12.9	59.5
17	75 53.8	44.3	327 31.0	10.3	1 10.5	13.0	59.5
18	90 53.8	N19 44.8	342 00.3	10.2	N 0 57.5	13.0	59.5
19	105 53.8	45.4	356 29.5	10.3	0 44.5	13.0	59.5
20	120 53.7	45.9	10 58.7	10.3	0 31.5	12.9	59.5
21	135 53.7 ··	46.4	25 28.0	10.2	0 18.6	13.0	59.5
22	150 53.7	47.0	39 57.2	10.2	N 0 05.6	13.0	59.5
23	165 53.6	47.5	54 26.4	10.2	S 0 07.4	13.0	59.5
20 00	180 53.6	N19 48.1	68 55.6	10.2	S 0 20.4	13.0	59.5
01	195 53.6	48.6	83 24.8	10.2	0 33.4	13.0	59.5
02	210 53.5	49.1	97 54.0	10.2	0 46.4	13.0	59.5
03	225 53.5 ··	49.6	112 23.2	10.2	0 59.4	13.0	59.5
04	240 53.5	50.2	126 52.4	10.1	1 12.4	13.0	59.5
05	255 53.5	50.7	141 21.5	10.2	1 25.4	13.0	59.5
06	270 53.4	N19 51.2	155 50.7	10.1	S 1 38.4	13.0	59.5
T 07	285 53.4	51.8	170 19.8	10.1	1 51.4	12.9	59.5
U 08	300 53.4	52.3	184 48.9	10.1	2 04.3	13.0	59.5
E 09	315 53.3 ··	52.8	199 18.0	10.1	2 17.3	12.9	59.5
S 10	330 53.3	53.4	213 47.1	10.1	2 30.2	13.0	59.5
D 11	345 53.3	53.9	228 16.2	10.1	2 43.2	12.9	59.5
A 12	0 53.2	N19 54.4	242 45.3	10.0	S 2 56.1	12.9	59.5
Y 13	15 53.2	54.9	257 14.3	10.1	3 09.0	12.9	59.5
14	30 53.2	55.5	271 43.4	10.0	3 21.9	12.9	59.5
15	45 53.1 ··	56.0	286 12.4	10.0	3 34.8	12.8	59.5
16	60 53.1	56.5	300 41.4	10.0	3 47.6	12.8	59.5
17	75 53.1	57.0	315 10.4	9.9	4 00.4	12.8	59.5
18	90 53.0	N19 57.6	329 39.3	9.9	S 4 13.2	12.8	59.5
19	105 53.0	58.1	344 08.2	10.0	4 26.0	12.8	59.5
20	120 53.0	58.6	358 37.2	9.8	4 38.8	12.7	59.5
21	135 52.9 ··	59.1	13 06.0	9.9	4 51.5	12.7	59.5
22	150 52.9	19 59.6	27 34.9	9.9	5 04.2	12.7	59.5
23	165 52.9	20 00.2	42 03.8	9.8	5 16.9	12.7	59.5
21 00	180 52.8	N20 00.7	56 32.6	9.8	S 5 29.6	12.6	59.5
01	195 52.8	01.2	71 01.4	9.7	5 42.2	12.6	59.5
02	210 52.8	01.7	85 30.1	9.8	5 54.8	12.5	59.5
03	225 52.7 ··	02.2	99 58.9	9.7	6 07.3	12.6	59.5
04	240 52.7	02.8	114 27.6	9.7	6 19.9	12.4	59.5
05	255 52.6	03.3	128 56.3	9.6	6 32.3	12.5	59.5
06	270 52.6	N20 03.8	143 24.9	9.7	S 6 44.8	12.4	59.5
W 07	285 52.6	04.3	157 53.6	9.6	6 57.2	12.4	59.5
E 08	300 52.5	04.8	172 22.2	9.5	7 09.6	12.3	59.5
D 09	315 52.5 ··	05.3	186 50.7	9.6	7 21.9	12.3	59.5
N 10	330 52.5	05.8	201 19.3	9.5	7 34.2	12.2	59.5
E 11	345 52.4	06.4	215 47.8	9.5	7 46.4	12.2	59.5
S 12	0 52.4	N20 06.9	230 16.3	9.4	S 7 58.6	12.1	59.5
D 13	15 52.4	07.4	244 44.7	9.4	8 10.7	12.1	59.5
A 14	30 52.3	07.9	259 13.1	9.4	8 22.8	12.1	59.5
Y 15	45 52.3 ··	08.4	273 41.5	9.4	8 34.9	12.0	59.5
16	60 52.2	08.9	288 09.9	9.3	8 46.9	11.9	59.5
17	75 52.2	09.4	302 38.2	9.3	8 58.8	11.9	59.5
18	90 52.2	N20 09.9	317 06.5	9.2	S 9 10.7	11.8	59.5
19	105 52.1	10.4	331 34.7	9.2	9 22.5	11.8	59.5
20	120 52.1	10.9	346 02.9	9.2	9 34.3	11.7	59.5
21	135 52.0 ··	11.5	0 31.1	9.1	9 46.0	11.7	59.5
22	150 52.0	12.0	14 59.2	9.2	9 57.7	11.6	59.5
23	165 52.0	12.5	29 27.4	9.0	10 09.3	11.6	59.5
	S.D. 15.8	d 0.5	S.D. 16.2		16.2		16.2

Moonrise

Lat.	Twilight Naut.	Civil	Sunrise	19	20	21	22
°	h m	h m	h m	h m	h m	h m	h m
N 72	□	□	□	12 37	14 40	16 47	19 05
N 70	□	□	□	12 40	14 35	16 32	18 35
68	////	////	01 21	12 42	14 30	16 21	18 13
66	////	00 27	02 05	12 44	14 27	16 11	17 56
64	////	01 32	02 34	12 45	14 24	16 03	17 43
62	////	01 32	02 55	12 47	14 21	15 56	17 31
60	////	02 05	03 13	12 48	14 19	15 50	17 21
N 58	00 24	02 29	03 27	12 49	14 17	15 45	17 13
56	01 23	02 48	03 40	12 50	14 15	15 40	17 05
54	01 54	03 04	03 50	12 51	14 13	15 36	16 59
52	02 16	03 17	04 00	12 52	14 12	15 33	16 53
50	02 34	03 28	04 09	12 53	14 11	15 29	16 47
45	02 57	03 52	04 27	12 54	14 08	15 22	16 36
N 40	03 32	04 10	04 41	12 55	14 05	15 16	16 26
35	03 51	04 25	04 53	12 57	14 03	15 11	16 18
30	04 06	04 38	05 04	12 58	14 02	15 06	16 11
20	04 30	04 59	05 22	12 59	13 59	14 58	15 59
N 10	04 49	05 16	05 38	13 01	13 56	14 52	15 48
0	05 05	05 31	05 53	13 02	13 54	14 45	15 39
S 10	05 19	05 45	06 07	13 04	13 51	14 39	15 29
20	05 33	05 59	06 23	13 06	13 49	14 32	15 18
30	05 46	06 15	06 40	13 07	13 46	14 25	15 07
35	05 52	06 23	06 50	13 08	13 44	14 21	15 00
40	06 00	06 33	07 02	13 10	13 42	14 16	14 52
45	06 07	06 43	07 16	13 11	13 40	14 10	14 43
S 50	06 16	06 56	07 32	13 13	13 38	14 04	14 33
52	06 20	07 02	07 40	13 13	13 36	14 01	14 28
54	06 24	07 08	07 49	13 14	13 35	13 57	14 22
56	06 29	07 15	07 58	13 15	13 34	13 54	14 16
58	06 33	07 23	08 10	13 16	13 32	13 50	14 10
S 60	06 39	07 31	08 22	13 17	13 31	13 45	14 02

Moonset

Lat.	Sunset	Twilight Civil	Naut.	19	20	21	22
°		h m		h m	h m	h m	h m
N 72	□	□	□	01 32	01 17	01 02	00 44
N 70	□	□	□	01 26	01 18	01 10	01 01
68	22 37	////	////	01 21	01 19	01 17	01 15
66	21 51	////	////	01 17	01 20	01 23	01 26
64	21 22	23 50	////	01 14	01 20	01 27	01 35
62	20 59	22 25	////	01 11	01 21	01 31	01 43
60	20 42	21 50	////	01 08	01 21	01 35	01 50
N 58	20 27	21 26	23 49	01 06	01 22	01 38	01 57
56	20 14	21 07	22 33	01 03	01 22	01 41	02 02
54	20 03	20 51	22 01	01 01	01 23	01 44	02 07
52	19 54	20 37	21 39	01 00	01 23	01 46	02 12
50	19 45	20 26	21 21	00 58	01 23	01 48	02 16
45	19 27	20 02	20 47	00 55	01 24	01 53	02 25
N 40	19 12	19 43	20 22	00 52	01 24	01 57	02 32
35	19 00	19 28	20 03	00 49	01 25	02 01	02 38
30	18 49	19 15	19 47	00 47	01 25	02 04	02 44
20	18 31	18 54	19 23	00 43	01 26	02 09	02 54
N 10	18 15	18 37	19 04	00 39	01 26	02 14	03 02
0	18 00	18 22	18 48	00 36	01 27	02 18	03 10
S 10	17 45	18 08	18 33	00 32	01 27	02 22	03 19
20	17 30	17 53	18 20	00 28	01 28	02 27	03 27
30	17 12	17 38	18 07	00 24	01 28	02 32	03 37
35	17 02	17 29	18 00	00 22	01 28	02 35	03 43
40	16 51	17 20	17 53	00 19	01 29	02 39	03 49
45	16 37	17 09	17 45	00 16	01 29	02 43	03 57
S 50	16 20	16 57	17 36	00 12	01 30	02 48	04 06
52	16 12	16 51	17 32	00 10	01 30	02 50	04 11
54	16 04	16 44	17 28	00 08	01 30	02 53	04 15
56	15 54	16 37	17 24	00 06	01 30	02 55	04 20
58	15 43	16 29	17 19	00 03	01 30	02 58	04 26
S 60	15 30	16 21	17 14	00 00	01 31	03 02	04 33

Day	SUN Eqn. of Time 00ʰ	12ʰ	Mer. Pass.	MOON Mer. Pass. Upper	Lower	Age	Phase
	m s	m s	h m	h m	h m	d	
19	03 37	03 36	11 56	19 15	06 49	08	
20	03 34	03 33	11 56	20 06	07 40	09	◗
21	03 31	03 30	11 57	20 58	08 32	10	

1975 AUGUST 29, 30, 31 (FRI., SAT., SUN.)

G.M.T.	ARIES G.H.A.	VENUS −3.3 G.H.A.	Dec.	MARS +0.3 G.H.A.	Dec.	JUPITER −2.3 G.H.A.	Dec.	SATURN +0.4 G.H.A.	Dec.	STARS Name	S.H.A.	Dec.
29 00	336 34.8	184 55.3 N 2	33.7	269 43.2 N20	37.9	313 26.8 N 8	02.0	216 28.4 N20	35.3	Acamar	315 39.7	S40 23.8
01	351 37.3	199 59.2	34.1	284 44.1	38.1	328 29.4	02.0	231 30.6	35.3	Achernar	335 47.4	S57 21.3
02	6 39.8	215 03.2	34.6	299 45.1	38.4	343 32.0	01.9	246 32.8	35.2	Acrux	173 41.6	S62 58.0
03	21 42.2	230 07.1 ··	35.1	314 46.1 ··	38.6	358 34.5 ··	01.9	261 34.9 ··	35.2	Adhara	255 35.0	S28 56.2
04	36 44.7	245 11.0	35.5	329 47.0	38.9	13 37.1	01.8	276 37.1	35.1	Aldebaran	291 21.9	N16 27.7
05	51 47.2	260 14.9	36.0	344 48.0	39.2	28 39.7	01.8	291 39.3	35.1			
06	66 49.6	275 18.8 N 2	36.5	359 49.0 N20	39.4	43 42.3 N 8	01.7	306 41.4 N20	35.0	Alioth	166 45.9	N56 05.7
07	81 52.1	290 22.8	36.9	14 49.9	39.7	58 44.8	01.7	321 43.6	35.0	Alkaid	153 21.5	N49 26.3
08	96 54.6	305 26.7	37.4	29 50.9	40.0	73 47.4	01.6	336 45.8	34.9	Al Na'ir	28 18.7	S47 04.6
F 09	111 57.0	320 30.6 ··	37.9	44 51.9 ··	40.2	88 50.0 ··	01.6	351 47.9 ··	34.8	Alnilam	276 15.2	S 1 12.9
R 10	126 59.5	335 34.5	38.3	59 52.8	40.5	103 52.6	01.5	6 50.1	34.8	Alphard	218 24.2	S 8 33.1
I 11	142 01.9	350 38.4	38.8	74 53.8	40.7	118 55.1	01.4	21 52.3	34.7			
D 12	157 04.4	5 42.3 N 2	39.3	89 54.8 N20	41.0	133 57.7 N 8	01.4	36 54.4 N20	34.7	Alphecca	126 35.1	N26 48.0
A 13	172 06.9	20 46.2	39.8	104 55.7	41.3	149 00.3	01.3	51 56.6	34.6	Alpheratz	358 12.5	N28 57.5
Y 14	187 09.3	35 50.1	40.2	119 56.7	41.5	164 02.8	01.3	66 58.8	34.6	Altair	62 35.6	N 8 48.5
15	202 11.8	50 54.0 ··	40.7	134 57.7 ··	41.8	179 05.4 ··	01.2	82 01.0 ··	34.5	Ankaa	353 43.2	S42 26.0
16	217 14.3	65 58.0	41.2	149 58.6	42.0	194 08.0	01.2	97 03.1	34.5	Antares	113 01.0	S26 22.7
17	232 16.7	81 01.9	41.7	164 59.6	42.3	209 10.6	01.1	112 05.3	34.4			
18	247 19.2	96 05.8 N 2	42.2	180 00.6 N20	42.6	224 13.1 N 8	01.1	127 07.5 N20	34.4	Arcturus	146 21.7	N19 18.7
19	262 21.7	111 09.7	42.7	195 01.5	42.8	239 15.7	01.0	142 09.6	34.3	Atria	108 28.2	S68 59.3
20	277 24.1	126 13.6	43.1	210 02.5	43.1	254 18.3	01.0	157 11.8	34.3	Avior	234 30.1	S59 25.8
21	292 26.6	141 17.5 ··	43.6	225 03.5 ··	43.3	269 20.9 ··	00.9	172 14.0 ··	34.2	Bellatrix	279 02.5	N 6 19.8
22	307 29.1	156 21.4	44.1	240 04.5	43.6	284 23.4	00.9	187 16.2	34.2	Betelgeuse	271 32.1	N 7 24.2
23	322 31.5	171 25.3	44.6	255 05.4	43.9	299 26.0	00.8	202 18.3	34.1			
30 00	337 34.0	186 29.2 N 2	45.1	270 06.4 N20	44.1	314 28.6 N 8	00.7	217 20.5 N20	34.1	Canopus	264 09.0	S52 40.7
01	352 36.4	201 33.0	45.6	285 07.4	44.4	329 31.2	00.7	232 22.7	34.0	Capella	281 16.4	N45 58.3
02	7 38.9	216 36.9	46.1	300 08.4	44.6	344 33.8	00.6	247 24.8	34.0	Deneb	49 50.4	N45 11.9
03	22 41.4	231 40.8 ··	46.5	315 09.3 ··	44.9	359 36.3 ··	00.6	262 27.0 ··	33.9	Denebola	183 02.8	N14 42.5
04	37 43.8	246 44.7	47.0	330 10.3	45.1	14 38.9	00.5	277 29.2	33.9	Diphda	349 24.0	S18 06.9
05	52 46.3	261 48.6	47.5	345 11.3	45.4	29 41.5	00.5	292 31.4	33.8			
06	67 48.8	276 52.5 N 2	48.0	0 12.2 N20	45.7	44 44.1 N 8	00.4	307 33.5 N20	33.7	Dubhe	194 27.0	N61 53.0
07	82 51.2	291 56.4	48.5	15 13.2	45.9	59 46.7	00.4	322 35.7	33.7	Elnath	278 48.5	N28 35.2
S 08	97 53.7	307 00.3	49.0	30 14.2	46.2	74 49.2	00.3	337 37.9	33.6	Eltanin	90 59.1	N51 29.9
A 09	112 56.2	322 04.1 ··	49.5	45 15.2 ··	46.4	89 51.8 ··	00.3	352 40.0 ··	33.6	Enif	34 14.6	N 9 46.0
T 10	127 58.6	337 08.0	50.0	60 16.1	46.7	104 54.4	00.2	7 42.2	33.5	Fomalhaut	15 54.8	S29 44.8
U 11	143 01.1	352 11.9	50.5	75 17.1	46.9	119 57.0	00.2	22 44.4	33.5			
R 12	158 03.6	7 15.8 N 2	51.0	90 18.1 N20	47.2	134 59.6 N 8	00.1	37 46.6 N20	33.4	Gacrux	172 33.0	S56 58.8
D 13	173 06.0	22 19.7	51.5	105 19.1	47.4	150 02.1	00.0	52 48.7	33.4	Gienah	176 21.8	S17 24.4
A 14	188 08.5	37 23.5	52.0	120 20.1	47.7	165 04.7	8 00.0	67 50.9	33.3	Hadar	149 28.5	S60 15.6
Y 15	203 10.9	52 27.4 ··	52.5	135 21.0 ··	48.0	180 07.3	7 59.9	82 53.1 ··	33.3	Hamal	328 32.6	N23 20.9
16	218 13.4	67 31.3	53.0	150 22.0	48.2	195 09.9	59.9	97 55.2	33.2	Kaus Aust.	84 21.2	S34 23.8
17	233 15.9	82 35.1	53.5	165 23.0	48.5	210 12.5	59.8	112 57.4	33.2			
18	248 18.3	97 39.0 N 2	54.0	180 24.0 N20	48.7	225 15.0 N 7	59.7	127 59.6 N20	33.1	Kochab	137 19.3	N74 15.6
19	263 20.8	112 42.9	54.5	195 24.9	49.0	240 17.6	59.7	143 01.8	33.1	Markab	14 06.2	N15 04.7
20	278 23.3	127 46.7	55.0	210 25.9	49.2	255 20.2	59.6	158 03.9	33.0	Menkar	314 44.6	N 3 59.8
21	293 25.7	142 50.6 ··	55.5	225 26.9 ··	49.5	270 22.8 ··	59.6	173 06.1 ··	33.0	Menkent	148 41.2	S36 15.2
22	308 28.2	157 54.5	56.1	240 27.9	49.7	285 25.4	59.5	188 08.3	32.9	Miaplacidus	221 46.5	S69 37.0
23	323 30.7	172 58.3	56.6	255 28.9	50.0	300 28.0	59.5	203 10.5	32.9			
31 00	338 33.1	188 02.2 N 2	57.1	270 29.8 N20	50.2	315 30.6 N 7	59.3	218 12.6 N20	32.8	Mirfak	309 20.9	N49 46.4
01	353 35.6	203 06.0	57.6	285 30.8	50.5	330 33.1	59.3	233 14.8	32.8	Nunki	76 33.2	S26 19.6
02	8 38.0	218 09.9	58.1	300 31.8	50.7	345 35.7	59.3	248 17.0	32.7	Peacock	54 03.2	S56 48.8
03	23 40.5	233 13.7 ··	58.6	315 32.8 ··	51.0	0 38.3 ··	59.2	263 19.1 ··	32.7	Pollux	244 02.6	N28 05.1
04	38 43.0	248 17.6	59.1	330 33.8	51.2	15 40.9	59.2	278 21.3	32.6	Procyon	245 29.6	N 5 17.3
05	53 45.4	263 21.4	2 59.6	345 34.8	51.5	30 43.5	59.1	293 23.5	32.6			
06	68 47.9	278 25.3 N 3	00.2	0 35.7 N20	51.7	45 46.1 N 7	59.0	308 25.7 N20	32.5	Rasalhague	96 32.6	N12 34.9
07	83 50.4	293 29.1	00.7	15 36.7	52.0	60 48.7	59.0	323 27.8	32.4	Regulus	208 13.9	N12 05.2
08	98 52.8	308 33.0	01.2	30 37.7	52.2	75 51.2	58.9	338 30.0	32.4	Rigel	281 39.4	S 8 13.6
S 09	113 55.3	323 36.8 ··	01.7	45 38.7 ··	52.5	90 53.8 ··	58.9	353 32.2 ··	32.3	Rigil Kent.	140 30.7	S60 44.3
U 10	128 57.8	338 40.6	02.2	60 39.7	52.7	105 56.4	58.8	8 34.4	32.3	Sabik	102 45.0	S15 41.7
N 11	144 00.2	353 44.5	02.7	75 40.7	53.0	120 59.0	58.8	23 36.5	32.2			
D 12	159 02.7	8 48.3 N 3	03.3	90 41.6 N20	53.2	136 01.6 N 7	58.7	38 38.7 N20	32.2	Schedar	350 12.4	N56 24.3
A 13	174 05.2	23 52.1	03.8	105 42.6	53.5	151 04.2	58.7	53 40.9	32.1	Shaula	97 00.3	S37 05.3
Y 14	189 07.6	38 56.0	04.3	120 43.6	53.7	166 06.8	58.6	68 43.1	32.1	Sirius	258 58.9	S16 40.8
15	204 10.1	53 59.8 ··	04.8	135 44.6 ··	54.0	181 09.4 ··	58.6	83 45.2 ··	32.0	Spica	159 01.4	S11 02.1
16	219 12.5	69 03.6	05.4	150 45.6	54.2	196 12.0	58.5	98 47.4	32.0	Suhail	223 13.7	S43 20.0
17	234 15.0	84 07.4	05.9	165 46.6	54.5	211 14.5	58.4	113 49.6	31.9			
18	249 17.5	99 11.3 N 3	06.4	180 47.6 N20	54.7	226 17.1 N 7	58.4	128 51.8 N20	31.9	Vega	80 57.9	N38 46.0
19	264 19.9	114 15.1	06.9	195 48.5	55.0	241 19.7	58.3	143 53.9	31.8	Zuben'ubi	137 36.9	S15 56.5
20	279 22.4	129 18.9	07.5	210 49.5	55.2	256 22.3	58.3	158 56.1	31.8			
21	294 24.9	144 22.7 ··	08.0	225 50.5 ··	55.5	271 24.9 ··	58.2	173 58.3 ··	31.7		S.H.A.	Mer. Pass.
22	309 27.3	159 26.5	08.5	240 51.5	55.7	286 27.5	58.2	189 00.5	31.7	Venus	208 55.2	11 31
23	324 29.8	174 30.4	09.0	255 52.5	56.0	301 30.1	58.1	204 02.6	31.6	Mars	292 32.4	5 59
										Jupiter	336 54.6	3 02
Mer. Pass.	1 29.5	v 3.9 d 0.5		v 1.0 d 0.3		v 2.6 d 0.1		v 2.2 d 0.1		Saturn	239 46.5	9 29

G.M.T.	SUN G.H.A.	SUN Dec.	MOON G.H.A.	v	MOON Dec.	d	H.P.
29 00	179 41.9	N 9 39.6	285 08.4	11.1	N18 51.7	4.9	55.5
01	194 42.1	38.8	299 38.5	11.1	18 56.6	4.9	55.5
02	209 42.3	37.9	314 08.6	11.0	19 01.5	4.8	55.5
03	224 42.5	.. 37.0	328 38.6	11.0	19 06.3	4.7	55.6
04	239 42.6	36.1	343 08.6	10.9	19 11.0	4.6	55.6
05	254 42.8	35.2	357 38.5	10.8	19 15.6	4.5	55.6
06	269 43.0	N 9 34.3	12 08.3	10.8	N19 20.1	4.4	55.6
07	284 43.2	33.5	26 38.1	10.7	19 24.5	4.4	55.7
08	299 43.4	32.6	41 07.8	10.6	19 28.9	4.2	55.7
F 09	314 43.6	.. 31.7	55 37.4	10.6	19 33.1	4.1	55.7
R 10	329 43.8	30.8	70 07.0	10.5	19 37.2	4.1	55.8
I 11	344 43.9	29.9	84 36.5	10.5	19 41.3	3.9	55.8
D 12	359 44.1	N 9 29.0	99 06.0	10.4	N19 45.2	3.9	55.8
A 13	14 44.3	28.1	113 35.4	10.3	19 49.1	3.7	55.8
Y 14	29 44.5	27.3	128 04.7	10.3	19 52.8	3.7	55.9
15	44 44.7	.. 26.4	142 34.0	10.2	19 56.5	3.5	55.9
16	59 44.9	25.5	157 03.2	10.2	20 00.0	3.5	55.9
17	74 45.1	24.6	171 32.4	10.1	20 03.5	3.3	56.0
18	89 45.3	N 9 23.7	186 01.5	10.0	N20 06.8	3.3	56.0
19	104 45.4	22.8	200 30.5	10.0	20 10.1	3.1	56.0
20	119 45.6	21.9	214 59.5	9.9	20 13.2	3.1	56.1
21	134 45.8	.. 21.0	229 28.4	9.8	20 16.3	2.9	56.1
22	149 46.0	20.1	243 57.2	9.8	20 19.2	2.8	56.1
23	164 46.2	19.3	258 26.0	9.7	20 22.0	2.8	56.2
30 00	179 46.4	N 9 18.4	272 54.7	9.7	N20 24.8	2.6	56.2
01	194 46.6	17.5	287 23.4	9.6	20 27.4	2.5	56.2
02	209 46.8	16.6	301 52.0	9.6	20 29.9	2.5	56.3
03	224 46.9	.. 15.7	316 20.6	9.5	20 32.4	2.3	56.3
04	239 47.1	14.8	330 49.1	9.4	20 34.7	2.2	56.3
05	254 47.3	13.9	345 17.5	9.4	20 36.9	2.1	56.4
06	269 47.5	N 9 13.0	359 45.9	9.3	N20 39.0	1.9	56.4
07	284 47.7	12.1	14 14.2	9.3	20 40.9	1.9	56.4
S 08	299 47.9	11.2	28 42.5	9.2	20 42.8	1.8	56.5
A 09	314 48.1	.. 10.3	43 10.7	9.2	20 44.6	1.6	56.5
T 10	329 48.3	09.5	57 38.9	9.1	20 46.2	1.6	56.5
U 11	344 48.5	08.6	72 07.0	9.0	20 47.8	1.4	56.6
R 12	359 48.6	N 9 07.7	86 35.0	9.0	N20 49.2	1.3	56.6
D 13	14 48.8	06.8	101 03.0	9.0	20 50.5	1.2	56.6
A 14	29 49.0	05.9	115 31.0	8.8	20 51.7	1.1	56.7
Y 15	44 49.2	.. 05.0	129 58.8	8.9	20 52.8	1.0	56.7
16	59 49.4	04.1	144 26.7	8.8	20 53.8	0.9	56.7
17	74 49.6	03.2	158 54.5	8.7	20 54.7	0.7	56.8
18	89 49.8	N 9 02.3	173 22.2	8.7	N20 55.4	0.6	56.8
19	104 50.0	01.4	187 49.9	8.6	20 56.0	0.5	56.9
20	119 50.2	9 00.5	202 17.5	8.6	20 56.5	0.4	56.9
21	134 50.4	8 59.6	216 45.1	8.5	20 56.9	0.3	56.9
22	149 50.5	58.7	231 12.6	8.5	20 57.2	0.2	57.0
23	164 50.7	57.8	245 40.1	8.4	20 57.4	0.1	57.0
31 00	179 50.9	N 8 56.9	260 07.5	8.4	N20 57.4	0.1	57.0
01	194 51.1	56.0	274 34.9	8.4	20 57.3	0.2	57.1
02	209 51.3	55.1	289 02.3	8.3	20 57.1	0.3	57.1
03	224 51.5	.. 54.2	303 29.6	8.2	20 56.8	0.4	57.2
04	239 51.7	53.3	317 56.8	8.2	20 56.4	0.6	57.2
05	254 51.9	52.4	332 24.0	8.2	20 55.8	0.7	57.2
06	269 52.1	N 8 51.5	346 51.2	8.1	N20 55.1	0.8	57.3
07	284 52.3	50.6	1 18.3	8.1	20 54.3	0.9	57.3
08	299 52.5	49.8	15 45.4	8.1	20 53.4	1.1	57.3
S 09	314 52.7	.. 48.9	30 12.5	8.0	20 52.3	1.1	57.4
U 10	329 52.8	48.0	44 39.5	7.9	20 51.2	1.3	57.4
N 11	344 53.0	47.1	59 06.4	7.9	20 49.9	1.5	57.5
D 12	359 53.2	N 8 46.2	73 33.3	7.9	N20 48.4	1.4	57.5
A 13	14 53.4	45.3	88 00.2	7.9	20 46.9	1.7	57.5
Y 14	29 53.6	44.4	102 27.1	7.8	20 45.2	1.8	57.6
15	44 53.8	.. 43.5	116 53.9	7.8	20 43.4	1.9	57.6
16	59 54.0	42.6	131 20.7	7.7	20 41.5	2.0	57.7
17	74 54.2	41.7	145 47.4	7.7	20 39.5	2.2	57.7
18	89 54.4	N 8 40.8	160 14.1	7.7	N20 37.3	2.3	57.7
19	104 54.6	39.9	174 40.8	7.6	20 35.0	2.4	57.8
20	119 54.8	39.0	189 07.4	7.6	20 32.6	2.6	57.8
21	134 55.0	.. 38.1	203 34.0	7.6	20 30.0	2.6	57.9
22	149 55.2	37.2	218 00.6	7.5	20 27.4	2.8	57.9
23	164 55.4	36.3	232 27.1	7.6	20 24.6	3.0	57.9
	S.D. 15.9	d 0.9	S.D. 15.2		15.4		15.7

Lat.	Twilight Naut.	Civil	Sunrise	Moonrise 29	30	31	1
N 72	////	02 09	03 47	□	□	□	□
N 70	////	02 43	04 03	17 44	□	□	21 50
68	00 59	03 07	04 16	19 20	19 50	20 59	22 39
66	01 51	03 26	04 26	19 59	20 38	21 42	23 10
64	02 22	03 40	04 35	20 26	21 08	22 11	23 33
62	02 44	03 52	04 42	20 47	21 31	22 33	23 51
60	03 02	04 02	04 48	21 04	21 50	22 51	24 06
N 58	03 16	04 11	04 54	21 19	22 05	23 06	24 19
56	03 28	04 19	04 59	21 31	22 19	23 18	24 30
54	03 38	04 25	05 03	21 42	22 30	23 29	24 40
52	03 47	04 31	05 07	21 52	22 40	23 39	24 48
50	03 55	04 37	05 11	22 00	22 49	23 48	24 56
45	04 11	04 48	05 18	22 19	23 08	24 06	00 06
N 40	04 24	04 57	05 25	22 33	23 24	24 22	00 22
35	04 34	05 05	05 30	22 46	23 37	24 34	00 34
30	04 42	05 11	05 35	22 57	23 49	24 45	00 45
20	04 55	05 21	05 44	23 16	24 08	00 08	01 04
N 10	05 05	05 30	05 51	23 33	24 25	00 25	01 21
0	05 12	05 36	05 58	23 48	24 42	00 42	01 37
S 10	05 18	05 43	06 04	24 04	00 04	00 58	01 52
20	05 23	05 49	06 11	24 21	00 21	01 15	02 09
30	05 27	05 54	06 19	24 40	00 40	01 35	02 28
35	05 28	05 57	06 23	24 51	00 51	01 46	02 39
40	05 29	06 00	06 28	00 07	01 04	02 00	02 52
45	05 30	06 04	06 33	00 21	01 20	02 15	03 07
S 50	05 30	06 07	06 40	00 38	01 38	02 35	03 25
52	05 30	06 09	06 43	00 46	01 47	02 44	03 34
54	05 30	06 11	06 47	00 55	01 57	02 54	03 43
56	05 30	06 13	06 50	01 05	02 09	03 06	03 54
58	05 30	06 15	06 55	01 16	02 22	03 19	04 07
S 60	05 29	06 17	06 59	01 30	02 37	03 35	04 21

Lat.	Sunset	Twilight Civil	Naut.	Moonset 29	30	31	1
N 72	20 11	21 46	////	□	□	□	□
N 70	19 56	21 14	////	17 20	□	□	18 55
68	19 44	20 51	22 51	15 45	17 04	17 49	18 06
66	19 34	20 33	22 04	15 06	16 17	17 06	17 35
64	19 25	20 19	21 35	14 39	15 46	16 37	17 11
62	19 18	20 08	21 14	14 19	15 23	16 14	16 51
60	19 12	19 57	20 57	14 02	15 04	15 56	16 37
N 58	19 06	19 49	20 44	13 47	14 49	15 41	16 24
56	19 02	19 41	20 32	13 35	14 36	15 29	16 12
54	18 57	19 35	20 22	13 25	14 24	15 17	16 02
52	18 53	19 29	20 13	13 15	14 14	15 07	15 54
50	18 50	19 24	20 05	13 07	14 05	14 59	15 46
45	18 42	19 13	19 49	12 49	13 46	14 40	15 28
N 40	18 36	19 04	19 37	12 34	13 31	14 24	15 14
35	18 31	18 56	19 27	12 22	13 18	14 11	15 02
30	18 26	18 50	19 19	12 11	13 06	14 00	14 52
20	18 18	18 40	19 06	11 53	12 47	13 41	14 34
N 10	18 11	18 32	18 57	11 37	12 30	13 24	14 18
0	18 04	18 25	18 49	11 22	12 14	13 08	14 03
S 10	17 58	18 19	18 43	11 07	11 58	12 52	13 49
20	17 51	18 13	18 39	10 51	11 41	12 35	13 33
30	17 43	18 08	18 35	10 32	11 21	12 15	13 15
35	17 39	18 05	18 34	10 22	11 10	12 03	13 03
40	17 34	18 02	18 33	10 10	10 56	11 50	12 51
45	17 29	17 58	18 32	09 55	10 41	11 35	12 37
S 50	17 22	17 55	18 32	09 38	10 22	11 15	12 19
52	17 19	17 53	18 32	09 29	10 13	11 06	12 10
54	17 16	17 52	18 33	09 20	10 03	10 56	12 01
56	17 12	17 50	18 33	09 10	09 51	10 44	11 50
58	17 08	17 48	18 34	08 58	09 38	10 31	11 38
S 60	17 03	17 45	18 34	08 44	09 23	10 15	11 24

Day	SUN Eqn. of Time 00h	12h	Mer. Pass.	MOON Mer. Pass. Upper	Lower	Age	Phase
29	01 13	01 04	12 01	05 10	17 35	22	◑
30	00 55	00 46	12 01	06 01	18 28	23	
31	00 37	00 27	12 00	06 55	19 22	24	

POLARIS (POLE STAR) TABLES, 1975

FOR DETERMINING LATITUDE FROM SEXTANT ALTITUDE AND FOR AZIMUTH

L.H.A. ARIES	240°–249°	250°–259°	260°–269°	270°–279°	280°–289°	290°–299°	300°–309°	310°–319°	320°–329°	330°–339°	340°–349°	350°–359°
	a_0	a_0	a_0	a_0	a_0	a_0	a_0	a_0	a_0	a_0	a_0	a_0
0	1 43·8	1 39·1	1 33·1	1 26·1	1 18·3	1 09·9	1 01·1	0 52·3	0 43·6	0 35·4	0 27·9	0 21·3
1	43·4	38·5	32·5	25·4	17·5	09·0	1 00·2	51·4	42·8	34·6	27·2	20·7
2	43·0	38·0	31·8	24·6	16·7	08·2	0 59·4	50·5	41·9	33·8	26·5	20·1
3	42·5	37·4	31·1	23·9	15·8	07·3	58·5	49·6	41·1	33·1	25·8	19·6
4	42·1	36·8	30·4	23·1	15·0	06·4	57·6	48·8	40·3	32·3	25·1	19·0
5	1 41·6	1 36·2	1 29·7	1 22·3	1 14·2	1 05·5	0 56·7	47·9	0 39·4	0 31·5	0 24·5	0 18·5
6	41·1	35·6	29·0	21·5	13·3	04·7	55·8	47·0	38·6	30·8	23·8	17·9
7	40·6	35·0	28·3	20·7	12·5	03·8	54·9	46·2	37·8	30·0	23·2	17·4
8	40·1	34·4	27·6	19·9	11·6	02·9	54·0	45·3	37·0	29·3	22·5	16·9
9	39·6	33·8	26·9	19·1	10·8	02·0	53·2	44·5	36·2	28·6	21·9	16·4
10	1 39·1	1 33·1	1 26·1	1 18·3	1 09·9	1 01·1	0 52·3	0 43·6	0 35·4	0 27·9	0 21·3	0 15·9
Lat.	a_1	a_1	a_1	a_1	a_1	a_1	a_1	a_1	a_1	a_1	a_1	a_1
0	0·5	0·4	0·3	0·2	0·2	0·2	0·2	0·2	0·2	0·3	0·4	0·4
10	·5	·4	·4	·3	·3	·2	·2	·2	·3	·3	·4	·5
20	·5	·5	·4	·4	·3	·3	·3	·3	·3	·4	·4	·5
30	·5	·5	·5	·4	·4	·4	·4	·4	·4	·4	·5	·5
40	0·6	0·5	0·5	0·5	0·5	0·5	0·5	0·5	0·5	0·5	0·5	0·6
45	·6	·6	·6	·5	·5	·5	·5	·5	·5	·5	·6	·6
50	·6	·6	·6	·6	·6	·6	·6	·6	·6	·6	·6	·6
55	·6	·6	·7	·7	·7	·7	·7	·7	·7	·7	·6	·6
60	·7	·7	·7	·8	·8	·8	·8	·8	·8	·7	·7	·7
62	0·7	0·7	0·8	0·8	0·8	0·9	0·9	0·8	0·8	0·8	0·7	0·7
64	·7	·7	·8	·9	0·9	0·9	0·9	0·9	·9	·8	·8	·7
66	·7	·8	·9	0·9	1·0	1·0	1·0	1·0	0·9	·9	·8	·7
68	0·7	0·8	0·9	1·0	1·0	1·1	1·1	1·1	1·0	0·9	0·9	0·8
Month	a_2	a_2	a_2	a_2	a_2	a_2	a_2	a_2	a_2	a_2	a_2	a_2
Jan.	0·4	0·4	0·4	0·5	0·5	0·5	0·6	0·6	0·6	0·7	0·7	0·7
Feb.	·3	·3	·3	·3	·3	·4	·4	·4	·5	·5	·6	·6
Mar.	·3	·3	·3	·3	·3	·3	·3	·3	·3	·4	·4	·5
Apr.	0·4	0·4	0·3	0·3	0·3	0·2	0·2	0·2	0·2	0·3	0·3	0·3
May	·6	·5	·5	·4	·3	·3	·3	·2	·2	·2	·2	·2
June	·7	·7	·6	·5	·5	·4	·4	·3	·3	·3	·2	·2
July	0·8	0·8	0·8	0·7	0·6	0·6	0·5	0·5	0·4	0·4	0·3	0·3
Aug.	·9	·9	·9	·8	·8	·8	·7	·7	·6	·5	·5	·4
Sept.	·9	·9	·9	·9	·9	·9	·9	·8	·8	·7	·7	·6
Oct.	0·8	0·8	0·9	0·9	0·9	0·9	0·9	0·9	0·9	0·9	0·9	0·8
Nov.	·6	·7	·8	·8	·9	·9	1·0	1·0	1·0	1·0	1·0	1·0
Dec.	0·5	0·5	0·6	0·7	0·8	0·9	0·9	1·0	1·0	1·0	1·1	1·1
Lat.						AZIMUTH						
0	0·5	0·6	0·7	0·8	0·8	0·8	0·8	0·8	0·8	0·7	0·6	0·5
20	0·5	0·6	0·7	0·8	0·9	0·9	0·9	0·9	0·8	0·8	0·7	0·5
40	0·6	0·7	0·9	1·0	1·1	1·1	1·1	1·1	1·0	0·9	0·8	0·7
50	0·7	0·9	1·0	1·2	1·3	1·3	1·3	1·3	1·2	1·1	1·0	0·8
55	0·8	1·0	1·2	1·3	1·4	1·5	1·5	1·4	1·4	1·3	1·1	0·9
60	0·9	1·1	1·3	1·5	1·6	1·7	1·7	1·7	1·6	1·4	1·3	1·0
65	1·1	1·3	1·6	1·8	1·9	2·0	2·0	2·0	1·9	1·7	1·5	1·2

Latitude = Apparent altitude (corrected for refraction) − 1° + a_0 + a_1 + a_2

The table is entered with L.H.A. Aries to determine the column to be used; each column refers to a range of 10°. a_0 is taken, with mental interpolation, from the upper table with the units of L.H.A. Aries in degrees as argument; a_1, a_2 are taken, without interpolation, from the second and third tables with arguments latitude and month respectively. a_0, a_1, a_2 are always positive. The final table gives the azimuth of *Polaris*.

CONVERSION OF ARC TO TIME

0°–59°		60°–119°		120°–179°		180°–239°		240°–299°		300°–359°		′	0′·00	0′·25	0′·50	0′·75
°	h m	°	h m	°	h m	°	h m	°	h m	°	h m	′	m s	m s	m s	m s
0	0 00	60	4 00	120	8 00	180	12 00	240	16 00	300	20 00	0	0 00	0 01	0 02	0 03
1	0 04	61	4 04	121	8 04	181	12 04	241	16 04	301	20 04	1	0 04	0 05	0 06	0 07
2	0 08	62	4 08	122	8 08	182	12 08	242	16 08	302	20 08	2	0 08	0 09	0 10	0 11
3	0 12	63	4 12	123	8 12	183	12 12	243	16 12	303	20 12	3	0 12	0 13	0 14	0 15
4	0 16	64	4 16	124	8 16	184	12 16	244	16 16	304	20 16	4	0 16	0 17	0 18	0 19
5	0 20	65	4 20	125	8 20	185	12 20	245	16 20	305	20 20	5	0 20	0 21	0 22	0 23
6	0 24	66	4 24	126	8 24	186	12 24	246	16 24	306	20 24	6	0 24	0 25	0 26	0 27
7	0 28	67	4 28	127	8 28	187	12 28	247	16 28	307	20 28	7	0 28	0 29	0 30	0 31
8	0 32	68	4 32	128	8 32	188	12 32	248	16 32	308	20 32	8	0 32	0 33	0 34	0 35
9	0 36	69	4 36	129	8 36	189	12 36	249	16 36	309	20 36	9	0 36	0 37	0 38	0 39
10	0 40	70	4 40	130	8 40	190	12 40	250	16 40	310	20 40	10	0 40	0 41	0 42	0 43
11	0 44	71	4 44	131	8 44	191	12 44	251	16 44	311	20 44	11	0 44	0 45	0 46	0 47
12	0 48	72	4 48	132	8 48	192	12 48	252	16 48	312	20 48	12	0 48	0 49	0 50	0 51
13	0 52	73	4 52	133	8 52	193	12 52	253	16 52	313	20 52	13	0 52	0 53	0 54	0 55
14	0 56	74	4 56	134	8 56	194	12 56	254	16 56	314	20 56	14	0 56	0 57	0 58	0 59
15	1 00	75	5 00	135	9 00	195	13 00	255	17 00	315	21 00	15	1 00	1 01	1 02	1 03
16	1 04	76	5 04	136	9 04	196	13 04	256	17 04	316	21 04	16	1 04	1 05	1 06	1 07
17	1 08	77	5 08	137	9 08	197	13 08	257	17 08	317	21 08	17	1 08	1 09	1 10	1 11
18	1 12	78	5 12	138	9 12	198	13 12	258	17 12	318	21 12	18	1 12	1 13	1 14	1 15
19	1 16	79	5 16	139	9 16	199	13 16	259	17 16	319	21 16	19	1 16	1 17	1 18	1 19
20	1 20	80	5 20	140	9 20	200	13 20	260	17 20	320	21 20	20	1 20	1 21	1 22	1 23
21	1 24	81	5 24	141	9 24	201	13 24	261	17 24	321	21 24	21	1 24	1 25	1 26	1 27
22	1 28	82	5 28	142	9 28	202	13 28	262	17 28	322	21 28	22	1 28	1 29	1 30	1 31
23	1 32	83	5 32	143	9 32	203	13 32	263	17 32	323	21 32	23	1 32	1 33	1 34	1 35
24	1 36	84	5 36	144	9 36	204	13 36	264	17 36	324	21 36	24	1 36	1 37	1 38	1 39
25	1 40	85	5 40	145	9 40	205	13 40	265	17 40	325	21 40	25	1 40	1 41	1 42	1 43
26	1 44	86	5 44	146	9 44	206	13 44	266	17 44	326	21 44	26	1 44	1 45	1 46	1 47
27	1 48	87	5 48	147	9 48	207	13 48	267	17 48	327	21 48	27	1 48	1 49	1 50	1 51
28	1 52	88	5 52	148	9 52	208	13 52	268	17 52	328	21 52	28	1 52	1 53	1 54	1 55
29	1 56	89	5 56	149	9 56	209	13 56	269	17 56	329	21 56	29	1 56	1 57	1 58	1 59
30	2 00	90	6 00	150	10 00	210	14 00	270	18 00	330	22 00	30	2 00	2 01	2 02	2 03
31	2 04	91	6 04	151	10 04	211	14 04	271	18 04	331	22 04	31	2 04	2 05	2 06	2 07
32	2 08	92	6 08	152	10 08	212	14 08	272	18 08	332	22 08	32	2 08	2 09	2 10	2 11
33	2 12	93	6 12	153	10 12	213	14 12	273	18 12	333	22 12	33	2 12	2 13	2 14	2 15
34	2 16	94	6 16	154	10 16	214	14 16	274	18 16	334	22 16	34	2 16	2 17	2 18	2 19
35	2 20	95	6 20	155	10 20	215	14 20	275	18 20	335	22 20	35	2 20	2 21	2 22	2 23
36	2 24	96	6 24	156	10 24	216	14 24	276	18 24	336	22 24	36	2 24	2 25	2 26	2 27
37	2 28	97	6 28	157	10 28	217	14 28	277	18 28	337	22 28	37	2 28	2 29	2 30	2 31
38	2 32	98	6 32	158	10 32	218	14 32	278	18 32	338	22 32	38	2 32	2 33	2 34	2 35
39	2 36	99	6 36	159	10 36	219	14 36	279	18 36	339	22 36	39	2 36	2 37	2 38	2 39
40	2 40	100	6 40	160	10 40	220	14 40	280	18 40	340	22 40	40	2 40	2 41	2 42	2 43
41	2 44	101	6 44	161	10 44	221	14 44	281	18 44	341	22 44	41	2 44	2 45	2 46	2 47
42	2 48	102	6 48	162	10 48	222	14 48	282	18 48	342	22 48	42	2 48	2 49	2 50	2 51
43	2 52	103	6 52	163	10 52	223	14 52	283	18 52	343	22 52	43	2 52	2 53	2 54	2 55
44	2 56	104	6 56	164	10 56	224	14 56	284	18 56	344	22 56	44	2 56	2 57	2 58	2 59
45	3 00	105	7 00	165	11 00	225	15 00	285	19 00	345	23 00	45	3 00	3 01	3 02	3 03
46	3 04	106	7 04	166	11 04	226	15 04	286	19 04	346	23 04	46	3 04	3 05	3 06	3 07
47	3 08	107	7 08	167	11 08	227	15 08	287	19 08	347	23 08	47	3 08	3 09	3 10	3 11
48	3 12	108	7 12	168	11 12	228	15 12	288	19 12	348	23 12	48	3 12	3 13	3 14	3 15
49	3 16	109	7 16	169	11 16	229	15 16	289	19 16	349	23 16	49	3 16	3 17	3 18	3 19
50	3 20	110	7 20	170	11 20	230	15 20	290	19 20	350	23 20	50	3 20	3 21	3 22	3 23
51	3 24	111	7 24	171	11 24	231	15 24	291	19 24	351	23 24	51	3 24	3 25	3 26	3 27
52	3 28	112	7 28	172	11 28	232	15 28	292	19 28	352	23 28	52	3 28	3 29	3 30	3 31
53	3 32	113	7 32	173	11 32	233	15 32	293	19 32	353	23 32	53	3 32	3 33	3 34	3 35
54	3 36	114	7 36	174	11 36	234	15 36	294	19 36	354	23 36	54	3 36	3 37	3 38	3 39
55	3 40	115	7 40	175	11 40	235	15 40	295	19 40	355	23 40	55	3 40	3 41	3 42	3 43
56	3 44	116	7 44	176	11 44	236	15 44	296	19 44	356	23 44	56	3 44	3 45	3 46	3 47
57	3 48	117	7 48	177	11 48	237	15 48	297	19 48	357	23 48	57	3 48	3 49	3 50	3 51
58	3 52	118	7 52	178	11 52	238	15 52	298	19 52	358	23 52	58	3 52	3 53	3 54	3 55
59	3 56	119	7 56	179	11 56	239	15 56	299	19 56	359	23 56	59	3 56	3 57	3 58	3 59

The above table is for converting expressions in arc to their equivalent in time ; its main use in this Almanac is for the conversion of longitude for application to L.M.T. (*added* if *west*, *subtracted* if *east*) to give G.M.T. or vice versa, particularly in the case of sunrise, sunset, etc.

i

52ᵐ

52ᵐ s	SUN PLANETS	ARIES	MOON	v or d / Corrⁿ	v or d / Corrⁿ	v or d / Corrⁿ
00	13 00·0	13 02·1	12 24·5	0·0 0·0	6·0 5·3	12·0 10·5
01	13 00·3	13 02·4	12 24·7	0·1 0·1	6·1 5·3	12·1 10·6
02	13 00·5	13 02·6	12 24·9	0·2 0·2	6·2 5·4	12·2 10·7
03	13 00·8	13 02·9	12 25·2	0·3 0·3	6·3 5·5	12·3 10·8
04	13 01·0	13 03·1	12 25·4	0·4 0·4	6·4 5·6	12·4 10·9
05	13 01·3	13 03·4	12 25·7	0·5 0·4	6·5 5·7	12·5 10·9
06	13 01·5	13 03·6	12 25·9	0·6 0·5	6·6 5·8	12·6 11·0
07	13 01·8	13 03·9	12 26·1	0·7 0·6	6·7 5·9	12·7 11·1
08	13 02·0	13 04·1	12 26·4	0·8 0·7	6·8 6·0	12·8 11·2
09	13 02·3	13 04·4	12 26·6	0·9 0·8	6·9 6·0	12·9 11·3
10	13 02·5	13 04·6	12 26·9	1·0 0·9	7·0 6·1	13·0 11·4
11	13 02·8	13 04·9	12 27·1	1·1 1·0	7·1 6·2	13·1 11·5
12	13 03·0	13 05·1	12 27·3	1·2 1·1	7·2 6·3	13·2 11·6
13	13 03·3	13 05·4	12 27·6	1·3 1·1	7·3 6·4	13·3 11·6
14	13 03·5	13 05·6	12 27·8	1·4 1·2	7·4 6·5	13·4 11·7
15	13 03·8	13 05·9	12 28·0	1·5 1·3	7·5 6·6	13·5 11·8
16	13 04·0	13 06·1	12 28·3	1·6 1·4	7·6 6·7	13·6 11·9
17	13 04·3	13 06·4	12 28·5	1·7 1·5	7·7 6·7	13·7 12·0
18	13 04·5	13 06·6	12 28·8	1·8 1·6	7·8 6·8	13·8 12·1
19	13 04·8	13 06·9	12 29·0	1·9 1·7	7·9 6·9	13·9 12·2
20	13 05·0	13 07·1	12 29·2	2·0 1·8	8·0 7·0	14·0 12·3
21	13 05·3	13 07·4	12 29·5	2·1 1·8	8·1 7·1	14·1 12·3
22	13 05·5	13 07·7	12 29·7	2·2 1·9	8·2 7·2	14·2 12·4
23	13 05·8	13 07·9	12 30·0	2·3 2·0	8·3 7·3	14·3 12·5
24	13 06·0	13 08·2	12 30·2	2·4 2·1	8·4 7·4	14·4 12·6
25	13 06·3	13 08·4	12 30·4	2·5 2·2	8·5 7·4	14·5 12·7
26	13 06·5	13 08·7	12 30·7	2·6 2·3	8·6 7·5	14·6 12·8
27	13 06·8	13 08·9	12 30·9	2·7 2·4	8·7 7·6	14·7 12·9
28	13 07·0	13 09·2	12 31·1	2·8 2·5	8·8 7·7	14·8 13·0
29	13 07·3	13 09·4	12 31·4	2·9 2·5	8·9 7·8	14·9 13·0
30	13 07·5	13 09·7	12 31·6	3·0 2·6	9·0 7·9	15·0 13·1
31	13 07·8	13 09·9	12 31·9	3·1 2·7	9·1 8·0	15·1 13·2
32	13 08·0	13 10·2	12 32·1	3·2 2·8	9·2 8·1	15·2 13·3
33	13 08·3	13 10·4	12 32·3	3·3 2·9	9·3 8·1	15·3 13·4
34	13 08·5	13 10·7	12 32·6	3·4 3·0	9·4 8·2	15·4 13·5
35	13 08·8	13 10·9	12 32·8	3·5 3·1	9·5 8·3	15·5 13·6
36	13 09·0	13 11·2	12 33·1	3·6 3·2	9·6 8·4	15·6 13·7
37	13 09·3	13 11·4	12 33·3	3·7 3·2	9·7 8·5	15·7 13·7
38	13 09·5	13 11·7	12 33·5	3·8 3·3	9·8 8·6	15·8 13·8
39	13 09·8	13 11·9	12 33·8	3·9 3·4	9·9 8·7	15·9 13·9
40	13 10·0	13 12·2	12 34·0	4·0 3·5	10·0 8·8	16·0 14·0
41	13 10·3	13 12·4	12 34·2	4·1 3·6	10·1 8·8	16·1 14·1
42	13 10·5	13 12·7	12 34·5	4·2 3·7	10·2 8·9	16·2 14·2
43	13 10·8	13 12·9	12 34·7	4·3 3·8	10·3 9·0	16·3 14·3
44	13 11·0	13 13·2	12 35·0	4·4 3·9	10·4 9·1	16·4 14·4
45	13 11·3	13 13·4	12 35·2	4·5 3·9	10·5 9·2	16·5 14·4
46	13 11·5	13 13·7	12 35·4	4·6 4·0	10·6 9·3	16·6 14·5
47	13 11·8	13 13·9	12 35·7	4·7 4·1	10·7 9·4	16·7 14·6
48	13 12·0	13 14·2	12 35·9	4·8 4·2	10·8 9·5	16·8 14·7
49	13 12·3	13 14·4	12 36·2	4·9 4·3	10·9 9·5	16·9 14·8
50	13 12·5	13 14·7	12 36·4	5·0 4·4	11·0 9·6	17·0 14·9
51	13 12·8	13 14·9	12 36·6	5·1 4·5	11·1 9·7	17·1 15·0
52	13 13·0	13 15·2	12 36·9	5·2 4·6	11·2 9·8	17·2 15·1
53	13 13·3	13 15·4	12 37·1	5·3 4·6	11·3 9·9	17·3 15·1
54	13 13·5	13 15·7	12 37·4	5·4 4·7	11·4 10·0	17·4 15·2
55	13 13·8	13 15·9	12 37·6	5·5 4·8	11·5 10·1	17·5 15·3
56	13 14·0	13 16·2	12 37·8	5·6 4·9	11·6 10·2	17·6 15·4
57	13 14·3	13 16·4	12 38·1	5·7 5·0	11·7 10·2	17·7 15·5
58	13 14·5	13 16·7	12 38·3	5·8 5·1	11·8 10·3	17·8 15·6
59	13 14·8	13 16·9	12 38·5	5·9 5·2	11·9 10·4	17·9 15·7
60	13 15·0	13 17·2	12 38·8	6·0 5·3	12·0 10·5	18·0 15·8

53ᵐ

53ᵐ s	SUN PLANETS	ARIES	MOON	v or d / Corrⁿ	v or d / Corrⁿ	v or d / Corrⁿ
00	13 15·0	13 17·2	12 38·8	0·0 0·0	6·0 5·4	12·0 10·7
01	13 15·3	13 17·4	12 39·0	0·1 0·1	6·1 5·4	12·1 10·8
02	13 15·5	13 17·7	12 39·3	0·2 0·2	6·2 5·5	12·2 10·9
03	13 15·8	13 17·9	12 39·5	0·3 0·3	6·3 5·6	12·3 11·0
04	13 16·0	13 18·2	12 39·7	0·4 0·4	6·4 5·7	12·4 11·1
05	13 16·3	13 18·4	12 40·0	0·5 0·4	6·5 5·8	12·5 11·1
06	13 16·5	13 18·7	12 40·2	0·6 0·5	6·6 5·9	12·6 11·2
07	13 16·8	13 18·9	12 40·5	0·7 0·6	6·7 6·0	12·7 11·3
08	13 17·0	13 19·2	12 40·7	0·8 0·7	6·8 6·1	12·8 11·4
09	13 17·3	13 19·4	12 41·0	0·9 0·8	6·9 6·2	12·9 11·5
10	13 17·5	13 19·7	12 41·2	1·0 0·9	7·0 6·2	13·0 11·6
11	13 17·8	13 19·9	12 41·4	1·1 1·0	7·1 6·3	13·1 11·7
12	13 18·0	13 20·2	12 41·6	1·2 1·1	7·2 6·4	13·2 11·8
13	13 18·3	13 20·4	12 41·9	1·3 1·2	7·3 6·5	13·3 11·9
14	13 18·5	13 20·7	12 42·1	1·4 1·2	7·4 6·6	13·4 11·9
15	13 18·8	13 20·9	12 42·4	1·5 1·3	7·5 6·7	13·5 12·0
16	13 19·0	13 21·2	12 42·6	1·6 1·4	7·6 6·8	13·6 12·1
17	13 19·3	13 21·4	12 42·8	1·7 1·5	7·7 6·9	13·7 12·2
18	13 19·5	13 21·7	12 43·1	1·8 1·6	7·8 7·0	13·8 12·3
19	13 19·8	13 21·9	12 43·3	1·9 1·7	7·9 7·0	13·9 12·4
20	13 20·0	13 22·2	12 43·6	2·0 1·8	8·0 7·1	14·0 12·5
21	13 20·3	13 22·4	12 43·8	2·1 1·9	8·1 7·2	14·1 12·6
22	13 20·5	13 22·7	12 44·0	2·2 2·0	8·2 7·3	14·2 12·7
23	13 20·8	13 22·9	12 44·3	2·3 2·1	8·3 7·4	14·3 12·8
24	13 21·0	13 23·2	12 44·5	2·4 2·1	8·4 7·5	14·4 12·8
25	13 21·3	13 23·4	12 44·7	2·5 2·2	8·5 7·6	14·5 12·9
26	13 21·5	13 23·7	12 45·0	2·6 2·3	8·6 7·7	14·6 13·0
27	13 21·8	13 23·9	12 45·2	2·7 2·4	8·7 7·8	14·7 13·1
28	13 22·0	13 24·2	12 45·5	2·8 2·5	8·8 7·8	14·8 13·2
29	13 22·3	13 24·4	12 45·7	2·9 2·6	8·9 7·9	14·9 13·3
30	13 22·5	13 24·7	12 45·9	3·0 2·7	9·0 8·0	15·0 13·4
31	13 22·8	13 24·9	12 46·2	3·1 2·8	9·1 8·1	15·1 13·5
32	13 23·0	13 25·2	12 46·4	3·2 2·9	9·2 8·2	15·2 13·6
33	13 23·3	13 25·4	12 46·7	3·3 2·9	9·3 8·3	15·3 13·6
34	13 23·5	13 25·7	12 46·9	3·4 3·0	9·4 8·4	15·4 13·7
35	13 23·8	13 26·0	12 47·1	3·5 3·1	9·5 8·5	15·5 13·8
36	13 24·0	13 26·2	12 47·4	3·6 3·2	9·6 8·6	15·6 13·9
37	13 24·3	13 26·5	12 47·6	3·7 3·3	9·7 8·6	15·7 14·0
38	13 24·5	13 26·7	12 47·9	3·8 3·4	9·8 8·7	15·8 14·1
39	13 24·8	13 27·0	12 48·1	3·9 3·5	9·9 8·8	15·9 14·2
40	13 25·0	13 27·2	12 48·3	4·0 3·6	10·0 8·9	16·0 14·3
41	13 25·3	13 27·5	12 48·6	4·1 3·7	10·1 9·0	16·1 14·4
42	13 25·5	13 27·7	12 48·8	4·2 3·7	10·2 9·1	16·2 14·4
43	13 25·8	13 28·0	12 49·0	4·3 3·8	10·3 9·2	16·3 14·5
44	13 26·0	13 28·2	12 49·3	4·4 3·9	10·4 9·3	16·4 14·6
45	13 26·3	13 28·5	12 49·5	4·5 4·0	10·5 9·4	16·5 14·7
46	13 26·5	13 28·7	12 49·8	4·6 4·1	10·6 9·5	16·6 14·8
47	13 26·8	13 29·0	12 50·0	4·7 4·2	10·7 9·5	16·7 14·9
48	13 27·0	13 29·2	12 50·2	4·8 4·3	10·8 9·6	16·8 15·0
49	13 27·3	13 29·5	12 50·5	4·9 4·3	10·9 9·7	16·9 15·1
50	13 27·5	13 29·7	12 50·7	5·0 4·5	11·0 9·8	17·0 15·2
51	13 27·8	13 30·0	12 51·0	5·1 4·5	11·1 9·9	17·1 15·2
52	13 28·0	13 30·2	12 51·2	5·2 4·6	11·2 10·0	17·2 15·3
53	13 28·3	13 30·5	12 51·4	5·3 4·7	11·3 10·1	17·3 15·4
54	13 28·5	13 30·7	12 51·7	5·4 4·8	11·4 10·2	17·4 15·5
55	13 28·8	13 31·0	12 51·9	5·5 4·9	11·5 10·3	17·5 15·6
56	13 29·0	13 31·2	12 52·1	5·6 5·0	11·6 10·3	17·6 15·6
57	13 29·3	13 31·5	12 52·4	5·7 5·1	11·7 10·4	17·7 15·8
58	13 29·5	13 31·7	12 52·6	5·8 5·2	11·8 10·5	17·8 15·9
59	13 29·8	13 32·0	12 52·9	5·9 5·3	11·9 10·6	17·9 16·0
60	13 30·0	13 32·2	12 53·1	6·0 5·4	12·0 10·7	18·0 16·1

54	SUN PLANETS	ARIES	MOON	v or Corrⁿ d		v or Corrⁿ d		v or Corrⁿ d	
s	° ′	° ′	° ′	′	′	′	′	′	′
00	13 30.0	13 32.2	12 53.1	0.0	0.0	6.0	5.5	12.0	10.9
01	13 30.3	13 32.5	12 53.3	0.1	0.1	6.1	5.5	12.1	11.0
02	13 30.5	13 32.7	12 53.6	0.2	0.2	6.2	5.6	12.2	11.1
03	13 30.8	13 33.0	12 53.8	0.3	0.3	6.3	5.7	12.3	11.2
04	13 31.0	13 33.2	12 54.1	0.4	0.4	6.4	5.8	12.4	11.3
05	13 31.3	13 33.5	12 54.3	0.5	0.5	6.5	5.9	12.5	11.4
06	13 31.5	13 33.7	12 54.5	0.6	0.5	6.6	6.0	12.6	11.4
07	13 31.8	13 34.0	12 54.8	0.7	0.6	6.7	6.1	12.7	11.5
08	13 32.0	13 34.2	12 55.0	0.8	0.7	6.8	6.2	12.8	11.6
09	13 32.3	13 34.5	12 55.2	0.9	0.8	6.9	6.3	12.9	11.7
10	13 32.5	13 34.7	12 55.5	1.0	0.9	7.0	6.4	13.0	11.8
11	13 32.8	13 35.0	12 55.7	1.1	1.0	7.1	6.4	13.1	11.9
12	13 33.0	13 35.2	12 56.0	1.2	1.1	7.2	6.5	13.2	12.0
13	13 33.3	13 35.5	12 56.2	1.3	1.2	7.3	6.6	13.3	12.1
14	13 33.5	13 35.7	12 56.4	1.4	1.3	7.4	6.7	13.4	12.2
15	13 33.8	13 36.0	12 56.7	1.5	1.4	7.5	6.8	13.5	12.3
16	13 34.0	13 36.2	12 56.9	1.6	1.5	7.6	6.9	13.6	12.4
17	13 34.3	13 36.5	12 57.2	1.7	1.5	7.7	7.0	13.7	12.4
18	13 34.5	13 36.7	12 57.4	1.8	1.6	7.8	7.1	13.8	12.5
19	13 34.8	13 37.0	12 57.6	1.9	1.7	7.9	7.2	13.9	12.6
20	13 35.0	13 37.2	12 57.9	2.0	1.8	8.0	7.3	14.0	12.7
21	13 35.3	13 37.5	12 58.1	2.1	1.9	8.1	7.4	14.1	12.8
22	13 35.5	13 37.7	12 58.3	2.2	2.0	8.2	7.4	14.2	12.9
23	13 35.8	13 38.0	12 58.6	2.3	2.1	8.3	7.5	14.3	13.0
24	13 36.0	13 38.2	12 58.8	2.4	2.2	8.4	7.6	14.4	13.1
25	13 36.3	13 38.5	12 59.1	2.5	2.3	8.5	7.7	14.5	13.2
26	13 36.5	13 38.7	12 59.3	2.6	2.4	8.6	7.8	14.6	13.3
27	13 36.8	13 39.0	12 59.5	2.7	2.5	8.7	7.9	14.7	13.4
28	13 37.0	13 39.2	12 59.8	2.8	2.5	8.8	8.0	14.8	13.4
29	13 37.3	13 39.5	13 00.0	2.9	2.6	8.9	8.1	14.9	13.5
30	13 37.5	13 39.7	13 00.3	3.0	2.7	9.0	8.2	15.0	13.6
31	13 37.8	13 40.0	13 00.5	3.1	2.8	9.1	8.3	15.1	13.7
32	13 38.0	13 40.2	13 00.7	3.2	2.9	9.2	8.4	15.2	13.8
33	13 38.3	13 40.5	13 01.0	3.3	3.0	9.3	8.4	15.3	13.9
34	13 38.5	13 40.7	13 01.2	3.4	3.1	9.4	8.5	15.4	14.0
35	13 38.8	13 41.0	13 01.5	3.5	3.2	9.5	8.6	15.5	14.1
36	13 39.0	13 41.2	13 01.7	3.6	3.3	9.6	8.7	15.6	14.2
37	13 39.3	13 41.5	13 01.9	3.7	3.4	9.7	8.8	15.7	14.3
38	13 39.5	13 41.7	13 02.2	3.8	3.5	9.8	8.9	15.8	14.4
39	13 39.8	13 42.0	13 02.4	3.9	3.5	9.9	9.0	15.9	14.4
40	13 40.0	13 42.2	13 02.6	4.0	3.6	10.0	9.1	16.0	14.5
41	13 40.3	13 42.5	13 02.9	4.1	3.7	10.1	9.2	16.1	14.6
42	13 40.5	13 42.7	13 03.1	4.2	3.8	10.2	9.3	16.2	14.7
43	13 40.8	13 43.0	13 03.4	4.3	3.9	10.3	9.4	16.3	14.8
44	13 41.0	13 43.2	13 03.6	4.4	4.0	10.4	9.4	16.4	14.9
45	13 41.3	13 43.5	13 03.8	4.5	4.1	10.5	9.5	16.5	15.3
46	13 41.5	13 43.7	13 04.1	4.6	4.2	10.6	9.6	16.6	15.1
47	13 41.8	13 44.0	13 04.3	4.7	4.3	10.7	9.7	16.7	15.2
48	13 42.0	13 44.3	13 04.6	4.8	4.4	10.8	9.8	16.8	15.3
49	13 42.3	13 44.5	13 04.8	4.9	4.5	10.9	9.9	16.9	15.4
50	13 42.5	13 44.8	13 05.0	5.0	4.5	11.0	10.0	17.0	15.4
51	13 42.8	13 45.0	13 05.3	5.1	4.6	11.1	10.1	17.1	15.5
52	13 43.0	13 45.3	13 05.5	5.2	4.7	11.2	10.2	17.2	15.6
53	13 43.3	13 45.5	13 05.7	5.3	4.8	11.3	10.3	17.3	15.7
54	13 43.5	13 45.8	13 06.0	5.4	4.9	11.4	10.4	17.4	15.8
55	13 43.8	13 46.0	13 06.2	5.5	5.0	11.5	10.4	17.5	15.9
56	13 44.0	13 46.3	13 06.5	5.6	5.1	11.6	10.5	17.6	16.0
57	13 44.3	13 46.5	13 06.7	5.7	5.2	11.7	10.6	17.7	16.1
58	13 44.5	13 46.8	13 06.9	5.8	5.3	11.8	10.7	17.8	16.2
59	13 44.8	13 47.0	13 07.2	5.9	5.4	11.9	10.8	17.9	16.3
60	13 45.0	13 47.3	13 07.4	6.0	5.5	12.0	10.9	18.0	16.4

55	SUN PLANETS	ARIES	MOON	v or Corrⁿ d		v or Corrⁿ d		v or Corrⁿ d	
s	° ′	° ′	° ′	′	′	′	′	′	′
00	13 45.0	13 47.3	13 07.4	0.0	0.0	6.0	5.6	12.0	11.1
01	13 45.3	13 47.5	13 07.7	0.1	0.1	6.1	5.6	12.1	11.2
02	13 45.5	13 47.8	13 07.9	0.2	0.2	6.2	5.7	12.2	11.3
03	13 45.8	13 48.0	13 08.1	0.3	0.3	6.3	5.8	12.3	11.4
04	13 46.0	13 48.3	13 08.4	0.4	0.4	6.4	5.9	12.4	11.5
05	13 46.3	13 48.5	13 08.6	0.5	0.5	6.5	6.0	12.5	11.6
06	13 46.5	13 48.8	13 08.8	0.6	0.6	6.6	6.1	12.6	11.7
07	13 46.8	13 49.0	13 09.1	0.7	0.6	6.7	6.2	12.7	11.7
08	13 47.0	13 49.3	13 09.3	0.8	0.7	6.8	6.3	12.8	11.8
09	13 47.3	13 49.5	13 09.6	0.9	0.8	6.9	6.4	12.9	11.9
10	13 47.5	13 49.8	13 09.8	1.0	0.9	7.0	6.5	13.0	12.0
11	13 47.8	13 50.0	13 10.1	1.1	1.0	7.1	6.6	13.1	12.1
12	13 48.0	13 50.3	13 10.3	1.2	1.1	7.2	6.7	13.2	12.2
13	13 48.3	13 50.5	13 10.5	1.3	1.2	7.3	6.8	13.3	12.3
14	13 48.5	13 50.8	13 10.8	1.4	1.3	7.4	6.8	13.4	12.4
15	13 48.8	13 51.0	13 11.0	1.5	1.4	7.5	6.9	13.5	12.5
16	13 49.0	13 51.3	13 11.2	1.6	1.5	7.6	7.0	13.6	12.6
17	13 49.3	13 51.5	13 11.5	1.7	1.6	7.7	7.1	13.7	12.7
18	13 49.5	13 51.8	13 11.7	1.8	1.7	7.8	7.2	13.8	12.8
19	13 49.8	13 52.0	13 12.0	1.9	1.8	7.9	7.3	13.9	12.9
20	13 50.0	13 52.3	13 12.2	2.0	1.9	8.0	7.4	14.0	13.0
21	13 50.3	13 52.5	13 12.4	2.1	1.9	8.1	7.5	14.1	13.0
22	13 50.5	13 52.8	13 12.7	2.2	2.0	8.2	7.6	14.2	13.1
23	13 50.8	13 53.0	13 12.9	2.3	2.1	8.3	7.7	14.3	13.2
24	13 51.0	13 53.3	13 13.1	2.4	2.2	8.4	7.8	14.4	13.3
25	13 51.3	13 53.5	13 13.4	2.5	2.3	8.5	7.9	14.5	13.4
26	13 51.5	13 53.8	13 13.6	2.6	2.4	8.6	8.0	14.6	13.5
27	13 51.8	13 54.0	13 13.9	2.7	2.5	8.7	8.0	14.7	13.6
28	13 52.0	13 54.3	13 14.1	2.8	2.6	8.8	8.1	14.8	13.7
29	13 52.3	13 54.5	13 14.3	2.9	2.7	8.9	8.2	14.9	13.8
30	13 52.5	13 54.8	13 14.6	3.0	2.8	9.0	8.3	15.0	13.9
31	13 52.8	13 55.0	13 14.8	3.1	2.9	9.1	8.4	15.1	14.0
32	13 53.0	13 55.3	13 15.1	3.2	3.0	9.2	8.5	15.2	14.1
33	13 53.3	13 55.5	13 15.3	3.3	3.1	9.3	8.6	15.3	14.2
34	13 53.5	13 55.8	13 15.5	3.4	3.1	9.4	8.7	15.4	14.2
35	13 53.8	13 56.0	13 15.8	3.5	3.2	9.5	8.8	15.5	14.3
36	13 54.0	13 56.3	13 16.0	3.6	3.3	9.6	8.9	15.6	14.4
37	13 54.3	13 56.5	13 16.2	3.7	3.4	9.7	9.0	15.7	14.5
38	13 54.5	13 56.8	13 16.5	3.8	3.5	9.8	9.1	15.8	14.6
39	13 54.8	13 57.0	13 16.7	3.9	3.6	9.9	9.2	15.9	14.7
40	13 55.0	13 57.3	13 17.0	4.0	3.7	10.0	9.3	16.0	14.8
41	13 55.3	13 57.5	13 17.2	4.1	3.8	10.1	9.3	16.1	14.9
42	13 55.5	13 57.8	13 17.4	4.2	3.9	10.2	9.4	16.2	15.0
43	13 55.8	13 58.0	13 17.7	4.3	4.0	10.3	9.5	16.3	15.1
44	13 56.0	13 58.3	13 17.9	4.4	4.1	10.4	9.6	16.4	15.2
45	13 56.3	13 58.5	13 18.2	4.5	4.2	10.5	9.7	16.5	15.3
46	13 56.5	13 58.8	13 18.4	4.6	4.3	10.6	9.8	16.6	15.4
47	13 56.8	13 59.0	13 18.6	4.7	4.3	10.7	9.9	16.7	15.4
48	13 57.0	13 59.3	13 18.9	4.8	4.4	10.8	10.0	16.8	15.5
49	13 57.3	13 59.5	13 19.1	4.9	4.5	10.9	10.1	16.9	15.6
50	13 57.5	13 59.8	13 19.3	5.0	4.6	11.0	10.2	17.0	15.7
51	13 57.8	14 00.0	13 19.6	5.1	4.7	11.1	10.3	17.1	15.8
52	13 58.0	14 00.3	13 19.8	5.2	4.8	11.2	10.4	17.2	15.9
53	13 58.3	14 00.5	13 20.1	5.3	4.9	11.3	10.5	17.3	16.0
54	13 58.5	14 00.8	13 20.3	5.4	4.9	11.4	10.5	17.4	16.1
55	13 58.8	14 01.0	13 20.5	5.5	5.1	11.5	10.6	17.5	16.2
56	13 59.0	14 01.3	13 20.8	5.6	5.2	11.6	10.7	17.6	16.3
57	13 59.3	14 01.5	13 21.0	5.7	5.2	11.7	10.8	17.7	16.4
58	13 59.5	14 01.8	13 21.3	5.8	5.4	11.8	10.9	17.8	16.5
59	13 59.8	14 02.0	13 21.5	5.9	5.5	11.9	11.0	17.9	16.6
60	14 00.0	14 02.3	13 21.7	6.0	5.6	12.0	11.1	18.0	16.7

ALTITUDE CORRECTION TABLES 0°–35°—MOON

App. Alt.	0°–4° Corrⁿ	5°–9° Corrⁿ	10°–14° Corrⁿ	15°–19° Corrⁿ	20°–24° Corrⁿ	25°–29° Corrⁿ	30°–34° Corrⁿ	App. Alt.
00	0 33·8	5 58·2	10 62·1	15 62·8	20 62·2	25 60·8	30 58·9	00
10	35·9	58·5	62·2	62·8	62·1	60·7	58·8	10
20	37·8	58·7	62·2	62·8	62·1	60·7	58·8	20
30	39·6	58·9	62·3	62·8	62·1	60·7	58·7	30
40	41·2	59·1	62·3	62·8	62·0	60·6	58·6	40
50	42·6	59·3	62·4	62·7	62·0	60·6	58·5	50
00	1 44·0	6 59·5	11 62·4	16 62·7	21 62·0	26 60·5	31 58·5	00
10	45·2	59·7	62·4	62·7	61·9	60·4	58·4	10
20	46·3	59·9	62·5	62·7	61·9	60·4	58·3	20
30	47·3	60·0	62·5	62·7	61·9	60·3	58·2	30
40	48·3	60·2	62·5	62·7	61·8	60·3	58·2	40
50	49·2	60·3	62·6	62·7	61·8	60·2	58·1	50
00	2 50·0	7 60·5	12 62·6	17 62·7	22 61·7	27 60·1	32 58·0	00
10	50·8	60·6	62·6	62·6	61·7	60·1	57·9	10
20	51·4	60·7	62·6	62·6	61·6	60·0	57·8	20
30	52·1	60·9	62·7	62·6	61·6	59·9	57·8	30
40	52·7	61·0	62·7	62·6	61·5	59·9	57·7	40
50	53·3	61·1	62·7	62·6	61·5	59·8	57·6	50
00	3 53·8	8 61·2	13 62·7	18 62·5	23 61·5	28 59·7	33 57·5	00
10	54·3	61·3	62·7	62·5	61·4	59·7	57·4	10
20	54·8	61·4	62·7	62·5	61·4	59·6	57·4	20
30	55·2	61·5	62·8	62·5	61·3	59·6	57·3	30
40	55·6	61·6	62·8	62·4	61·3	59·5	57·2	40
50	56·0	61·6	62·8	62·4	61·2	59·4	57·1	50
00	4 56·4	9 61·7	14 62·8	19 62·4	24 61·2	29 59·3	34 57·0	00
10	56·7	61·8	62·8	62·3	61·1	59·3	56·9	10
20	57·1	61·9	62·8	62·3	61·1	59·2	56·9	20
30	57·4	61·9	62·8	62·3	61·0	59·1	56·8	30
40	57·7	62·0	62·8	62·2	60·9	59·1	56·7	40
50	57·9	62·1	62·8	62·2	60·9	59·0	56·6	50

H.P.	L U	L U	L U	L U	L U	L U	L U	H.P.
54·0	0·3 0·9	0·3 0·9	0·4 1·0	0·5 1·1	0·6 1·2	0·7 1·3	0·9 1·5	54·0
54·3	0·7 1·1	0·7 1·2	0·7 1·2	0·8 1·3	0·9 1·4	1·1 1·5	1·2 1·7	54·3
54·6	1·1 1·4	1·1 1·4	1·1 1·4	1·2 1·5	1·3 1·6	1·4 1·7	1·5 1·8	54·6
54·9	1·4 1·6	1·5 1·6	1·5 1·6	1·6 1·7	1·6 1·8	1·8 1·9	1·9 2·0	54·9
55·2	1·8 1·8	1·8 1·8	1·9 1·9	1·9 1·9	2·0 2·0	2·1 2·1	2·2 2·2	55·2
55·5	2·2 2·0	2·2 2·0	2·3 2·1	2·3 2·1	2·4 2·2	2·4 2·3	2·5 2·4	55·5
55·8	2·6 2·2	2·6 2·2	2·6 2·3	2·7 2·3	2·7 2·4	2·8 2·4	2·9 2·5	55·8
56·1	3·0 2·4	3·0 2·5	3·0 2·5	3·0 2·5	3·1 2·6	3·1 2·6	3·2 2·7	56·1
56·4	3·4 2·7	3·4 2·7	3·4 2·7	3·4 2·7	3·4 2·8	3·5 2·8	3·5 2·9	56·4
56·7	3·7 2·9	3·7 2·9	3·8 2·9	3·8 2·9	3·8 3·0	3·8 3·0	3·9 3·0	56·7
57·0	4·1 3·1	4·1 3·1	4·1 3·1	4·1 3·1	4·2 3·1	4·2 3·2	4·2 3·2	57·0
57·3	4·5 3·3	4·5 3·3	4·5 3·3	4·5 3·3	4·5 3·3	4·5 3·4	4·6 3·4	57·3
57·6	4·9 3·5	4·9 3·5	4·9 3·5	4·9 3·5	4·9 3·6	4·9 3·6	4·9 3·6	57·6
57·9	5·3 3·8	5·3 3·8	5·2 3·8	5·2 3·7	5·2 3·7	5·2 3·7	5·2 3·7	57·9
58·2	5·6 4·0	5·6 4·0	5·6 4·0	5·6 4·0	5·6 3·9	5·6 3·9	5·6 3·9	58·2
58·5	6·0 4·2	6·0 4·2	6·0 4·2	6·0 4·2	6·0 4·1	5·9 4·1	5·9 4·1	58·5
58·8	6·4 4·4	6·4 4·4	6·3 4·4	6·3 4·4	6·3 4·3	6·3 4·3	6·2 4·2	58·8
59·1	6·8 4·6	6·8 4·6	6·7 4·6	6·7 4·6	6·7 4·5	6·6 4·5	6·6 4·4	59·1
59·4	7·2 4·8	7·1 4·8	7·1 4·8	7·1 4·8	7·0 4·7	7·0 4·7	6·9 4·6	59·4
59·7	7·5 5·1	7·5 5·0	7·5 5·0	7·5 5·0	7·4 4·9	7·3 4·8	7·2 4·7	59·7
60·0	7·9 5·3	7·9 5·3	7·9 5·2	7·8 5·2	7·8 5·1	7·7 5·0	7·6 4·9	60·0
60·3	8·3 5·5	8·3 5·5	8·2 5·4	8·2 5·4	8·1 5·3	8·0 5·2	7·9 5·1	60·3
60·6	8·7 5·7	8·7 5·7	8·6 5·7	8·6 5·6	8·5 5·5	8·4 5·4	8·2 5·3	60·6
60·9	9·1 5·9	9·0 5·9	9·0 5·8	8·9 5·8	8·8 5·7	8·7 5·6	8·6 5·4	60·9
61·2	9·5 6·2	9·4 6·1	9·4 6·1	9·3 6·0	9·2 5·9	9·1 5·8	8·9 5·6	61·2
61·5	9·8 6·4	9·8 6·3	9·7 6·3	9·7 6·2	9·5 6·1	9·4 5·9	9·2 5·8	61·5

DIP

Ht. of Eye (m)	Corrⁿ	Ht. of Eye (ft.)	Ht. of Eye (m)	Corrⁿ	Ht. of Eye (ft.)
2·4	−2·8	8·0	9·5	−5·5	31·5
2·6	−2·9	8·6	9·9	−5·6	32·7
2·8	−3·0	9·2	10·3	−5·7	33·9
3·0	−3·1	9·8	10·6	−5·8	35·1
3·2	−3·2	10·5	11·0	−5·9	36·3
3·4	−3·3	11·2	11·4	−6·0	37·6
3·6	−3·4	11·9	11·8	−6·1	38·9
3·8	−3·5	12·6	12·2	−6·2	40·1
4·0	−3·6	13·3	12·6	−6·3	41·5
4·3	−3·7	14·1	13·0	−6·4	42·8
4·5	−3·8	14·9	13·4	−6·5	44·2
4·7	−3·9	15·7	13·8	−6·6	45·5
5·0	−4·0	16·5	14·2	−6·7	46·9
5·2	−4·1	17·4	14·7	−6·8	48·4
5·5	−4·2	18·3	15·1	−6·9	49·8
5·8	−4·3	19·1	15·5	−7·0	51·3
6·1	−4·4	20·1	16·0	−7·1	52·8
6·3	−4·5	21·0	16·5	−7·2	54·3
6·6	−4·6	22·0	16·9	−7·3	55·8
6·9	−4·7	22·9	17·4	−7·4	57·4
7·2	−4·8	23·9	17·9	−7·5	58·9
7·5	−4·9	24·9	18·4	−7·6	60·5
7·9	−5·0	26·0	18·8	−7·7	62·1
8·2	−5·1	27·1	19·3	−7·8	63·8
8·5	−5·2	28·1	19·8	−7·9	65·4
8·8	−5·3	29·2	20·4	−8·0	67·1
9·2	−5·4	30·4	20·9	−8·1	68·8
9·5		31·5	21·4		70·5

MOON CORRECTION TABLE

The correction is in two parts; the first correction is taken from the upper part of the table with argument apparent altitude, and the second from the lower part, with argument H.P., in the same column as that from which the first correction was taken. Separate corrections are given in the lower part for lower (L) and upper (U) limbs. All corrections are to be **added** to apparent altitude, *but 30′ is to be subtracted from the altitude of the upper limb.*

For corrections for pressure and temperature see page A4.

For bubble sextant observations ignore dip, take the mean of upper and lower limb corrections and subtract 15′ from the altitude.

App. Alt. = Apparent altitude = Sextant altitude corrected for index error and dip.

Appendix 7
Sight reduction tables, extracts from AP 3270, or HO 249

Vol: 1
Selected stars

LAT 50°N

LHA ♈	Hc Zn	Hc Zn	Hc Zn	Hc Zn	Hc Zn	Hc Zn	Hc Zn
	◆Mirfak	Alpheratz	◆ALTAIR	Rasalhague	◆ARCTURUS	Alkaid	Kochab
270	15 18 025	20 42 069	42 56 142	52 12 190	36 06 257	50 18 295	58 49 337
271	15 35 026	21 18 070	43 20 143	52 04 192	35 29 257	49 43 295	58 34 337
272	15 52 026	21 54 071	43 43 144	51 55 194	34 51 258	49 08 295	58 19 337
273	16 09 027	22 31 071	44 05 145	51 46 195	34 13 259	48 33 296	58 04 337
274	16 27 028	23 07 072	44 27 147	51 35 197	33 35 260	47 59 296	57 49 337
275	16 45 028	23 44 073	44 48 148	51 24 198	32 57 261	47 24 297	57 33 336
276	17 03 029	24 21 073	45 08 149	51 11 200	32 19 262	46 50 297	57 18 336
277	17 22 029	24 58 074	45 27 151	50 58 201	31 41 262	46 15 298	57 02 336
278	17 41 030	25 35 075	45 45 152	50 43 203	31 03 263	45 41 298	56 47 336
279	18 00 031	26 12 075	46 03 153	50 28 204	30 24 264	45 07 299	56 31 336
280	18 20 031	26 50 076	46 20 155	50 11 206	29 46 265	44 34 299	56 15 336
281	18 40 032	27 27 077	46 36 156	49 54 207	29 08 266	44 00 299	55 59 336
282	19 01 032	28 05 077	46 51 157	49 36 209	28 29 266	43 26 300	55 43 336
283	19 21 033	28 42 078	47 06 159	49 17 210	27 51 267	42 53 300	55 27 335
284	19 42 033	29 20 079	47 19 160	48 57 211	27 12 268	42 20 301	55 11 335
	◆Mirfak	Alpheratz	◆ALTAIR	Rasalhague	◆ARCTURUS	Alkaid	Kochab
285	20 04 034	29 58 080	47 32 162	48 37 213	26 34 269	41 47 301	54 55 335
286	20 25 035	30 36 080	47 43 163	48 16 214	25 55 270	41 14 302	54 39 335
287	20 47 035	31 14 081	47 54 165	47 54 216	25 16 270	40 41 302	54 23 335
288	21 10 036	31 52 082	48 04 166	47 31 217	24 38 271	40 09 303	54 07 335
289	21 32 036	32 30 082	48 13 168	47 07 218	23 59 272	39 36 303	53 50 335
290	21 55 037	33 09 083	48 21 169	46 43 220	23 21 273	39 04 304	53 34 335
291	22 19 037	33 47 084	48 28 170	46 18 221	22 42 273	38 32 304	53 18 335
292	22 42 038	34 25 084	48 33 172	45 53 222	22 04 274	38 00 305	53 02 335
293	23 06 038	35 04 085	48 38 173	45 26 223	21 25 275	37 29 305	52 45 335
294	23 30 039	35 42 086	48 42 175	45 00 225	20 47 276	36 57 306	52 29 335
295	23 55 040	36 21 087	48 45 176	44 32 226	20 09 276	36 26 306	52 13 335
296	24 19 040	36 59 087	48 47 178	44 04 227	19 30 277	35 55 307	51 57 335
297	24 44 041	37 38 088	48 48 179	43 36 228	18 52 278	35 24 307	51 40 335
298	25 10 041	38 16 089	48 48 181	43 07 229	18 14 279	34 54 308	51 24 335
299	25 35 042	38 55 090	48 47 182	42 37 230	17 36 279	34 23 308	51 08 335
	CAPELLA	◆Alpheratz	Enif	ALTAIR	◆Rasalhague	Alphecca	◆Kochab
300	12 25 028	39 33 090	44 28 143	48 45 184	42 07 232	34 59 271	50 52 335
301	12 44 029	40 12 091	44 51 144	48 42 185	41 37 233	34 20 272	50 36 335
302	13 02 029	40 51 092	45 13 146	48 37 187	41 06 234	33 42 273	50 19 335
303	13 21 030	41 29 093	45 34 147	48 32 188	40 35 235	33 03 274	50 03 335
304	13 41 031	42 08 094	45 55 148	48 26 190	40 03 236	32 25 274	49 47 335
305	14 01 031	42 46 094	46 15 150	48 19 191	39 31 237	31 46 275	49 31 336
306	14 21 032	43 25 095	46 34 151	48 11 193	38 58 238	31 08 276	49 15 336
307	14 41 032	44 03 096	46 52 152	48 02 194	38 25 239	30 30 276	48 59 336
308	15 02 033	44 41 097	47 09 154	47 52 196	37 52 240	29 51 277	48 44 336
309	15 23 034	45 19 098	47 26 155	47 41 197	37 18 241	29 13 278	48 28 336
310	15 45 034	45 58 099	47 42 157	47 29 199	36 44 242	28 35 279	48 12 336
311	16 07 035	46 36 099	47 57 158	47 16 200	36 10 243	27 57 279	47 56 336
312	16 29 036	47 14 100	48 11 159	47 03 201	35 36 244	27 19 280	47 41 336
313	16 52 036	47 52 101	48 24 161	46 48 203	35 01 245	26 41 281	47 25 336
314	17 15 037	48 29 102	48 36 162	46 33 204	34 26 246	26 03 281	47 10 336
	CAPELLA	◆Hamal	Alpheratz	Enif	◆ALTAIR	VEGA	◆Kochab
315	17 38 037	26 14 084	49 07 103	48 47 164	46 16 206	62 17 260	46 55 337
316	18 01 038	26 52 085	49 45 104	48 57 165	45 5_ 207	63 39 261	46 39 337

Extracts from Vol: 3 of AP 3270 or HO 249

N. Lat. { LHA greater than 180°........ Zn=Z / LHA less than 180°........ Zn=360—Z }

DECLINATION (0°-14...

LHA	0° Hc	d	Z	1° Hc	d	Z	2° Hc	d	Z	3° Hc	d	Z	4° Hc	d	Z	5° Hc	d	Z	6° Hc	d	Z
0	40 00	+60	180	41 00	+60	180	42 00	+60	180	43 00	+60	180	44 00	+60	180	45 00	+60	180	46 00	+60	18
1	40 00	60	179	41 00	60	179	42 00	60	179	43 00	60	179	44 00	60	179	45 00	60	179	46 00	60	1
2	39 58	60	177	40 58	60	177	41 58	60	177	42 58	60	177	43 58	60	177	44 58	60	177	45 58	60	1
3	39 56	60	176	40 56	60	176	41 56	60	176	42 56	60	176	43 56	59	175	44 56	60	176	45 56	60	1
4	39 53	60	175	40 53	60	175	41 53	60	175	42 53	60	175	43 53	59	175	44 52	60	174	45 52	60	1
5	39 49	+60	174	40 49	+60	173	41 49	+60	173	42 49	+59	173	43 48	+60	173	44 48	+60	173	45 48	+60	1
6	39 44	60	172	40 44	60	172	41 44	60	172	42 44	59	172	43 43	60	172	44 43	60	172	45 43	59	1
7	39 39	59	171	40 38	60	171	41 38	60	171	42 38	59	171	43 37	60	170	44 37	60	170	45 37	59	1
8	39 32	60	170	40 32	59	170	41 31	60	169	42 31	59	169	43 30	60	169	44 30	60	169	45 29	60	16
9	39 25	59	168	40 24	60	168	41 24	59	168	42 23	60	168	43 23	59	168	44 22	59	167	45 21	60	16
10	39 16	+60	167	40 16	+59	167	41 15	+59	167	42 14	+59	167	43 14	+59	166	44 13	+59	166	45 12	+60	1
11	39 07	60	166	40 07	57	166	41 06	59	165	42 05	59	165	43 04	59	165	44 03	59	165	45 02	59	1
12	38 57	60	165	39 57	59	164	40 56	59	164	41 55	59	164	42 54	59	164	43 53	59	163	44 52	59	1
13	38 47	59	163	39 46	59	163	40 45	59	163	41 44	58	163	42 42	59	162	43 41	59	162	44 40	59	1
14	38 35	59	162	39 34	59	162	40 33	58	161	41 31	59	161	42 30	59	161	43 29	58	161	44 27	59	1
15	38 23	+59	161	39 22	+58	160	40 20	+59	160	41 19	+59	160	42 17	+59	160	43 16	+58	159	44 14	+58	15
16	38 10	58	160	39 08	59	159	40 07	58	159	41 05	58	159	42 03	58	159	43 01	59	158	44 00	58	15
17	37 56	58	158	38 54	58	158	39 52	58	158	40 50	59	157	41 49	58	157	42 47	58	157	43 45	57	15
18	37 41	58	157	38 39	58	157	39 37	58	156	40 35	58	156	41 33	58	156	42 31	58	155	43 29	58	15
19	37 26	58	156	38 24	57	156	39 21	58	155	40 19	58	155	41 17	57	154	42 14	58	154	43 12	57	15
20	37 10	+57	155	38 07	+58	154	39 05	+57	154	40 02	+58	154	41 00	+57	153	41 57	+57	153	42 54	+58	15
21	36 53	57	153	37 50	57	153	38 47	58	153	39 45	57	152	40 42	57	152	41 39	57	152	42 36	57	15
22	36 35	57	152	37 32	57	152	38 29	57	151	39 26	57	151	40 23	57	151	41 20	57	150	42 17	57	15
23	36 17	57	151	37 14	57	151	38 11	56	150	39 07	57	150	40 04	57	149	41 01	56	149	41 57	57	14
24	35 58	56	150	36 54	57	149	37 51	57	149	38 48	56	149	39 44	56	148	40 40	57	148	41 37	56	14
25	35 38	+56	149	36 34	+57	148	37 31	+56	148	38 27	+56	147	39 23	+57	147	40 20	+56	147	41 16	+55	14
26	35 18	56	148	36 14	56	147	37 10	56	147	38 06	56	146	39 02	56	146	39 58	56	145	40 54	55	14
27	34 56	57	146	35 53	56	146	36 48	56	146	37 44	56	145	38 40	56	145	39 36	55	144	40 31	56	14
28	34 35	55	145	35 31	56	145	36 26	56	144	37 22	55	144	38 17	56	144	39 13	55	143	40 08	55	14
29	34 13	55	144	35 08	55	144	36 03	56	143	36 59	55	143	37 54	55	142	38 49	55	142	39 44	55	14
30	33 50	+55	143	34 45	+55	143	35 40	+55	142	36 35	+55	142	37 30	+55	141	38 25	+54	141	39 19	+55	1
31	33 26	55	142	34 21	55	141	35 16	55	141	36 11	54	140	37 05	55	140	38 00	54	139	38 54	55	1
32	33 02	55	141	33 57	54	140	34 51	54	140	35 46	54	139	36 40	55	139	37 35	54	138	38 29	54	1
33	32 37	55	140	33 32	54	139	34 26	55	139	35 21	54	138	36 15	54	138	37 09	53	137	38 02	54	1
34	32 12	54	139	33 06	55	138	34 01	54	138	34 55	53	137	35 48	54	137	36 42	54	136	37 36	53	1
35	31 46	+54	138	32 40	+54	137	33 34	+54	137	34 28	+54	136	35 22	+53	135	36 15	+53	135	37 08	+53	1
36	31 20	54	137	32 14	54	136	33 07	54	136	34 01	53	135	34 54	54	134	35 47	53	134	36 40	53	1
37	30 53	54	136	31 47	53	135	32 40	54	134	33 33	53	134	34 26	53	133	35 19	53	133	36 12	53	1
38	30 26	54	134	31 19	53	134	32 12	53	133	33 05	53	133	33 58	53	132	34 51	52	132	35 43	53	1
39	29 58	53	133	30 51	53	133	31 44	53	132	32 37	52	132	33 29	53	131	34 22	52	131	35 14	52	1
40	29 30	+53	132	30 23	+52	132	31 15	+53	131	32 08	+52	131	33 00	+52	130	33 52	+52	130	34 44	+52	1
41	29 01	53	131	29 54	52	130	30 46	52	130	31 38	52	130	32 30	52	129	33 22	52	129	34 14	52	1
42	28 32	52	130	29 24	52	130	30 16	52	129	31 08	52	129	32 00	52	128	32 52	51	128	33 43	52	1
43	28 03	52	129	28 55	51	129	29 46	52	128	30 38	52	128	31 30	51	127	32 21	51	127	33 12	51	1
44	27 33	51	128	28 24	52	128	29 16	51	127	30 07	52	127	30 59	51	126	31 50	51	126	32 41	51	1
45	27 02	+52	128	27 54	+51	127	28 45	+51	126	29 36	+51	126	30 27	+51	125	31 18	+51	125	32 09	+50	1
46	26 31	52	127	27 23	51	126	28 14	51	125	29 05	51	125	29 56	50	124	30 46	51	124	31 37	50	1
47	26 00	51	126	26 51	51	125	27 42	51	124	28 33	50	124	29 23	51	123	30 14	50	123	31 04	50	1
48	25 29	51	125	26 19	51	124	27 10	51	123	28 01	50	123	28 51	50	122	29 41	50	122	30 31	50	1
49	24 57	50	124	25 47	51	123	26 38	50	123	27 28	50	122	28 18	50	121	29 08	50	121	29 58	50	1
50	24 24	+51	123	25 15	+50	122	26 05	+50	122	26 55	+50	121	27 45	+50	121	28 35	+49	120	29 24	+50	1
51	23 52	50	122	24 42	50	121	25 32	50	121	26 22	50	120	27 12	49	119	28 01	49	119	28 50	49	1
52	23 19	50	121	24 09	50	120	24 59	49	120	25 48	50	119	26 38	49	118	27 27	49	118	28 16	49	1
53	22 46	49	120	23 35	50	120	24 25	49	119	25 14	50	118	26 04	49	118	26 53	49	117	27 42	49	1
54	22 12	50	119	23 02	49	119	23 51	49	118	24 40	49	117	25 29	49	117	26 18	49	116	27 07	49	1
55	21 38	+50	118	22 28	+49	118	23 17	+49	117	24 06	+49	116	24 55	+49	116	25 44	+48	115	26 32	+49	1
56	21 04	49	117	21 53	49	117	22 42	49	116	23 31	49	116	24 20	49	115	25 08	49	114	25 57	48	1
57	20 30	49	116	21 19	48	116	22 07	49	115	22 56	49	115	23 45	48	114	24 33	48	113	25 21	48	1
58	19 55	49	116	20 44	49	115	21 32	49	114	22 21	48	114	23 09	49	113	23 58	48	112	24 46	48	1
59	19 20	49	115	20 09	48	114	20 57	49	114	21 46	48	113	22 34	48	112	23 22	48	112	24 10	48	1
60	18 45	+48	114	19 33	+49	113	20 22	+48	113	21 10	+48	113	21 58	+48	111	22 46	+48	111	23 34	+47	1
61	18 09	49	113	18 58	48	112	19 46	48	112	20 34	48	111	21 22	48	111	22 10	47	110	22 57	48	1
62	17 34	48	112	18 22	48	112	19 10	48	111	19 58	48	110	20 46	47	110	21 33	48	109	22 21	47	1
63	16 58	48	111	17 46	48	111	18 34	48	110	19 22	47	109	20 09	48	109	20 57	47	108	21 44	47	1
64	16 22	48	111	17 10	48	110	17 58	47	109	18 45	48	109	19 33	47	108	20 20	47	107	21 07	47	1
65	15 46	+48	110	16 34	+47	109	17 21	+48	108	18 09	+47	108	18 56	+47	107	19 43	+47	106	20 30	+47	1
66	15 09	48	109	15 57	47	108	16 44	48	108	17 32	47	107	18 19	47	106	19 06	47	106	19 53	47	1
67	14 33	47	108	15 20	48	107	16 08	47	107	16 55	47	106	17 42	47	105	18 29	47	105	19 16	46	1
68	13 56	47	107	14 43	47	107	15 31	47	106	16 18	47	105	17 05	46	105	17 51	47	104	18 38	47	1
69	13 19	47	106	14 06	47	106	14 53	47	105	15 40	47	105	16 27	47	104	17 14	47	103	18 01	46	1

S. Lat. { LHA greater than 180°.......Zn=180—Z / LHA less than 180°...........Zn=180+Z }

DECLINATION (0°-14...

SAME NAME AS LATITUDE   LAT 50°

LAT 50°

LHA	7° Hc d Z	8° Hc d Z	9° Hc d Z	10° Hc d Z	11° Hc d Z	12° Hc d Z	13° Hc d Z	14° Hc d Z
360	00 +60 180	48 00 60 180	49 00 60 180	50 00 60 180	51 00 60 180	52 00 60 180	53 00 59 178	54 00 +60 180
359	00 60 179	48 00 60 179	49 00 60 179	50 00 60 179	51 00 60 178	52 00 60 178	53 59 59 178	53 59 60 178
358	58 60 177	47 58 60 177	48 58 60 177	49 58 60 177	50 58 60 177	51 58 60 177	52 58 60 177	53 58 60 177
357	56 60 176	47 56 59 176	48 55 60 176	49 55 60 175	50 55 60 175	51 55 60 175	52 55 60 175	53 55 60 175
356	52 60 174	47 52 60 174	48 52 60 174	49 52 60 174	50 52 60 174	51 52 59 174	52 52 60 174	53 51 60 173
355	48 +60 173	47 48 +59 173	48 47 +60 173	49 47 +60 172	50 47 +60 172	51 47 +59 172	52 46 +60 172	53 46 +60 172
354	42 60 171	47 42 60 171	48 42 60 171	49 42 59 171	50 41 60 171	51 41 60 171	52 41 59 170	53 40 60 170
353	36 60 170	47 36 60 170	48 35 60 170	49 35 59 169	50 34 60 169	51 34 60 169	52 34 59 169	53 33 59 169
352	29 59 168	47 28 60 168	48 28 59 168	49 27 60 168	50 27 59 168	51 26 59 167	52 25 60 167	53 25 59 167
351	21 59 167	47 20 58 167	48 19 60 167	49 19 59 166	50 18 59 166	51 17 59 166	52 16 60 166	53 16 59 165
350	12 +59 166	47 11 +59 165	48 10 +59 165	49 09 +59 165	50 08 +59 165	51 07 +59 164	52 06 +59 164	53 05 +59 164
349	01 60 164	47 01 59 164	48 00 59 164	48 59 58 163	49 57 59 163	50 56 59 163	51 55 59 163	52 54 59 162
348	51 58 163	46 49 59 163	47 48 59 162	48 47 59 162	49 46 59 162	50 44 59 161	51 43 59 161	52 42 58 161
347	39 58 161	46 37 59 161	47 36 59 161	48 35 58 160	49 33 59 160	50 32 58 160	51 30 59 159	52 28 58 159
346	26 58 160	46 24 59 160	47 23 58 159	48 21 58 159	49 19 59 159	50 18 58 158	51 16 58 158	52 14 58 158
345	12 +59 159	46 11 +58 158	47 09 +58 158	48 07 +58 158	49 05 +58 157	50 03 +58 157	51 01 +58 156	51 59 +57 156
344	58 58 157	45 56 58 157	46 54 58 157	47 52 58 156	48 50 57 156	49 47 58 156	50 45 57 155	51 42 58 154
343	42 58 156	45 40 58 156	46 38 58 155	47 36 57 155	48 33 58 154	49 31 57 154	50 28 57 153	51 25 58 153
342	26 58 155	45 24 57 154	46 21 58 154	47 19 57 153	48 16 57 153	49 13 57 153	50 10 57 152	51 07 57 152
341	09 58 153	45 07 57 153	46 04 57 152	47 01 57 152	47 58 57 152	48 55 57 151	49 52 57 151	50 49 56 150
340	52 +57 152	44 49 +57 152	45 46 +57 151	46 43 +56 151	47 39 +57 150	48 36 +56 150	49 32 +57 149	50 29 +56 149
339	33 57 151	44 30 57 150	45 27 56 150	46 23 57 149	47 20 56 149	48 16 56 148	49 12 56 148	50 08 56 147
338	14 56 149	44 10 57 149	45 07 56 148	46 03 56 148	46 59 56 147	47 55 56 147	48 51 56 146	49 47 56 146
337	54 56 148	43 50 56 148	44 46 56 147	45 42 56 147	46 38 56 146	47 34 56 146	48 29 56 145	49 25 55 144
336	33 56 147	43 29 56 146	44 25 56 146	45 21 55 145	46 16 56 145	47 12 55 144	48 07 55 144	49 02 55 143
335	11 +56 146	43 07 +56 145	44 03 +55 145	44 58 +56 144	45 54 +55 143	46 49 +55 143	47 44 +54 142	48 38 +55 142
334	49 56 144	42 45 55 144	43 40 55 143	44 35 55 143	45 30 55 142	46 25 55 142	47 20 54 141	48 14 54 140
333	26 56 143	42 22 55 143	43 17 54 142	44 11 55 141	45 06 55 141	46 01 54 140	46 55 54 140	47 49 54 139
332	03 55 142	41 58 55 141	42 53 54 141	43 47 55 140	44 42 54 140	45 36 54 139	46 30 54 138	47 24 53 138
331	39 54 141	41 33 54 140	42 28 54 140	43 22 54 139	44 16 54 138	45 10 54 138	46 04 53 137	46 57 54 136
330	14 +54 140	41 08 +54 139	42 02 +54 138	42 56 +54 138	43 50 +54 137	44 44 +53 137	45 37 +53 136	46 30 +53 135
329	49 54 138	40 43 54 138	41 37 53 137	42 30 54 137	43 24 53 136	44 17 53 135	45 10 53 135	46 03 53 134
328	23 53 137	40 16 54 137	41 10 53 136	42 03 54 135	42 57 53 135	43 50 52 134	44 42 53 133	45 35 52 133
327	56 54 136	39 50 53 135	40 43 53 135	41 36 53 134	42 29 53 134	43 22 52 133	44 14 52 132	45 06 52 132
326	29 53 135	39 22 53 134	40 15 53 134	41 08 53 133	42 01 52 132	42 53 52 132	43 45 52 131	44 37 52 130
325	01 +53 134	38 54 +53 133	39 47 +53 133	40 40 +52 132	41 32 +52 131	42 24 +52 131	43 16 +52 130	44 08 +51 129
324	33 53 133	38 26 52 132	39 18 53 131	40 11 52 131	41 03 52 130	41 55 51 129	42 46 51 129	43 37 51 128
323	05 52 132	37 57 52 131	38 49 52 130	39 41 52 130	40 33 51 129	41 24 52 128	42 16 51 128	43 07 51 127
322	36 52 130	37 28 52 130	38 20 51 129	39 11 52 129	40 03 51 128	40 54 51 127	41 45 51 127	42 36 50 126
321	06 52 129	36 58 51 129	37 49 52 128	38 41 51 127	39 32 51 127	40 23 51 126	41 14 50 125	42 04 50 125
320	36 +51 128	36 27 +52 128	37 19 +51 127	38 10 +51 126	39 01 +51 126	39 52 +50 125	40 42 +50 124	41 32 +50 124
319	05 52 127	35 57 51 127	36 48 51 126	37 39 50 125	38 29 51 125	39 20 50 124	40 10 50 123	41 00 50 123
318	35 51 126	35 26 50 126	36 16 51 125	37 07 50 124	37 57 51 124	38 48 50 123	39 38 49 122	40 27 50 121
317	03 51 125	34 54 51 125	35 45 50 124	36 35 50 123	37 25 50 123	38 15 50 122	39 05 49 121	39 54 49 120
316	32 50 124	34 22 50 124	35 12 51 123	36 03 49 122	36 52 50 122	37 42 50 121	38 32 49 120	39 21 49 119
315	59 +51 123	33 50 +50 123	34 40 +50 121	35 30 +49 121	36 19 +50 120	37 09 +49 120	37 58 +49 119	38 47 +48 118
314	27 50 122	33 17 50 122	34 07 50 121	34 57 49 120	35 46 49 120	36 35 49 119	37 24 49 118	38 13 48 117
313	51 50 121	32 44 50 121	33 34 49 120	34 23 49 119	35 12 49 119	36 01 49 118	36 50 48 117	37 38 49 116
312	21 50 120	32 11 49 120	33 00 49 119	33 49 49 118	34 38 49 118	35 27 48 117	36 15 49 116	37 04 48 115
311	48 49 119	31 37 49 119	32 26 49 118	33 15 49 117	34 04 48 117	34 52 49 116	35 41 48 115	36 29 47 114
310	14 +49 118	31 03 +49 118	31 52 +49 117	32 41 +48 116	33 29 +49 116	34 18 +48 115	35 06 +47 114	35 53 +48 113
309	40 49 117	30 29 48 117	31 17 49 116	32 06 48 115	32 54 48 115	33 42 48 114	34 30 48 113	35 18 47 113
308	05 49 117	29 54 49 116	30 43 48 115	31 31 48 115	32 19 48 114	33 07 48 113	33 55 47 112	34 42 47 112
307	31 48 116	29 19 48 115	30 08 48 114	30 56 48 114	31 44 48 113	32 32 47 112	33 19 47 111	34 06 47 111
306	56 48 115	28 44 48 114	29 32 48 113	30 20 48 113	31 08 48 112	31 56 47 111	32 43 47 111	33 30 47 110
305	21 +48 114	28 09 +48 113	28 57 +48 112	29 45 +47 112	30 32 +48 111	31 20 +47 110	32 07 +47 110	32 54 +46 109
304	45 48 113	27 33 48 112	28 21 48 112	29 09 47 111	29 56 47 110	30 43 47 109	31 30 47 109	32 17 46 108
303	09 48 112	26 57 48 111	27 45 48 111	28 33 47 110	29 20 47 109	30 07 47 109	30 54 46 108	31 40 46 107
302	34 47 111	26 21 48 110	27 09 47 110	27 56 47 109	28 43 47 108	29 30 47 108	30 17 46 107	31 03 46 106
301	58 47 110	25 45 47 110	26 32 48 109	27 20 47 108	28 07 46 108	28 53 47 107	29 40 46 106	30 26 46 105
300	21 +48 109	25 09 +47 109	25 56 +47 108	26 43 +47 107	27 30 +46 107	28 16 +47 106	29 03 +46 105	29 49 +46 104
299	45 47 109	24 32 47 108	25 19 47 107	26 06 47 106	26 53 46 106	27 39 46 105	28 25 46 104	29 11 46 104
298	08 47 108	23 55 47 107	24 42 47 106	25 29 46 106	26 15 47 105	27 02 46 104	27 48 46 104	28 34 46 103
297	31 47 107	23 18 47 106	24 05 47 105	24 52 46 105	25 38 46 104	26 24 46 103	27 10 46 103	27 56 46 102
296	54 47 106	22 41 47 105	23 28 46 105	24 14 47 104	25 01 46 103	25 47 46 103	26 33 45 102	27 18 46 101
295	17 +47 105	22 04 +46 104	22 50 +47 104	23 37 +46 103	24 23 +46 102	25 09 +46 102	25 55 +45 101	26 40 +45 100
294	40 46 104	21 26 47 104	22 13 46 103	22 59 46 102	23 45 46 102	24 31 46 101	25 17 45 100	26 02 46 99
293	02 47 104	20 49 46 103	21 35 46 103	22 21 46 102	23 07 46 101	23 53 46 100	24 39 45 99	25 24 45 99
292	25 46 103	20 11 46 102	20 57 47 101	21 44 45 101	22 30 45 100	23 15 46 99	24 01 45 99	24 46 45 98
291	47 46 102	19 33 46 101	20 20 46 101	21 06 45 100	21 51 46 99	22 37 46 98	23 23 45 98	24 08 45 97

SAME NAME AS LATITUDE

N. Lat. { LHA greater than 180°....... Zn=Z
{ LHA less than 180°........... Zn=360—Z

DECLINATION (0°-1...

LHA	0° Hc	d	Z	1° Hc	d	Z	2° Hc	d	Z	3° Hc	d	Z	4° Hc	d	Z	5° Hc	d	Z	6° Hc	d
	° ′	′	°	° ′	′	°	° ′	′	°	° ′	′	°	° ′	′	°	° ′	′	°	° ′	′
70	12 42	+47	106	13 29	+47	105	14 16	+47	104	15 03	+47	104	15 50	+46	103	16 36	+47	102	17 23	+46
71	12 05	47	105	12 52	47	104	13 39	46	104	14 25	47	103	15 12	47	102	15 59	46	102	16 45	46
72	11 27	47	104	12 14	47	103	13 01	47	103	13 48	46	102	14 34	47	101	15 21	46	101	16 07	46
73	10 50	47	103	11 37	46	103	12 23	47	102	13 10	46	101	13 56	47	101	14 43	46	100	15 29	46
74	10 12	47	102	10 59	47	102	11 46	46	101	12 32	47	101	13 19	46	100	14 05	46	99	14 51	46
75	09 35	+46	102	10 21	+47	101	11 08	+46	100	11 54	+46	100	12 40	+47	99	13 27	+46	98	14 13	+46
76	08 57	46	101	09 43	47	100	10 30	46	100	11 16	46	99	12 02	47	98	12 49	46	98	13 35	46
77	08 19	46	100	09 05	47	99	09 52	46	99	10 38	46	98	11 24	46	97	12 10	46	97	12 56	46
78	07 41	46	99	08 27	46	99	09 13	47	98	10 00	46	97	10 46	46	97	11 32	46	96	12 18	46
79	07 03	46	99	07 49	46	98	08 35	46	97	09 21	47	97	10 08	46	96	10 54	45	95	11 39	46
80	06 25	+46	98	07 11	+46	97	07 57	+46	96	08 43	+46	96	09 29	46	95	10 15	+46	95	11 01	+46
81	05 46	46	97	06 32	47	96	07 19	46	96	08 05	46	95	08 51	46	94	09 37	46	94	10 23	45
82	05 08	46	96	05 54	46	96	06 40	46	95	07 26	46	94	08 12	46	93	08 58	46	93	09 44	46
83	04 30	46	95	05 16	46	95	06 02	46	94	06 48	46	93	07 34	46	93	08 20	45	92	09 05	46
84	03 51	46	95	04 37	46	94	05 23	46	93	06 09	46	93	06 55	46	92	07 41	46	91	08 27	46
85	03 13	+46	94	03 59	+46	93	04 45	+46	93	05 31	+46	92	06 17	+45	92	07 02	+46	91	07 48	+46
86	02 34	46	93	03 20	46	92	04 06	46	92	04 52	46	91	05 38	46	91	06 24	46	90	07 10	45
87	01 56	46	92	02 42	46	92	03 28	46	91	04 14	45	90	04 59	46	90	05 45	46	89	06 31	46
88	01 17	46	92	02 03	46	91	02 49	46	90	03 35	46	90	04 21	46	89	05 07	46	88	05 53	45
89	00 39	46	91	01 25	45	90	02 10	46	89	02 56	46	89	03 42	46	88	04 28	46	88	05 14	46
90	00 00	+46	90	00 46	+46	89	01 32	+46	89	02 18	+46	88	03 04	+46	87	03 50	+46	87	04 36	+45
91	−0 39	46	89	00 07	46	89	00 53	46	88	01 39	46	87	02 25	46	87	03 11	46	86	03 57	46
92	−1 17	46	88	−0 31	46	88	00 15	46	87	01 01	46	87	01 47	46	86	02 33	46	85	03 19	46
93	−1 56	46	88	−1 10	46	87	−0 24	46	86	00 22	46	86	01 08	46	85	01 54	46	84	02 40	46
94	−2 34	46	87	−1 48	46	86	−1 02	46	86	−0 16	46	85	00 30	46	84	01 16	46	84	02 02	46
95	−3 13	+46	86	−2 27	+46	86	−1 41	+46	85	−0 55	+47	84	−0 08	+46	84	00 38	+46	83	01 24	+46
96	−3 51	46	85	−3 05	46	85	−2 19	46	84	−1 33	46	83	−0 47	46	83	−0 01	47	82	00 46	46
97	−4 30	47	85	−3 43	46	84	−2 57	46	83	−2 11	46	83	−1 25	46	82	−0 39	46	81	00 07	47
98	−5 08	46	84	−4 22	46	83	−3 36	46	83	−2 49	46	82	−2 03	46	81	−1 17	46	81	−0 31	47
99	−5 46	46	83	−5 00	46	82	−4 14	46	82	−3 28	47	81	−2 41	46	81	−1 55	46	80	−1 09	47
100				−5 38	+46	82	−4 52	+46	81	−4 06	+47	80	−3 19	+46	80	−2 33	+47	79	−1 46	+47
101							−5 30	46	80	−4 44	47	80	−3 57	46	79	−3 11	47	78	−2 24	46
102							−6 08	47	79	−5 21	46	79	−4 35	47	78	−3 48	46	78	−3 02	47
103										−5 59	46	78	−5 13	47	77	−4 26	47	77	−3 39	46
104													−5 50	47	77	−5 03	46	76	−4 17	46
105																−5 41	+47	75	−4 54	+47
106																			−5 31	47
107																			−6 08	47

S. Lat. { LHA greater than 180°.......Zn=180—Z
{ LHA less than 180°...........Zn=180+Z

DECLINATION (0°-1...

SAME NAME AS LATITUDE

7°			8°			9°			10°			11°			12°			13°			14°			
	d	Z	Hc	d	Z	Hc	d	Z	Hc	d	Z	Hc	d	Z	Hc	d	Z	Hc	d	Z	Hc	d	Z	LHA
′	′	°	° ′	′	°	° ′	′	°	° ′	′	°	° ′	′	°	° ′	′	°	° ′	′	°	° ′	′	°	
9	+47	101	18 56	+46	100	19 42	+46	100	20 28	+45	99	21 13	+46	98	21 59	+45	98	22 44	+46	97	23 30	+45	96	290
1	47	100	18 18	46	100	19 04	45	99	19 49	46	98	20 35	46	98	21 21	45	97	22 06	45	96	22 51	45	95	289
3	46	99	17 39	46	99	18 25	46	98	19 11	46	97	19 57	45	97	20 42	46	96	21 28	45	95	22 13	45	95	288
5	46	99	17 01	46	98	17 47	46	97	18 33	46	97	19 19	45	96	20 04	45	95	20 49	45	95	21 34	45	94	287
7	46	98	16 23	46	97	17 09	46	97	17 55	45	96	18 40	46	95	19 26	45	94	20 11	45	94	20 56	45	93	286
9	+46	97	15 45	+46	96	16 31	+45	96	17 16	+46	95	18 02	+45	94	18 47	+45	94	19 32	+45	93	20 17	+45	92	285
1	45	96	15 06	46	96	15 52	46	95	16 38	45	94	17 23	46	94	18 09	45	93	18 54	45	92	19 39	45	92	284
2	46	96	14 28	46	95	15 14	45	94	15 59	46	94	16 45	45	93	17 30	45	92	18 15	45	91	19 00	45	91	283
4	46	95	13 50	45	94	14 35	46	93	15 21	45	93	16 06	45	92	16 51	46	91	17 37	45	91	18 22	45	90	282
5	46	94	13 11	46	93	13 57	45	93	14 42	46	92	15 28	45	91	16 13	45	91	16 58	45	90	17 43	45	89	281
7	+46	93	12 33	+45	93	13 18	+46	92	14 04	+45	91	14 49	+45	91	15 34	+46	90	16 20	+45	89	17 05	+44	88	280
8	46	92	11 54	46	92	12 40	45	91	13 25	46	90	14 11	45	90	14 56	45	89	15 41	45	88	16 26	45	88	279
0	45	92	11 15	46	91	12 01	46	90	12 47	45	90	13 32	45	89	14 17	45	88	15 02	45	88	15 47	45	87	278
1	46	91	10 37	45	90	11 22	46	90	12 08	45	89	12 53	46	88	13 39	45	88	14 24	45	87	15 09	45	86	277
3	45	90	09 58	46	89	10 44	45	89	11 29	46	88	12 15	45	87	13 00	45	87	13 45	46	86	14 31	45	85	276
4	+46	89	09 20	+45	89	10 05	+46	88	10 51	+45	87	11 36	+46	87	12 22	+45	86	13 07	+45	85	13 52	+45	85	275
5	46	89	08 41	46	88	09 27	45	87	10 12	46	87	10 58	45	86	11 43	46	85	12 29	45	85	13 14	45	84	274
7	46	88	08 03	45	87	08 48	46	87	09 34	45	86	10 19	46	85	11 05	45	85	11 50	45	84	12 35	46	83	273
8	46	87	07 24	46	86	08 10	45	86	08 55	46	85	09 41	45	84	10 26	46	84	11 12	45	83	11 57	45	82	272
0	46	86	06 46	45	86	07 31	46	85	08 17	46	84	09 03	45	84	09 48	46	83	10 34	45	82	11 19	45	82	271
1	+46	86	06 07	+46	85	06 53	+46	84	07 39	+45	84	08 24	+46	83	09 10	+45	82	09 55	+46	82	10 41	+45	81	270
3	46	85	05 29	46	84	06 15	45	83	07 00	46	83	07 46	46	82	08 32	45	82	09 17	46	81	10 03	45	80	269
5	45	84	04 50	46	83	05 36	46	83	06 22	46	82	07 08	46	81	07 54	45	81	08 39	46	80	09 25	45	79	268
6	46	83	04 12	46	83	04 58	46	82	05 44	46	81	06 30	46	81	07 16	45	80	08 01	46	79	08 47	46	79	267
3	46	82	03 34	46	82	04 20	46	81	05 06	46	81	05 52	46	80	06 38	45	79	07 23	46	79	08 09	46	78	266
0	+47	82	02 57	+45	81	03 42	+46	80	04 28	+46	80	05 14	+46	79	06 00	+46	79	06 46	+46	78	07 32	+45	77	265
2	46	81	02 18	46	80	03 04	46	80	03 50	46	79	04 36	46	78	05 22	46	78	06 08	46	77	06 54	46	76	264
4	46	80	01 40	46	80	02 26	46	79	03 12	46	78	03 58	46	78	04 44	47	77	05 31	46	76	06 17	46	76	263
6	46	79	01 02	46	79	01 48	46	78	02 34	47	77	03 21	46	77	04 07	46	76	04 53	46	76	05 39	46	75	262
2	46	79	00 24	47	78	01 11	46	77	01 57	46	77	02 43	47	76	03 30	46	76	04 16	46	75	05 02	46	74	261
0	+47	78	-0 13	+46	77	00 33	+46	77	01 19	+47	76	02 06	+46	75	02 52	+47	75	03 39	+46	74	04 25	+46	73	260
8	47	77	-0 51	47	76	-0 04	46	76	00 42	47	75	01 29	46	75	02 15	47	74	03 02	46	73	03 48	47	73	259
5	47	76	-1 28	46	76	-0 42	47	75	00 05	47	74	00 52	46	74	01 38	47	73	02 25	46	73	03 11	47	72	258
3	47	76	-2 06	47	75	-1 19	47	74	-0 32	47	74	00 15	46	73	01 01	47	72	01 48	47	72	02 35	47	71	257
0	47	75	-2 43	47	74	-1 56	47	74	-1 09	47	73	-0 22	47	72	00 25	47	72	01 12	46	71	01 58	47	70	256
7	+47	74	-3 20	+47	73	-2 33	+47	73	-1 46	+47	72	-0 59	+47	71	-0 12	+47	71	00 35	+47	70	01 22	+47	70	255
4	47	73	-3 57	47	73	-3 10	47	72	-2 23	48	71	-1 35	47	71	-0 48	47	70	-0 01	47	69	00 46	47	69	254
1	47	72	-4 34	48	72	-3 46	47	71	-2 59	47	71	-2 12	48	70	-1 24	47	69	-0 37	47	69	00 10	48	68	253
8	48	72	-5 10	47	71	-4 23	48	70	-3 35	47	70	-2 48	48	69	-2 00	47	69	-1 13	48	68	-0 25	47	67	252
		109	-5 47	48	70	-4 59	48	70	-4 11	47	69	-3 24	48	68	-2 36	47	68	-1 49	48	67	-1 01	48	67	251
					110	-5 35	+48	69	-4 47	+47	68	-4 00	+48	68	-3 12	+48	67	-2 24	+48	66	-1 36	+48	66	250
					111	-6 11	48	68	-5 23	48	67	-4 35	48	67	-3 47	48	66	-2 59	48	66	-2 11	48	65	249
								112	-5 59	48	67	-5 11	49	66	-4 22	48	65	-3 34	48	65	-2 46	48	64	248
											113	-5 46	49	65	-4 57	48	65	-4 09	48	64	-3 21	49	63	247
														114	-5 32	48	64	-4 44	49	63	-3 55	48	63	246
														115	-6 07	+49	63	-5 18	+49	62	-4 29	+48	62	245
																	116	-5 52	49	62	-5 03	49	61	244
																				117	-5 37	49	60	243
7°			8°			9°			10°			11°			12°			13°			14°			

LAT 50°

SAME NAME AS LATITUDE

LAT 50°

N. Lat. { LHA greater than 180°....... Zn=Z / LHA less than 180°.......... Zn=360—Z }

DECLINATION (0°-14°)

LHA	0° Hc	d	Z	1° Hc	d	Z	2° Hc	d	Z	3° Hc	d	Z	4° Hc	d	Z	5° Hc	d	Z	6° Hc	d
69	13 19	47	106	12 32	48	107	11 44	47	108	10 57	47	108	10 10	48	109	09 22	48	110	08 34	47
68	13 56	47	107	13 09	48	108	12 21	47	109	11 34	48	109	10 46	48	110	09 58	48	110	09 10	47
67	14 33	48	108	13 45	47	109	12 58	48	109	12 10	48	110	11 22	48	111	10 34	48	111	09 46	48
66	15 09	47	109	14 22	48	110	13 34	48	110	12 46	48	111	11 58	48	111	11 10	48	112	10 22	48
65	15 46	-48	110	14 58	-48	110	14 10	-48	111	13 22	-48	112	12 34	-48	112	11 46	-48	113	10 58	-49
64	16 22	48	111	15 34	48	111	14 46	48	112	13 58	48	112	13 10	49	113	12 21	48	114	11 33	49
63	16 58	48	111	16 10	48	112	15 22	49	113	14 33	48	113	13 45	49	114	12 56	49	114	12 08	49
62	17 34	48	112	16 46	49	113	15 57	48	113	15 09	49	114	14 20	48	115	13 32	49	115	12 43	49
61	18 09	48	113	17 21	48	114	16 33	49	114	15 44	49	115	14 55	49	116	14 06	49	116	13 17	49
60	18 45	-49	114	17 56	-48	115	17 08	-49	115	16 19	-49	116	15 30	-49	116	14 41	-49	117	13 52	-50
59	19 20	49	115	18 31	49	115	17 42	49	116	16 53	49	117	16 04	49	117	15 15	49	118	14 26	50
58	19 55	49	116	19 06	49	116	18 17	49	117	17 28	49	117	16 38	49	118	15 49	49	119	15 00	50
57	20 30	50	116	19 40	49	117	18 51	49	118	18 02	50	118	17 12	49	119	16 23	50	119	15 33	50
56	21 04	49	117	20 15	50	118	19 25	49	119	18 36	50	119	17 46	50	120	16 56	50	120	16 06	50
55	21 38	-49	118	20 49	-50	119	19 59	-50	119	19 09	-50	120	18 19	-50	121	17 29	-50	121	16 39	-50
54	22 12	50	119	21 22	50	120	20 32	50	120	19 42	50	121	18 52	50	122	18 02	50	122	17 12	50
53	22 46	50	120	21 56	50	121	21 06	51	121	20 15	50	122	19 25	50	122	18 35	51	123	17 44	50
52	23 19	50	121	22 29	50	122	21 38	50	122	20 48	50	123	19 58	51	123	19 07	51	124	18 16	51
51	23 52	51	122	23 01	50	122	22 11	51	123	21 20	51	124	20 30	51	124	19 39	51	125	18 48	51
50	24 24	-50	123	23 34	-51	123	22 43	-51	124	21 52	-51	125	21 01	-51	125	20 10	-51	126	19 19	-51
49	24 57	51	124	24 06	51	124	23 15	51	125	22 24	51	125	21 33	51	126	20 42	51	127	19 50	51
48	25 29	51	125	24 38	52	125	23 46	51	126	22 55	51	126	22 04	52	127	21 12	51	127	20 21	52
47	26 00	51	126	25 09	51	126	24 18	52	127	23 26	52	127	22 34	51	128	21 43	52	128	20 51	52
46	26 31	51	127	25 40	52	127	24 48	51	128	23 57	52	128	23 05	52	129	22 13	52	129	21 21	52
45	27 02	-52	128	26 10	-51	128	25 19	-52	129	24 27	-52	129	23 35	-53	130	22 42	-52	130	21 50	-52
44	27 33	52	128	26 41	52	129	25 49	53	130	24 56	52	130	24 04	52	131	23 12	53	131	22 19	52
43	28 03	53	129	27 10	52	130	26 18	52	131	25 26	53	131	24 33	52	132	23 41	53	132	22 48	53
42	28 32	53	130	27 40	53	131	26 47	52	132	25 55	53	132	25 02	53	133	24 09	53	133	23 16	53
41	29 01	52	131	28 09	53	132	27 16	53	133	26 23	53	133	25 30	53	134	24 37	53	134	23 44	54
40	29 30	-53	132	28 37	-53	133	27 44	-53	134	26 51	-53	134	25 58	-54	135	25 04	-53	135	24 11	-54
39	29 58	53	133	29 05	53	134	28 12	54	135	27 18	53	135	26 25	54	136	25 31	53	136	24 38	54
38	30 26	53	134	29 33	54	135	28 39	53	136	27 46	54	136	26 52	54	137	25 58	54	137	25 04	54
37	30 53	53	136	30 00	54	135	29 06	54	137	28 12	54	137	27 18	54	138	26 24	54	138	25 30	54
36	31 20	54	137	30 26	54	137	29 32	54	138	28 38	54	138	27 44	54	139	26 50	55	139	25 55	54
35	31 46	-54	138	30 52	-54	138	29 58	-54	139	29 04	-54	139	28 09	-54	140	27 15	-55	140	26 20	-55
34	32 12	54	139	31 18	55	139	30 23	54	140	29 29	55	140	28 34	55	141	27 39	55	141	26 44	55
33	32 37	55	140	31 43	55	140	30 48	55	141	29 53	55	141	28 58	55	142	28 03	55	142	27 08	55
32	33 02	55	141	32 07	55	141	31 12	55	142	30 17	55	142	29 22	55	143	28 27	56	143	27 31	55
31	33 26	55	142	32 31	55	142	31 36	55	143	30 40	55	143	29 45	56	144	28 49	55	144	27 54	56
30	33 50	-56	143	32 54	-55	144	31 59	-56	144	31 03	-55	144	30 08	-56	145	29 12	-56	145	28 16	-56
29	34 13	56	144	33 17	56	145	32 21	56	145	31 25	56	145	30 29	56	146	29 33	56	146	28 37	56
28	34 35	56	145	33 39	56	146	32 43	56	146	31 47	56	147	30 51	56	147	29 55	57	147	28 58	56
27	34 56	56	146	34 00	56	147	33 04	56	147	32 08	56	148	31 12	57	148	30 15	56	148	29 19	57
26	35 18	57	148	34 21	56	148	33 25	57	148	32 28	56	149	31 32	57	149	30 35	57	150	29 38	57
25	35 38	-57	149	34 41	-56	149	33 45	-57	150	32 48	-57	150	31 51	-57	150	30 54	-57	151	29 57	-57
24	35 58	57	150	35 01	57	150	34 04	57	151	33 07	57	151	32 10	57	151	31 13	57	152	30 16	58
23	36 17	57	151	35 20	58	151	34 22	57	152	33 25	57	152	32 28	57	153	31 31	58	153	30 33	57
22	36 35	57	152	35 38	58	153	34 40	57	153	33 43	57	153	32 46	58	154	31 48	58	154	30 50	57
21	36 53	58	153	35 55	57	154	34 58	58	154	34 00	58	154	33 02	57	155	32 05	58	155	31 07	58
20	37 10	-58	155	36 12	-58	155	35 14	-58	155	34 16	-58	156	33 18	-57	156	32 20	-58	156	31 23	-58
19	37 26	58	156	36 28	58	156	35 30	58	156	34 32	58	157	33 34	58	157	32 36	58	157	31 38	58
18	37 41	58	157	36 43	58	157	35 45	58	158	34 47	59	158	33 48	58	158	32 50	58	159	31 52	58
17	37 56	58	158	36 58	59	159	35 59	58	159	35 01	59	159	34 02	58	159	33 04	59	160	32 05	58
16	38 10	59	160	37 11	58	160	36 13	59	160	35 14	58	160	34 16	59	161	33 17	59	161	32 18	58
15	38 23	-59	161	37 24	-58	161	36 26	-59	161	35 27	-59	162	34 28	-59	162	33 29	-58	162	32 31	-59
14	38 35	59	162	37 36	58	162	36 38	59	163	35 39	59	163	34 40	59	163	33 41	59	163	32 42	59
13	38 47	59	163	37 48	59	164	36 49	59	164	35 50	59	164	34 51	59	164	33 52	59	164	32 53	60
12	38 57	59	165	37 58	59	165	36 59	59	165	36 00	59	165	35 01	59	165	34 02	60	166	33 02	59
11	39 07	59	166	38 08	59	166	37 09	59	166	36 10	60	166	35 10	59	167	34 11	59	167	33 12	60
10	39 16	-59	167	38 17	-59	167	37 18	-60	167	36 18	-59	168	35 19	-60	168	34 19	-60	168	33 20	-60
9	39 25	60	168	38 25	59	169	37 26	60	169	36 26	59	169	35 27	60	169	34 27	59	169	33 28	60
8	39 32	60	170	38 32	59	170	37 33	60	170	36 33	59	170	35 34	60	170	34 34	60	170	33 34	59
7	39 39	60	171	38 39	60	171	37 39	59	171	36 40	60	171	35 40	60	171	34 40	60	172	33 40	59
6	39 44	59	172	38 45	60	172	37 45	60	172	36 45	60	173	35 45	60	173	34 45	59	173	33 46	60
5	39 49	-60	174	38 49	-60	174	37 49	-59	174	36 50	-60	174	35 50	-60	174	34 50	-60	174	33 50	-60
4	39 53	60	175	38 53	60	175	37 53	60	175	36 53	60	175	35 53	59	175	34 54	60	175	33 54	60
3	39 56	60	176	38 56	60	176	37 56	60	176	36 56	60	176	35 56	60	176	34 56	60	176	33 56	60
2	39 58	60	177	38 58	60	177	37 58	60	178	36 58	60	178	35 58	60	178	34 58	60	178	33 58	60
1	40 00	60	179	39 00	60	179	38 00	60	179	37 00	60	179	36 00	60	179	35 00	60	179	34 00	60
0	40 00	-60	180	39 00	-60	180	38 00	-60	180	37 00	-60	180	36 00	-60	180	35 00	-60	180	34 00	-60

0° 1° 2° 3° 4° 5° 6°

S. Lat. { LHA greater than 180°........Zn=180—Z / LHA less than 180°...........Zn=180+Z }

DECLINATION (0°-14°)

CONTRARY NAME TO LATITUDE

7° (Hc d Z)	8° (Hc d Z)	9° (Hc d Z)	10° (Hc d Z)	11° (Hc d Z)	12° (Hc d Z)	13° (Hc d Z)	14° (Hc d Z)	LHA
07 47 48 111	06 59 48 111	06 11 48 112	05 23 48 113	04 35 48 113	03 47 48 114	02 59 48 114	02 11 48 115	291
08 23 48 112	07 35 48 112	06 47 48 113	05 59 48 113	05 11 49 114	04 22 48 115	03 34 48 115	02 46 48 116	292
08 58 48 112	08 10 48 113	07 22 48 114	06 34 48 114	05 46 49 115	04 57 48 115	04 09 48 116	03 21 49 117	293
09 34 48 113	08 46 49 114	07 57 48 114	07 09 48 115	06 21 49 116	05 32 48 116	04 44 49 117	03 55 48 117	294
10 09 -48 114	09 21 -49 115	08 32 -48 115	07 44 -49 116	06 55 -48 116	06 07 -49 117	05 18 -49 118	04 29 -48 118	295
10 44 48 115	09 56 49 116	09 07 49 116	08 18 48 117	07 30 49 117	06 41 49 118	05 52 49 118	05 03 49 119	296
11 19 48 116	10 31 49 116	09 42 49 117	08 53 49 117	08 04 49 118	07 15 49 119	06 26 49 119	05 37 49 120	297
11 54 49 116	11 05 49 117	10 16 49 118	09 27 49 118	08 38 49 119	07 49 49 119	07 00 50 120	06 10 49 121	298
12 28 49 117	11 39 49 118	10 50 49 118	10 01 49 119	09 12 50 120	08 22 49 120	07 33 50 121	06 43 49 121	299
13 02 -49 118	12 13 -49 119	11 24 -50 119	10 34 -49 120	09 45 -50 120	08 55 -49 121	08 06 -50 122	07 16 -50 122	300
13 36 49 119	12 47 49 120	11 57 49 120	11 08 50 121	10 18 50 121	09 28 49 122	08 39 50 122	07 49 50 123	301
14 10 50 120	13 20 49 120	12 31 50 121	11 41 50 122	10 51 50 122	10 01 50 123	09 11 50 123	08 21 50 124	302
14 43 50 121	13 53 49 121	13 04 50 122	12 14 51 122	11 23 50 123	10 33 50 123	09 43 50 124	08 53 50 125	303
15 16 50 122	14 26 50 122	13 36 50 123	12 46 50 123	11 56 51 124	11 05 50 124	10 15 51 125	09 24 50 125	304
15 49 -50 122	14 59 -50 123	14 09 -51 124	13 18 -50 124	12 28 -51 125	11 37 -51 125	10 46 -50 126	09 56 -51 126	305
16 22 51 123	15 31 50 124	14 41 51 124	13 50 51 125	12 59 51 125	12 08 50 126	11 18 51 127	10 27 51 127	306
16 54 51 124	16 03 51 125	15 12 51 125	14 21 51 126	13 30 51 126	12 39 51 127	11 48 51 127	10 57 51 128	307
17 25 50 125	16 35 51 126	15 44 51 126	14 53 52 127	14 01 51 127	13 10 51 128	12 19 51 128	11 28 52 129	308
17 57 51 126	17 06 51 126	16 15 52 127	15 23 51 128	14 32 51 128	13 41 52 129	12 49 52 129	11 57 51 130	309
18 28 -51 127	17 37 -52 127	16 45 -51 128	15 54 -52 128	15 02 -51 129	14 11 -52 129	13 19 -52 130	12 27 -52 130	310
18 59 52 128	18 07 51 128	17 16 52 129	16 24 52 129	15 32 52 130	14 40 52 130	13 48 52 131	12 56 52 131	311
19 29 52 129	18 37 52 129	17 45 51 130	16 54 53 130	16 01 52 131	15 09 52 131	14 17 52 132	13 25 52 132	312
19 59 52 129	19 07 52 130	18 15 52 131	17 23 52 131	16 31 53 132	15 38 52 132	14 46 53 133	13 53 52 133	313
20 29 53 130	19 36 52 131	18 44 53 131	17 52 53 132	16 59 52 132	16 07 53 133	15 14 53 133	14 21 53 134	314
20 58 -53 132	20 05 -52 132	19 13 -53 132	18 20 -52 132	17 28 -53 133	16 35 -53 134	15 42 -53 134	14 49 -53 135	315
21 27 53 132	20 34 53 133	19 41 53 133	18 48 53 134	17 55 53 134	17 02 53 135	16 09 53 135	15 16 53 136	316
21 55 53 133	21 02 53 134	20 09 53 134	19 16 53 135	18 23 53 135	17 30 54 136	16 36 53 136	15 43 54 137	317
22 23 54 134	21 30 53 135	20 37 54 135	19 43 53 136	18 50 54 136	17 56 53 137	17 03 54 137	16 09 54 138	318
22 50 53 135	21 57 53 136	21 04 54 136	20 10 54 137	19 16 53 137	18 23 54 138	17 29 54 138	16 35 54 138	319
23 17 -53 136	22 24 -54 137	21 30 -54 137	20 36 -54 137	19 42 -54 138	18 48 -54 138	17 54 -54 139	17 00 -54 139	320
23 44 54 137	22 50 54 138	21 56 54 138	21 02 54 138	20 08 54 139	19 14 54 139	18 20 54 140	17 25 54 140	321
24 10 54 138	23 16 54 138	22 22 55 139	21 27 54 139	20 33 54 140	19 39 54 140	18 44 54 141	17 50 55 141	322
24 36 54 139	23 41 54 139	22 47 55 140	21 52 55 140	20 58 55 141	20 03 54 141	19 08 54 142	18 14 55 142	323
25 01 55 140	24 06 55 140	23 11 54 141	22 17 55 141	21 22 55 142	20 27 55 142	19 32 55 143	18 37 55 143	324
25 25 -55 141	24 30 -54 141	23 36 -55 142	22 41 -55 142	21 46 -55 142	20 50 -55 143	19 55 -55 144	19 00 -55 144	325
25 49 55 142	24 54 55 142	23 59 55 143	23 04 55 143	22 09 56 144	21 13 55 144	20 18 55 145	19 23 56 145	326
26 13 55 143	25 18 56 143	24 22 55 144	23 27 56 144	22 31 55 145	21 36 56 145	20 40 56 145	19 44 55 146	327
26 36 56 144	25 40 55 144	24 45 56 145	23 49 56 145	22 53 55 146	21 58 56 146	21 02 56 146	20 06 56 147	328
26 58 56 145	26 02 55 145	25 07 56 146	24 11 56 146	23 15 56 147	22 19 56 147	21 23 56 147	20 27 56 148	329
27 20 -56 146	26 24 -56 146	25 28 -56 147	24 32 -56 147	23 36 -57 148	22 40 -57 148	21 43 -56 148	20 47 -56 149	330
27 41 56 147	26 45 56 148	25 49 56 148	24 53 57 148	23 56 56 149	23 00 57 149	22 03 56 149	21 07 57 150	331
28 02 56 148	27 06 57 149	26 09 56 149	25 13 57 149	24 16 57 150	23 19 56 150	22 23 57 150	21 26 57 151	332
28 22 57 149	27 25 57 150	26 29 57 150	25 32 57 150	24 35 57 151	23 38 57 151	22 41 57 151	21 44 57 152	333
28 41 56 150	27 45 57 151	26 48 57 151	25 51 57 151	24 54 57 152	23 57 57 152	23 00 57 152	22 02 57 153	334
29 00 -57 151	28 03 -57 152	27 06 -57 152	26 09 -57 152	25 12 -58 153	24 14 -57 153	23 17 -57 153	22 20 -58 154	335
29 18 57 152	28 21 57 153	27 24 58 153	26 26 57 153	25 29 57 154	24 32 58 154	23 34 57 154	22 37 58 155	336
29 36 57 153	28 39 58 154	27 41 58 154	26 43 57 155	25 46 58 155	24 48 57 155	23 51 58 155	22 53 58 156	337
29 53 58 155	28 55 57 155	27 57 57 155	27 00 58 155	26 02 58 156	25 04 58 156	24 06 58 156	23 08 58 157	338
30 09 58 156	29 11 58 156	28 13 58 156	27 15 58 157	26 17 58 157	25 19 58 157	24 21 58 157	23 23 58 158	339
30 25 -58 157	29 27 -59 157	28 28 -58 157	27 30 -58 158	26 32 -58 158	25 34 -58 158	24 36 -58 159	23 38 -59 159	340
30 39 58 158	29 41 58 158	28 43 58 159	27 45 59 159	26 46 58 159	25 48 58 159	24 50 59 160	23 51 58 160	341
30 54 59 159	29 55 58 159	28 57 59 160	27 58 58 160	27 00 59 160	26 01 58 160	25 03 59 161	24 04 58 161	342
31 07 59 160	30 08 58 160	29 10 59 161	28 11 59 161	27 13 59 161	26 14 59 161	25 15 59 162	24 17 59 162	343
31 20 59 161	30 21 59 162	29 22 59 162	28 23 58 162	27 25 59 162	26 26 59 163	25 27 59 163	24 28 59 163	344
31 32 -59 163	30 33 -59 163	29 34 -59 163	28 35 -59 163	27 36 -59 163	26 37 -59 164	25 38 -59 164	24 39 -59 164	345
31 43 59 164	30 44 59 164	29 45 59 164	28 46 59 164	27 47 59 164	26 48 59 165	25 49 59 165	24 50 60 165	346
31 53 59 165	30 54 59 165	29 55 59 165	28 56 59 165	27 57 59 166	26 58 60 166	25 58 59 166	24 59 59 166	347
32 03 59 166	31 04 59 166	30 05 60 166	29 05 59 166	28 06 59 167	27 07 60 167	26 07 59 167	25 08 59 167	348
32 12 59 167	31 13 60 167	30 13 59 167	29 14 59 168	28 15 60 168	27 15 59 168	26 16 60 168	25 16 59 168	349
32 20 -59 168	31 21 -60 168	30 21 -59 169	29 22 -60 169	28 22 -59 169	27 23 -60 169	26 23 -59 169	25 24 -60 169	350
32 28 60 169	31 28 60 170	30 29 60 170	29 29 59 170	28 30 60 170	27 30 60 170	26 30 59 170	25 31 60 170	351
32 35 60 171	31 35 60 171	30 35 60 171	29 36 60 171	28 36 60 171	27 36 59 171	26 37 60 171	25 37 60 171	352
32 41 60 172	31 41 60 172	30 41 60 172	29 41 59 172	28 42 60 172	27 42 60 172	26 42 60 172	25 42 59 173	353
32 46 60 173	31 46 60 173	30 46 60 173	29 46 60 173	28 46 59 173	27 47 60 173	26 47 60 173	25 47 60 174	354
32 50 -60 174	31 50 -60 174	30 50 -60 174	29 50 -59 174	28 51 -60 174	27 51 -60 175	26 51 -60 175	25 51 -60 175	355
32 54 60 175	31 54 60 175	30 54 60 175	29 54 60 175	28 54 60 176	27 54 60 176	26 54 60 176	25 54 60 176	356
32 56 59 177	31 57 60 177	30 57 60 177	29 57 60 177	28 57 60 177	27 57 60 177	26 57 60 177	25 57 60 177	357
32 58 60 178	31 58 60 178	30 58 60 178	29 59 60 178	28 59 60 178	27 59 60 178	26 59 60 178	25 59 60 178	358
33 00 60 179	32 00 60 179	31 00 60 179	30 00 60 179	29 00 60 179	28 00 60 179	27 00 60 179	26 00 60 179	359
33 00 -60 180	32 00 -60 180	31 00 -60 180	30 00 -60 180	29 00 -60 180	28 00 -60 180	27 00 -60 180	26 00 -60 180	360

CONTRARY NAME TO LATITUDE

LAT 50°

165

N. Lat. { LHA greater than 180°....... Zn=Z / LHA less than 180°.......... Zn=360−Z

DECLINATION (15°-29°)

LHA	15° Hc	d	Z	16° Hc	d	Z	17° Hc	d	Z	18° Hc	d	Z	19° Hc	d	Z	20° Hc	d	Z	21° Hc	d	Z
0	55 00	+60	180	56 00	+60	180	57 00	+60	180	58 00	+60	180	59 00	+60	180	60 00	+60	180	61 00	+60	180
1	54 59	60	178	55 59	60	178	56 59	60	178	57 59	60	178	58 59	60	178	59 59	60	178	60 59	60	178
2	54 58	60	177	55 58	60	177	56 58	60	177	57 58	60	176	58 58	60	176	59 58	59	176	60 57	60	176
3	54 55	60	175	55 55	60	175	56 55	60	175	57 55	59	175	58 54	60	175	59 54	60	174	60 54	60	174
4	54 51	60	173	55 51	60	173	56 51	59	173	57 50	60	173	58 50	60	173	59 50	60	173	60 50	59	172
5	54 46	+60	172	55 46	+59	171	56 45	+60	171	57 45	+60	171	58 45	+59	171	59 44	+60	171	60 44	+60	170
6	54 40	60	170	55 39	60	170	56 39	59	170	57 38	60	169	58 38	59	169	59 37	60	169	60 37	59	169
7	54 32	60	168	55 32	59	168	56 31	60	168	57 31	59	168	58 30	59	167	59 29	60	167	60 29	59	167
8	54 24	59	167	55 23	60	166	56 23	59	166	57 22	59	166	58 21	59	166	59 20	59	165	60 19	59	165
9	54 15	59	165	55 14	59	165	56 13	59	164	57 12	59	164	58 11	59	164	59 10	58	163	60 08	59	163
10	54 04	+59	163	55 03	+59	163	56 02	+59	163	57 01	+58	162	57 59	+59	162	58 58	+58	162	59 56	+59	161
11	53 53	58	162	54 51	59	161	55 50	58	161	56 48	59	161	57 47	58	160	58 45	58	160	59 43	59	159
12	53 40	58	160	54 38	59	160	55 37	58	159	56 35	58	159	57 33	58	159	58 31	58	158	59 29	58	158
13	53 26	59	159	54 25	58	158	55 23	58	158	56 21	58	157	57 19	57	157	58 16	58	158	59 14	57	156
14	53 12	58	157	54 10	58	157	55 08	57	156	56 05	58	156	57 03	57	155	58 00	58	155	58 58	57	154
15	52 56	+58	156	53 54	+58	155	54 52	+57	155	55 49	+57	154	56 46	+57	154	57 43	+57	153	58 40	+57	152
16	52 40	57	154	53 37	57	154	54 34	58	153	55 32	56	152	56 28	57	152	57 25	57	151	58 22	56	151
17	52 23	57	152	53 20	56	152	54 16	57	151	55 13	57	151	56 10	56	150	57 06	56	150	58 02	56	149
18	52 04	57	151	53 01	57	150	53 58	56	150	54 54	56	149	55 50	56	149	56 46	56	148	57 42	56	147
19	51 45	56	150	52 41	57	149	53 38	56	148	54 34	56	148	55 30	55	147	56 25	56	146	57 21	55	146
20	51 25	+56	148	52 21	+56	147	53 17	+56	147	54 13	+55	146	55 08	+56	146	56 04	+55	145	56 59	+54	144
21	51 04	56	147	52 00	56	146	52 56	55	145	53 51	55	145	54 46	55	144	55 41	55	143	56 36	54	143
22	50 43	55	145	51 38	55	145	52 33	55	144	53 28	55	143	54 23	54	143	55 17	55	142	56 12	54	141
23	50 20	55	144	51 15	55	143	52 10	55	143	53 05	54	142	53 59	54	141	54 53	54	140	55 47	54	140
24	49 57	55	142	50 52	54	142	51 46	54	141	52 40	54	140	53 34	54	140	54 28	54	139	55 22	53	138
25	49 33	+54	141	50 27	+55	140	51 22	+54	140	52 16	+53	139	53 09	+53	138	54 02	+54	137	54 56	+52	137
26	49 08	55	140	50 03	53	139	50 56	54	138	51 50	53	138	52 43	53	137	53 36	53	136	54 29	52	135
27	48 43	54	138	49 37	53	138	50 30	53	137	51 23	53	136	52 16	53	136	53 09	52	135	54 01	52	134
28	48 17	54	137	49 11	53	136	50 04	52	136	50 56	53	135	51 49	52	134	52 41	52	133	53 33	52	133
29	47 51	53	136	48 44	52	135	49 36	53	134	50 29	52	134	51 21	52	133	52 13	51	132	53 04	51	131
30	47 23	+53	135	48 16	+52	134	49 08	+53	133	50 01	+51	132	50 52	+52	132	51 44	+51	131	52 35	+51	130
31	46 56	52	133	47 48	52	133	48 40	52	132	49 32	51	131	50 23	51	130	51 14	51	129	52 05	50	129
32	46 27	52	132	47 19	52	131	48 11	51	131	49 02	51	130	49 53	51	129	50 44	51	128	51 35	50	127
33	45 58	52	131	46 50	51	130	47 41	51	129	48 32	51	129	49 23	51	128	50 14	50	127	51 04	49	126
34	45 29	51	130	46 20	51	129	47 11	51	128	48 02	50	127	48 52	51	127	49 43	49	126	50 32	49	125
35	44 59	+51	128	45 50	+51	128	46 41	+50	127	47 31	+50	126	48 21	+50	125	49 11	+49	125	50 00	+49	124
36	44 28	51	127	45 19	51	127	46 10	50	126	47 00	50	125	47 50	49	124	48 39	49	123	49 28	49	122
37	43 58	50	126	44 48	50	125	45 38	50	125	46 28	49	124	47 17	49	123	48 06	49	123	48 55	48	121
38	43 26	50	125	44 16	50	124	45 06	50	124	45 56	49	123	46 45	49	122	47 34	48	121	48 22	48	120
39	42 54	50	124	43 44	50	123	44 33	49	122	45 23	49	122	46 12	48	121	47 00	48	120	47 48	48	119
40	42 22	+50	123	43 12	+49	122	44 01	+49	121	44 50	+49	121	45 39	+48	120	46 27	+48	119	47 15	+47	118
41	41 50	49	122	42 39	49	121	43 28	49	120	44 17	48	119	45 05	48	119	45 53	47	118	46 40	47	117
42	41 17	49	121	42 06	48	120	42 54	49	119	43 43	48	118	44 31	47	118	45 18	48	117	46 06	47	116
43	40 43	49	120	41 32	48	119	42 20	49	118	43 09	47	117	43 56	48	116	44 44	47	116	45 31	46	115
44	40 10	48	119	40 58	48	118	41 46	48	117	42 34	47	117	43 22	47	115	44 09	47	115	44 56	46	114
45	39 35	+49	118	40 24	+48	117	41 12	+47	116	41 59	+48	115	42 47	+47	114	43 34	+46	114	44 20	+46	113
46	39 01	48	117	39 49	48	116	40 37	47	115	41 24	47	114	42 11	47	113	42 58	46	113	43 44	46	112
47	38 27	48	116	39 14	48	115	40 02	46	113	40 49	47	113	41 36	46	112	42 22	46	112	43 08	46	111
48	37 52	47	115	38 39	48	114	39 27	46	113	40 13	47	112	41 00	46	111	41 46	46	111	42 32	46	110
49	37 16	48	113	38 04	47	113	38 51	47	112	39 38	46	111	40 24	46	110	41 10	46	110	41 56	45	109
50	36 41	+47	113	37 28	+47	112	38 15	+47	111	39 02	+46	110	39 48	+46	110	40 34	+45	109	41 19	+45	108
51	36 05	47	112	36 52	47	111	37 39	46	110	38 25	46	109	39 11	46	109	39 57	45	108	40 42	45	107
52	35 29	47	111	36 16	47	110	37 03	46	109	37 49	46	108	38 35	45	108	39 20	45	107	40 05	45	106
53	34 53	47	110	35 40	46	109	36 26	46	108	37 12	46	108	37 58	45	107	38 43	45	106	39 28	45	105
54	34 17	46	109	35 03	46	108	35 49	46	107	36 35	46	107	37 21	45	106	38 06	45	105	38 51	44	104
55	33 40	+47	108	34 27	+46	107	35 13	+45	107	35 58	+46	106	36 44	+45	105	37 29	+44	104	38 13	+45	103
56	33 03	47	107	33 50	45	106	34 35	46	106	35 21	45	105	36 06	45	104	36 51	45	103	37 36	44	102
57	32 26	47	106	33 13	45	106	33 58	46	105	34 44	45	104	35 29	45	103	36 14	44	102	36 58	44	102
58	31 49	46	105	32 35	45	105	33 21	45	104	34 06	45	103	34 51	45	102	35 36	44	102	36 20	44	101
59	31 12	46	105	31 58	45	104	32 43	46	103	33 29	44	102	34 13	45	101	34 58	44	101	35 42	44	100
60	30 35	+45	104	31 20	+46	103	32 06	+45	102	32 51	+45	101	33 36	+44	101	34 20	+44	100	35 04	+44	99
61	29 57	46	103	30 43	45	102	31 28	45	102	32 13	45	101	32 58	44	100	33 42	44	99	34 26	44	98
62	29 20	45	102	30 05	45	101	30 50	45	101	31 35	45	100	32 20	44	99	33 04	44	98	33 48	44	97
63	28 42	45	101	29 27	45	100	30 12	45	100	30 57	44	99	31 41	45	98	32 26	44	97	33 10	43	97
64	28 04	45	100	28 49	45	100	29 34	45	99	30 19	44	98	31 03	44	97	31 47	44	97	32 31	44	96
65	27 26	+45	100	28 11	+45	99	28 56	+45	98	29 41	+44	97	30 25	+44	96	31 09	+44	96	31 53	+43	95
66	26 48	45	99	27 33	45	98	28 18	44	97	29 02	45	96	29 47	44	96	30 31	43	95	31 14	44	94
67	26 10	45	98	26 55	44	97	27 39	45	96	28 24	44	96	29 08	44	95	29 52	44	94	30 36	43	93
68	25 31	45	97	26 16	45	96	27 01	44	96	27 45	45	95	28 30	44	94	29 14	43	93	29 57	44	93
69	24 53	45	96	25 38	45	96	26 23	44	95	27 07	44	95	27 51	44	93	28 35	44	93	29 19	43	92

15° 16° 17° 18° 19° 20° 21°

S. Lat. { LHA greater than 180°....... Zn=180−Z / LHA less than 180°.......... Zn=180+Z

DECLINATION (15°-29°)

SAME NAME AS LATITUDE   **LAT 50°**

22° Hc	d	Z	23° Hc	d	Z	24° Hc	d	Z	25° Hc	d	Z	26° Hc	d	Z	27° Hc	d	Z	28° Hc	d	Z	29° Hc	d	Z	LHA
62 00	+60	180	63 00	+60	180	64 00	+60	180	65 00	+60	180	66 00	+60	180	67 00	+60	180	68 00	+60	180	69 00	+60	180	360
61 59	60	178	62 59	60	178	63 59	60	178	64 59	60	178	65 59	60	178	66 59	60	178	67 59	60	178	68 59	60	178	359
61 57	60	176	62 57	60	176	63 57	60	176	64 57	60	176	65 57	60	175	66 57	60	175	67 57	60	175	68 57	59	175	358
61 54	60	174	62 54	60	174	63 54	60	174	64 54	59	174	65 53	60	173	66 53	60	173	67 53	60	173	68 53	59	173	357
61 49	60	172	62 49	60	172	63 49	60	172	64 49	59	172	65 48	60	171	66 48	59	171	67 47	60	171	68 47	59	171	356
61 44	+59	170	62 43	+60	170	63 43	+59	170	64 42	+60	169	65 42	+59	169	66 41	+59	169	67 40	+59	168	68 40	+59	168	355
61 36	60	168	62 36	59	168	63 35	59	168	64 34	60	167	65 34	59	167	66 33	59	167	67 32	59	166	68 31	59	166	354
61 28	59	166	62 27	59	166	63 26	59	166	64 25	59	165	65 24	59	165	66 23	59	164	67 22	58	164	68 20	59	163	353
61 18	59	164	62 18	59	164	63 16	59	164	64 15	58	163	65 13	59	163	66 12	58	162	67 09	59	162	68 09	58	161	352
61 07	59	163	62 06	58	162	63 04	58	162	64 03	58	161	65 01	58	161	65 59	58	160	66 57	58	159	67 55	58	159	351
60 55	+58	161	61 53	+58	160	62 51	+59	160	63 50	+58	159	64 48	+57	159	65 45	+58	158	66 43	+58	157	67 41	+57	156	350
60 42	58	159	61 40	57	158	62 37	58	158	63 35	58	157	64 33	57	157	65 30	57	156	66 27	57	155	67 24	57	154	349
60 27	58	157	61 25	57	156	62 22	58	156	63 20	57	155	64 17	57	155	65 14	57	154	66 11	56	153	67 07	56	152	348
60 11	58	155	61 09	57	155	62 06	57	153	63 03	57	153	64 00	56	152	64 56	56	152	65 52	56	151	66 48	56	150	347
59 55	57	153	60 52	56	153	61 48	57	152	62 45	56	151	63 41	56	151	64 37	56	150	65 33	56	149	66 29	55	148	346
59 37	+56	152	60 33	+57	151	61 30	+56	150	62 26	+56	150	63 22	+55	149	64 17	+56	148	65 13	+54	147	66 07	+55	146	345
59 18	56	150	60 14	56	149	61 10	56	149	62 06	55	148	63 01	55	147	63 56	55	146	64 51	54	145	65 45	54	144	344
58 58	56	148	59 54	56	148	60 50	55	147	61 45	55	146	62 40	54	145	63 34	54	144	64 28	54	143	65 22	54	142	343
58 38	55	147	59 33	55	146	60 28	55	145	61 23	54	144	62 17	54	143	63 11	54	142	64 05	53	141	64 58	53	140	342
58 16	55	145	59 11	54	144	60 05	55	143	61 00	54	143	61 54	53	142	62 47	53	141	63 40	53	140	64 33	52	139	341
57 53	+55	143	58 48	+54	143	59 42	+54	142	60 36	+53	141	61 29	+53	140	62 22	+53	139	63 15	+52	138	64 07	+52	137	340
57 30	54	142	58 24	54	141	59 18	53	140	60 11	53	139	61 04	53	138	61 57	52	137	62 49	51	136	63 40	51	135	339
57 06	54	140	57 59	54	139	58 53	52	139	59 45	53	138	60 38	52	137	61 30	51	136	62 21	51	135	63 12	51	133	338
56 41	53	139	57 34	53	138	58 27	52	137	59 19	52	136	60 11	52	135	61 03	51	134	61 54	50	133	62 44	50	132	337
56 15	53	137	57 08	52	136	58 00	52	136	58 52	51	135	59 43	51	134	60 34	51	133	61 25	49	131	62 15	49	130	336
55 48	+53	136	56 41	+52	135	57 33	+51	134	58 24	+51	133	59 15	+51	132	60 06	+50	131	60 56	+49	130	61 45	+49	129	335
55 21	52	134	56 13	51	134	57 04	52	133	57 56	50	132	58 46	50	131	59 36	50	130	60 26	49	128	61 15	48	127	334
54 53	52	133	55 45	51	132	56 36	50	131	57 26	50	130	58 17	49	129	59 06	49	128	59 55	49	127	60 44	48	126	333
54 25	51	132	55 16	50	131	56 06	51	130	56 57	49	129	57 46	49	128	58 35	49	127	59 24	48	126	60 12	47	124	332
53 55	51	130	54 46	50	129	55 36	50	128	56 26	49	127	57 15	49	126	58 04	48	125	58 52	48	124	59 40	47	123	331
53 26	+50	129	54 16	+50	128	55 06	+49	127	55 55	+49	126	56 44	+48	125	57 32	+48	124	58 20	+47	123	59 07	+47	122	330
52 55	50	128	53 45	50	127	54 35	49	126	55 24	48	125	56 12	48	124	57 00	48	123	57 48	46	121	58 34	46	120	329
52 25	49	126	53 14	49	125	54 03	49	124	54 52	48	123	55 40	48	122	56 28	46	121	57 14	47	120	58 01	45	119	328
51 53	49	125	52 42	49	124	53 31	48	123	54 19	48	122	55 07	47	121	55 54	47	120	56 41	46	119	57 27	45	118	327
51 21	49	124	52 10	49	123	52 59	48	122	53 47	47	121	54 34	47	120	55 21	46	119	56 07	45	118	56 52	45	117	326
50 49	+49	122	51 38	+48	122	52 26	+47	121	53 13	+47	120	54 00	+47	119	54 47	+46	118	55 33	+45	117	56 18	+44	115	325
50 17	48	122	51 05	47	121	51 52	48	120	52 40	46	119	53 26	46	118	54 12	46	116	54 58	45	115	55 43	44	114	324
49 43	48	120	50 31	48	119	51 19	47	118	52 06	46	117	52 52	46	116	53 38	45	115	54 23	44	114	55 07	44	113	323
49 10	48	119	49 58	47	118	50 45	46	117	51 31	46	116	52 17	45	115	53 03	45	114	53 48	44	113	54 32	43	112	322
48 36	47	118	49 23	47	117	50 10	46	116	50 56	46	115	51 42	45	114	52 27	45	113	53 12	44	112	53 56	43	111	321
48 02	+47	116	48 49	+46	116	49 35	+46	115	50 21	+46	114	51 07	+45	113	51 52	+44	111	52 36	+44	111	53 20	+43	110	320
47 27	47	116	48 14	46	115	49 00	46	114	49 46	45	113	50 31	45	112	51 16	44	111	52 00	43	110	52 43	43	109	319
46 53	46	115	47 39	46	114	48 25	45	113	49 10	45	112	49 55	45	111	50 40	43	110	51 23	44	109	52 07	42	108	318
46 17	47	114	47 04	45	113	47 49	45	112	48 34	44	111	49 19	44	109	50 03	44	109	50 47	43	108	51 30	42	107	317
45 42	46	113	46 28	45	112	47 13	45	111	47 58	45	110	48 43	44	109	49 27	43	108	50 10	43	107	50 53	42	106	316
45 06	+46	112	45 52	+45	111	46 37	+45	110	47 22	+44	109	48 06	+44	108	48 50	+43	107	49 33	+42	105	50 15	+42	105	315
44 30	46	111	45 16	45	110	46 01	44	109	46 45	44	108	47 29	44	107	48 13	42	105	48 56	42	105	49 38	42	104	314
43 54	45	110	44 39	45	109	45 24	45	108	46 09	43	107	46 52	44	106	47 36	42	105	48 18	42	104	49 01	41	103	313
43 18	45	109	44 03	44	108	44 47	45	107	45 32	43	106	46 15	43	105	46 58	43	104	47 41	42	103	48 23	41	102	312
42 41	46	108	43 26	44	107	44 10	44	106	44 54	44	105	45 38	43	104	46 21	42	103	47 03	42	102	47 45	41	101	311
42 04	+45	107	42 49	+44	106	43 33	+44	105	44 17	+43	104	45 00	+43	103	45 43	+42	102	46 25	+42	101	47 07	+41	100	310
41 27	45	106	42 12	44	105	42 56	44	104	43 40	43	103	44 23	42	102	45 05	43	101	45 48	41	100	46 29	41	99	309
40 50	45	105	41 35	43	104	42 18	44	103	43 02	43	102	43 45	43	101	44 28	42	100	45 10	41	99	45 51	41	98	308
40 13	44	104	40 57	44	103	41 41	43	102	42 24	43	101	43 07	41	101	43 50	41	100	44 31	42	99	45 13	41	98	307
39 35	44	103	40 19	44	102	41 03	43	102	41 46	43	101	42 29	42	100	43 11	42	99	43 53	42	98	44 35	40	97	306
38 58	+44	102	39 42	+43	102	40 25	+43	101	41 08	+43	100	41 51	+42	99	42 33	+42	98	43 15	+41	97	43 56	+41	96	305
38 20	44	102	39 04	43	101	39 47	43	100	40 30	43	99	41 13	42	98	41 55	42	97	42 37	41	96	43 18	40	95	304
37 42	44	101	38 26	43	100	39 09	43	99	39 52	43	98	40 35	42	97	41 17	41	96	41 58	41	95	42 39	41	94	303
37 04	44	100	37 48	43	99	38 31	43	98	39 14	42	97	39 56	42	96	40 38	41	95	41 20	41	94	42 01	40	93	302
36 26	44	99	37 10	43	98	37 53	43	97	38 36	42	96	39 18	42	95	40 00	41	95	40 41	41	94	41 22	41	93	301
35 48	+44	98	36 32	+43	97	37 15	+42	96	37 57	+43	96	38 40	+41	95	39 21	+42	94	40 03	+41	93	40 44	+40	92	300
35 10	43	97	35 53	43	96	36 36	43	96	37 19	42	95	38 01	42	94	38 43	41	93	39 24	41	91	40 05	41	91	299
34 32	43	97	35 15	43	96	35 58	42	95	36 40	43	94	37 23	41	93	38 04	42	92	38 46	41	91	39 27	40	90	298
33 53	43	96	34 36	43	95	35 19	43	94	36 02	42	93	36 44	42	93	37 26	41	91	38 07	41	90	38 48	41	90	297
33 15	43	95	33 58	43	94	34 41	42	93	35 23	43	92	36 06	41	91	36 47	42	91	37 29	41	90	38 10	40	89	296
32 36	+44	94	33 20	+42	93	34 02	+43	92	34 45	+42	92	35 27	+42	91	36 09	+41	90	36 50	+41	89	37 31	+40	88	295
31 58	43	94	32 41	42	92	33 24	42	92	34 06	42	91	34 48	42	90	35 30	42	89	36 12	40	88	36 52	41	87	294
31 19	43	93	32 02	43	92	32 45	42	91	33 28	42	90	34 10	42	89	34 52	41	88	35 33	41	87	36 14	40	86	293
30 41	43	92	31 24	43	91	32 07	42	90	32 49	42	89	33 31	42	88	34 13	41	88	34 54	41	87	35 35	41	86	292
30 02	43	91	30 45	43	90	31 28	43	89	32 11	42	89	32 53	42	88	33 35	41	87	34 16	41	86	34 57	41	85	291

22°	23°	24°	25°	26°	27°	28°	29°

SAME NAME AS LATITUDE

N. Lat. { LHA greater than 180°....... Zn=Z / LHA less than 180°......... Zn=360−Z }

DECLINATION (15°–29°

LHA	Hc 15°	d	Z	Hc 16°	d	Z	Hc 17°	d	Z	Hc 18°	d	Z	Hc 19°	d	Z	Hc 20°	d	Z	Hc 21°	d	Z
70	24 15	+45	96	25 00	+44	95	25 44	+45	94	26 29	+44	93	27 13	+44	93	27 57	+43	92	28 40	+44	9
71	23 36	45	95	24 21	45	94	25 06	44	93	25 50	44	93	26 34	44	92	27 18	44	91	28 02	43	9
72	22 58	45	94	23 43	44	93	24 27	44	92	25 11	45	92	25 56	43	91	26 39	44	90	27 23	44	8
73	22 19	45	93	23 04	45	92	23 49	44	92	24 33	44	91	25 17	44	90	26 01	44	89	26 45	43	8
74	21 41	45	92	22 26	44	92	23 10	44	91	23 54	44	90	24 38	44	89	25 22	44	89	26 06	43	8
75	21 02	+45	92	21 47	+44	91	22 31	+45	90	23 16	+44	90	24 00	+44	89	24 44	+44	88	25 28	+43	8
76	20 24	44	91	21 08	45	90	21 53	44	89	22 37	44	89	23 21	44	88	24 05	44	87	24 49	43	8
77	19 45	45	90	20 30	44	89	21 14	45	89	21 59	44	88	22 43	44	87	23 27	44	86	24 11	43	8
78	19 07	44	89	19 51	45	89	20 36	44	88	21 20	44	87	22 04	44	86	22 48	44	86	23 32	44	8
79	18 28	45	89	19 13	44	88	19 57	45	87	20 42	44	86	21 26	44	86	22 10	44	85	22 54	43	8
80	17 49	+45	88	18 34	+45	87	19 19	+44	86	20 03	+44	86	20 47	+44	85	21 31	+44	84	22 15	+44	8
81	17 11	45	87	17 56	44	86	18 40	45	86	19 25	44	85	20 09	44	84	20 53	44	83	21 37	44	8
82	16 32	45	86	17 17	45	86	18 02	44	85	18 46	45	84	19 31	44	83	20 15	44	83	20 59	44	8
83	15 54	45	86	16 39	44	85	17 23	45	84	18 08	44	83	18 52	45	83	19 37	44	82	20 21	44	8
84	15 16	44	85	16 00	45	84	16 45	45	83	17 30	44	83	18 14	44	83	18 58	45	81	19 43	44	8
85	14 37	+45	84	15 22	+45	83	16 07	+45	83	16 52	+45	82	17 36	+44	81	18 20	+45	81	19 05	+44	8
86	13 59	44	83	14 44	45	83	15 29	44	82	16 13	45	81	16 58	44	80	17 42	45	80	18 27	44	7
87	13 21	45	83	14 06	44	82	14 51	44	81	15 35	45	80	16 20	45	80	17 05	44	79	17 49	44	7
88	12 42	45	82	13 27	45	81	14 12	45	80	14 57	45	80	15 42	45	79	16 27	44	78	17 11	45	7
89	12 04	45	81	12 49	45	80	13 34	45	80	14 19	45	79	15 04	45	79	15 49	45	78	16 34	44	7
90	11 26	+45	80	12 11	+46	80	12 57	+45	79	13 42	+45	78	14 27	+44	78	15 11	+45	77	15 56	+45	7
91	10 48	46	80	11 34	45	79	12 19	45	78	13 04	45	78	13 49	45	77	14 34	45	76	15 19	44	7
92	10 10	46	79	10 56	45	78	11 41	45	77	12 26	45	77	13 11	46	76	13 57	44	75	14 41	45	7
93	09 33	45	78	10 18	46	77	11 04	45	77	11 49	45	76	12 34	45	75	13 19	45	75	14 04	45	7
94	08 55	46	77	09 41	45	77	10 26	45	76	11 11	46	75	11 57	45	75	12 42	45	74	13 27	45	7
95	08 17	+46	77	09 03	+46	76	09 49	+45	75	10 34	+46	75	11 20	+45	74	12 05	+45	73	12 50	+46	7
96	07 40	46	76	08 26	45	75	09 11	46	75	09 57	46	74	10 43	45	73	11 28	46	73	12 14	45	7
97	07 03	46	75	07 49	45	74	08 34	46	74	09 20	46	73	10 06	46	73	10 52	45	72	11 37	46	7
98	06 25	46	74	07 11	46	74	07 57	46	73	08 43	46	72	09 29	46	72	10 15	46	71	11 01	45	7
99	05 48	47	74	06 35	46	73	07 21	46	73	08 07	46	72	08 53	46	72	09 39	46	70	10 25	45	7
100	05 11	+47	73	05 58	+46	72	06 44	+46	72	07 30	+46	71	08 16	+46	70	09 02	+46	70	09 48	+46	6
101	04 35	46	72	05 21	46	71	06 07	47	71	06 54	46	70	07 40	46	70	08 26	47	69	09 13	46	6
102	03 58	47	71	04 45	46	71	05 31	47	70	06 18	46	69	07 04	46	69	07 50	47	68	08 37	46	6
103	03 22	46	71	04 08	47	70	04 55	47	69	05 42	46	69	06 28	47	68	07 15	46	68	08 01	47	6
104	02 45	47	70	03 32	47	69	04 19	47	69	05 06	47	68	05 53	46	68	06 39	47	67	07 26	47	6
105	02 09	+47	69	02 56	+47	68	03 43	+47	68	04 30	+47	67	05 17	+47	67	06 04	‑47	66	06 51	+47	6
106	01 33	47	68	02 20	48	67	03 08	47	67	03 55	47	66	04 42	47	66	05 29	47	65	06 16	47	6
107	00 58	47	68	01 45	47	67	02 32	47	66	03 19	48	66	04 07	47	65	04 54	47	64	05 41	47	6
108	00 22	47	67	01 09	48	66	01 57	47	66	02 44	48	65	03 32	47	64	04 19	48	64	05 07	47	6
109	−0 13	47	66	00 34	48	65	01 22	48	65	02 10	47	64	02 57	48	64	03 45	47	63	04 32	48	6
110	−0 48	+47	65	−0 01	+48	65	00 47	+48	64	01 35	+48	63	02 23	+48	63	03 11	+47	62	03 58	+48	6
111	−1 23	48	64	−0 35	48	64	00 13	48	63	01 01	48	63	01 49	48	62	02 37	48	61	03 25	48	6
112	−1 58	48	64	−1 10	48	63	−0 22	49	62	00 27	48	62	01 15	48	61	02 03	48	61	02 51	48	6
113	−2 32	48	63	−1 44	48	62	−0 56	49	62	−0 07	48	61	00 41	48	61	01 29	49	60	02 18	48	5
114	−3 07	49	62	−2 18	48	62	−1 30	49	61	−0 41	49	60	00 08	48	60	00 56	49	59	01 45	48	5
115	−3 41	+49	61	−2 52	+49	61	−2 03	+49	60	−1 14	+48	60	−0 26	+49	59	00 23	+49	58	01 12	+49	5
116	−4 14	49	61	−3 25	49	60	−2 36	48	59	−1 48	49	59	−0 59	49	58	−0 10	49	58	00 39	49	5
117	−4 48	49	60	−3 59	49	59	−3 10	50	59	−2 20	49	58	−1 31	49	57	−0 42	49	57	00 07	49	5
118	−5 21	49	59	−4 32	50	58	−3 42	49	58	−2 53	49	57	−2 04	50	57	−1 14	49	56	−0 25	50	5
119	−5 54	50	58	−5 04	49	58	−4 15	50	57	−3 25	49	56	−2 36	50	56	−1 46	50	55	−0 56	49	5
120				−5 37	+50	57	−4 47	+50	56	−3 57	+50	56	−3 07	+49	55	−2 18	+50	55	−1 28	+50	5
121							−5 19	50	55	−4 29	50	55	−3 39	50	54	−2 49	50	54	−1 59	50	5
122							−5 51	51	55	−5 00	50	54	−4 10	50	54	−3 20	51	53	−2 30	51	5
123										−5 31	50	53	−4 41	51	53	−3 50	50	52	−3 00	51	5
124													−5 11	50	52	−4 21	51	51	−3 30	51	5
125													−5 42	+51	51	−4 51	+51	51	−4 00	+51	5
126																−5 20	51	50	−4 29	51	4
127																−5 50	52	49	−4 58	51	4
128																			−5 27	52	4
129																			−5 55	52	4
13																					

| | 15° | | | 16° | | | 17° | | | 18° | | | 19° | | | 20° | | | 21° | | |

S. Lat. { LHA greater than 180°......Zn=180−Z / LHA less than 180°.........Zn=180+Z }

DECLINATION (15°–29°

SAME NAME AS LATITUDE

	22°			23°			24°			25°			26°			27°			28°			29°		
	c	d	Z	Hc	d	Z	Hc	d	Z	Hc	d	Z	Hc	d	Z	Hc	d	Z	Hc	d	Z	Hc	d	Z	LHA
	24	+43	90	3007	+43	89	3050	+42	89	3132	+42	88	3214	+42	87	3256	+42	86	3338	+41	85	3419	+40	84	290
	45	43	89	2928	43	89	3011	43	88	3054	42	87	3136	42	86	3218	41	85	3259	41	84	3340	41	84	289
	07	43	89	2850	42	88	2932	43	87	3015	42	86	3057	42	85	3139	42	85	3221	41	84	3302	41	83	288
	28	43	88	2811	43	87	2854	42	86	2937	42	86	3019	42	85	3101	41	84	3142	42	83	3224	41	82	287
	49	44	87	2733	43	86	2816	42	86	2858	42	85	2940	42	84	3022	42	83	3104	42	82	3146	41	81	286
	11	+43	86	2654	+43	86	2737	+43	85	2820	+42	84	2902	+42	83	2944	+42	82	3026	+41	82	3107	+42	81	285
	32	44	86	2616	43	85	2659	42	84	2741	43	84	2824	42	83	2906	42	82	2948	41	81	3029	42	80	284
	54	44	85	2537	43	84	2620	43	83	2703	43	83	2746	42	82	2828	42	81	2910	42	80	2952	41	79	283
	16	43	84	2459	43	83	2542	43	83	2625	43	82	2708	42	81	2750	42	80	2832	42	79	2914	41	79	282
	37	44	83	2421	43	83	2504	43	82	2547	42	81	2629	43	80	2712	42	80	2754	42	79	2836	41	78	281
	59	+43	83	2342	+44	82	2426	+43	81	2509	+42	80	2551	+43	80	2634	+42	79	2716	+42	78	2758	+42	77	280
	21	43	82	2304	44	81	2348	43	80	2431	43	80	2514	42	79	2556	43	78	2639	42	77	2721	42	77	279
	43	43	81	2226	44	81	2310	43	80	2353	43	79	2436	43	78	2519	42	77	2601	42	77	2643	42	76	278
	05	43	81	2148	44	80	2232	43	79	2315	43	78	2358	43	78	2441	43	77	2524	42	76	2606	42	75	277
	27	43	80	2110	44	79	2154	43	78	2237	44	78	2321	42	77	2403	43	76	2446	43	75	2529	42	75	276
	49	+44	79	2033	+43	78	2116	+44	78	2200	+43	77	2243	+43	76	2326	+43	75	2409	+43	75	2452	+42	74	275
	11	44	78	1955	44	78	2039	43	77	2122	44	76	2206	43	75	2249	43	75	2332	43	73	2415	42	73	274
	33	44	78	1917	44	77	2001	44	76	2045	43	75	2128	44	75	2212	43	74	2255	43	73	2338	42	72	273
	56	44	77	1840	44	76	1924	44	75	2008	43	75	2051	44	74	2135	43	73	2218	43	73	2301	43	72	272
	18	44	76	1802	44	76	1846	44	75	1930	44	74	2014	44	73	2058	43	73	2141	44	72	2225	43	71	271
	41	+44	75	1725	+44	75	1809	+44	74	1853	+44	73	1937	+44	73	2021	+44	72	2105	+43	71	2148	+43	70	270
	03	45	75	1648	44	74	1732	45	73	1817	44	73	1901	44	72	1945	43	71	2028	44	70	2112	43	70	269
	26	45	74	1611	44	73	1655	45	73	1740	44	72	1824	44	71	1908	44	71	1952	44	70	2036	43	69	268
	49	45	73	1534	45	73	1619	44	72	1703	45	71	1748	44	71	1832	44	70	1916	44	69	2000	44	68	267
	12	45	73	1457	45	72	1542	45	71	1627	44	71	1711	45	70	1756	44	69	1840	44	68	1924	44	68	266
	36	+45	72	1421	+45	71	1506	+45	71	1551	+44	70	1635	+45	69	1720	+44	68	1804	+44	68	1848	+45	67	265
	59	45	71	1344	45	71	1429	45	70	1514	45	69	1559	45	68	1644	45	68	1729	44	67	1813	44	66	264
	23	45	70	1308	45	70	1353	45	69	1438	46	68	1524	44	68	1608	45	67	1653	45	66	1738	44	66	263
	46	46	70	1232	45	69	1317	46	68	1403	45	68	1448	45	67	1533	45	66	1618	45	66	1703	45	65	262
	10	46	69	1156	46	68	1242	45	68	1327	46	67	1413	45	66	1458	46	65	1543	45	65	1628	45	64	261
	34	+46	68	1120	+46	68	1206	+46	67	1252	+45	66	1337	+46	66	1423	+45	65	1508	+45	64	1553	+45	64	260
	59	46	68	1045	46	67	1131	45	66	1216	46	66	1302	46	65	1348	45	64	1433	46	64	1519	45	63	259
	23	46	67	1009	46	66	1055	46	65	1141	46	65	1227	46	64	1313	46	64	1359	46	63	1445	45	62	258
	48	46	66	0934	46	65	1020	47	65	1107	46	64	1153	46	64	1239	46	62	1325	46	62	1411	45	62	257
	13	46	65	0859	47	65	0946	46	64	1032	46	63	1118	47	63	1205	46	62	1251	46	62	1337	46	61	256
	38	+46	65	0824	+47	64	0911	+47	63	0958	+46	63	1044	+47	62	1131	+46	61	1217	+46	61	1303	+47	60	255
	03	47	64	0750	47	63	0837	47	63	0924	46	62	1010	47	61	1057	46	61	1143	47	60	1230	47	59	254
	28	47	63	0715	48	63	0803	47	62	0850	47	61	0937	46	61	1023	47	60	1110	47	59	1157	47	59	253
	54	47	62	0641	48	62	0729	47	61	0816	47	61	0903	47	60	0950	47	59	1037	47	59	1124	47	58	252
	20	47	62	0607	48	61	0655	47	61	0742	48	60	0830	47	59	0917	47	59	1004	47	58	1051	48	57	251
	46	+48	61	0534	+48	60	0622	+47	60	0709	+48	59	0757	+47	59	0844	+48	58	0932	+47	57	1019	+47	57	250
	13	47	60	0500	48	60	0548	48	59	0636	48	58	0724	48	58	0812	47	57	0859	48	57	0947	48	56	249
	39	48	59	0427	48	59	0515	48	58	0603	48	58	0651	48	57	0739	48	57	0827	48	55	0915	48	55	248
	06	48	59	0354	49	58	0443	48	58	0531	48	57	0619	48	56	0707	49	56	0756	48	55	0844	48	55	247
	33	49	58	0322	48	57	0410	49	57	0459	48	56	0547	49	56	0636	48	55	0724	48	54	0812	49	54	246
	01	+48	57	0249	+49	57	0338	+49	56	0427	+49	55	0516	+48	55	0604	+49	54	0653	+48	54	0741	+49	53	245
	28	49	56	0217	49	56	0306	49	55	0355	49	55	0444	49	54	0533	49	54	0622	49	53	0711	48	52	244
	56	50	56	0146	49	55	0235	49	55	0324	49	54	0413	49	53	0502	49	53	0551	49	52	0640	49	52	243
	25	49	55	0114	49	54	0203	50	54	0253	49	53	0342	50	53	0432	49	52	0521	49	52	0610	49	51	242
	07	50	54	0043	49	54	0132	50	53	0222	50	53	0312	49	52	0401	50	51	0451	49	51	0540	50	50	241
	38	+50	53	0012	+50	53	0102	+50	52	0152	+19	52	0241	+50	51	0331	+50	51	0421	+50	50	0511	+50	50	240
	09	50	53	−019	50	52	0031	50	51	0121	51	51	0212	50	50	0302	50	50	0352	50	49	0442	50	49	239
	39	50	52	−049	50	51	0001	51	51	0052	50	50	0142	50	50	0232	51	49	0323	50	49	0413	50	48	238
	09	50	51	−119	51	51	−028	50	50	0022	51	49	0113	50	49	0203	51	48	0254	50	48	0344	51	47	237
	39	51	50	−148	50	50	−058	51	49	−007	51	49	0044	51	48	0135	50	48	0225	51	47	0316	51	47	236
	09	+51	50	−218	+51	49	−127	+51	48	−036	+51	48	0015	+51	47	0106	+51	47	0157	+51	46	0248	+51	46	235
	38	51	49	−247	52	48	−155	51	48	−104	51	47	−013	51	47	0038	52	46	0130	51	46	0221	51	45	234
	07	52	48	−315	51	47	−224	52	47	−132	51	46	−041	52	45	0011	51	45	0102	52	45	0154	51	44	233
	35	52	47	−343	51	47	−252	52	46	−200	52	46	−108	51	45	−017	52	45	0035	52	44	0127	52	44	232
	03	52	46	−411	52	46	−319	52	45	−227	52	45	−135	52	44	−043	51	44	0008	52	43	0100	53	43	231
	31	+52	45	−439	+52	45	−347	+53	45	−254	+52	44	−202	+52	44	−110	+52	43	−018	+52	43	0034	+53	42	230
	131			−506	53	44	−413	53	44	−321	52	43	−229	53	43	−136	52	42	−044	53	42	0009	52	41	229
	132			−533	53	43	−440	53	43	−347	52	43	−255	52	42	−202	53	41	−109	53	41	−016	52	41	228
				133			−506	53	42	−413	53	42	−320	53	41	−227	53	41	−134	53	40	−041	53	40	227
				134			−532	53	41	−440	53	42	−345	53	41	−252	53	40	−159	53	40	−106	53	39	226
							135			−504	54	40	−410	53	40	−317	54	39	−223	53	39	−130	53	38	225
							136			−528	53	39	−435	54	39	−341	54	38	−247	53	38	−154	54	37	224
										137			−458	53	38	−405	54	38	−311	54	37	−217	54	37	223
										138			−522	54	37	−428	54	37	−334	54	36	−240	54	36	222
										139			−545	54	36	−451	55	36	−356	54	35	−302	54	35	221

| 22° | 23° | 24° | 25° | 26° | 27° | 28° | 29° | |

LAT 50°

SAME NAME AS LATITUDE   LAT 50°

N. Lat. { LHA greater than 180°....... Zn=Z / LHA less than 180°.......... Zn=360—Z }

DECLINATION (15°-2

LHA	15° Hc	d	Z	16° Hc	d	Z	17° Hc	d	Z	18° Hc	d	Z	19° Hc	d	Z	20° Hc	d	Z	21° Hc	d
69	01 23	48	116	00 35	48	116	-0 13	48	117	-1 01	48	117	-1 49	48	118	-2 37	48	119	-3 25	48
68	01 58	48	116	01 10	48	117	00 22	49	118	-0 27	48	118	-1 15	48	119	-2 03	48	119	-2 51	48
67	02 32	48	117	01 44	48	118	00 56	49	118	00 07	48	119	-0 41	48	119	-1 29	49	120	-2 18	48
66	03 07	49	118	02 18	48	118	01 30	49	119	00 41	49	120	-0 08	48	120	-0 56	49	121	-1 45	48
65	03 41	-49	119	02 52	-49	119	02 03	-49	120	01 14	-48	120	00 26	-49	121	-0 23	-49	122	-1 12	-49
64	04 14	49	119	03 25	49	120	02 36	48	121	01 48	49	121	00 59	49	122	00 10	49	122	-0 39	49
63	04 48	49	120	03 59	49	121	03 10	50	121	02 20	49	122	01 31	49	123	00 42	49	123	-0 07	49
62	05 21	49	121	04 32	50	122	03 42	49	122	02 53	49	123	02 04	50	123	01 14	49	124	00 25	50
61	05 54	50	122	05 04	49	122	04 15	50	123	03 25	49	124	02 36	50	124	01 46	50	125	00 56	49
60	06 26	-49	123	05 37	-50	123	04 47	-50	124	03 57	-50	124	03 07	-49	125	02 18	-50	125	01 28	-50
59	06 59	50	124	06 09	50	124	05 19	50	125	04 29	50	125	03 39	50	126	02 49	50	126	01 59	50
58	07 31	50	124	06 41	50	125	05 51	51	125	05 00	50	126	04 10	50	126	03 20	50	127	02 30	51
57	08 03	51	125	07 12	50	126	06 22	51	126	05 31	50	127	04 41	51	127	03 50	50	128	03 00	51
56	08 34	51	126	07 43	50	127	06 53	51	127	06 02	51	128	05 11	50	128	04 21	51	129	03 30	51
55	09 05	-51	127	08 14	-51	127	07 23	-50	128	06 33	-51	128	05 42	-51	129	04 51	-51	129	04 00	-51
54	09 36	51	128	08 45	51	128	07 54	51	129	07 03	52	129	06 11	51	130	05 20	51	130	04 29	51
53	10 06	51	128	09 15	51	129	08 24	52	130	07 32	51	130	06 41	51	131	05 50	52	131	04 58	51
52	10 36	51	129	09 45	52	130	08 53	51	130	08 02	52	131	07 10	51	131	06 19	52	132	05 27	52
51	11 06	52	130	10 14	52	131	09 22	51	131	08 31	52	132	07 39	52	132	06 47	52	133	05 55	52
50	11 35	-52	131	10 43	-52	132	09 51	-52	132	08 59	-52	133	08 07	-52	133	07 15	-52	134	06 23	-52
49	12 04	52	132	11 12	52	132	10 20	52	133	09 28	53	133	08 35	52	134	07 43	52	134	06 51	53
48	12 33	53	133	11 40	52	133	10 48	53	134	09 55	52	134	09 03	53	135	08 10	52	135	07 18	53
47	13 01	53	134	12 08	52	134	11 16	53	135	10 23	53	135	09 30	52	136	08 37	52	136	07 45	53
46	13 29	53	134	12 36	53	135	11 43	53	135	10 50	53	136	09 57	53	136	09 04	53	137	08 11	53
45	13 56	-53	135	13 03	-53	136	12 10	-53	136	11 17	-54	137	10 23	-53	137	09 30	-53	138	08 37	-53
44	14 23	53	136	13 30	54	137	12 36	53	137	11 43	54	138	10 49	53	138	09 56	53	139	09 03	54
43	14 49	53	137	13 56	54	138	13 02	53	138	12 09	54	138	11 15	54	139	10 21	53	139	09 28	54
42	15 15	53	138	14 22	54	138	13 28	54	139	12 34	54	139	11 40	54	140	10 46	54	140	09 52	54
41	15 41	54	139	14 47	54	139	13 53	54	140	12 59	54	140	12 05	54	141	11 11	54	141	10 17	54
40	16 06	-54	140	15 12	-54	140	14 18	-55	141	13 23	-54	141	12 29	-54	142	11 35	-55	142	10 40	-54
39	16 31	55	141	15 36	54	141	14 42	55	142	13 47	54	142	12 53	55	142	11 58	54	143	11 04	55
38	16 55	55	142	16 00	54	142	15 06	55	142	14 11	55	143	13 16	55	143	12 21	55	144	11 26	54
37	17 19	55	143	16 24	55	143	15 29	55	143	14 34	54	144	13 39	55	144	12 44	55	145	11 49	55
36	17 42	55	143	16 47	55	144	15 52	55	144	14 57	55	145	14 01	55	145	13 06	55	146	12 11	55
35	18 05	-56	144	17 09	-55	145	16 14	-55	145	15 19	-56	146	14 23	-55	146	13 28	-56	146	12 32	-55
34	18 27	56	145	17 31	55	146	16 36	56	146	15 40	55	147	14 45	56	147	13 49	56	147	12 53	56
33	18 49	56	146	17 53	56	147	16 57	56	147	16 01	56	147	15 05	56	148	14 09	56	148	13 13	56
32	19 10	56	147	18 14	56	148	17 18	56	148	16 22	56	149	15 26	56	149	14 30	57	149	13 33	56
31	19 31	57	148	18 34	56	149	17 38	56	149	16 42	57	149	15 45	56	150	14 49	56	150	13 53	57
30	19 51	-57	149	18 54	-56	150	17 58	-57	150	17 01	-56	150	16 05	-57	151	15 08	-56	151	14 12	-57
29	20 10	56	150	19 14	57	150	18 17	57	151	17 20	57	151	16 23	56	152	15 27	57	152	14 30	57
28	20 29	57	151	19 32	57	151	18 35	56	152	17 39	57	152	16 42	57	152	15 45	57	153	14 48	57
27	20 47	57	152	19 50	57	152	18 53	57	153	17 56	57	153	16 59	57	153	16 02	57	154	15 05	57
26	21 05	57	153	20 08	57	153	19 11	57	154	18 14	58	154	17 16	57	154	16 19	58	155	15 21	57
25	21 22	-57	154	20 25	-57	154	19 28	-58	155	18 30	-57	155	17 33	-58	155	16 35	-57	156	15 38	-58
24	21 39	58	155	20 41	57	155	19 44	58	156	18 46	57	156	17 49	58	156	16 51	58	157	15 53	58
23	21 55	58	156	20 57	58	156	19 59	57	157	19 02	58	157	18 04	58	157	17 06	58	157	16 08	58
22	22 10	58	157	21 12	57	157	20 15	58	158	19 17	59	158	18 18	58	158	17 20	58	158	16 22	58
21	22 25	58	158	21 27	58	158	20 29	58	159	19 31	58	159	18 33	59	159	17 34	58	159	16 36	58
20	22 39	-58	159	21 41	-58	159	20 43	-59	160	19 44	-58	160	18 46	-58	160	17 48	-59	160	16 49	-58
19	22 53	59	160	21 54	58	160	20 56	59	161	19 57	59	161	18 59	59	161	18 00	58	161	17 02	59
18	23 06	59	161	22 07	59	161	21 08	58	162	20 10	59	162	19 11	59	162	18 12	58	162	17 14	59
17	23 18	59	162	22 19	59	162	21 20	59	163	20 22	59	163	19 23	59	163	18 24	59	163	17 25	59
16	23 29	59	163	22 30	58	163	21 32	59	164	20 33	59	164	19 34	59	164	18 35	59	164	17 36	59
15	23 40	-59	164	22 41	-59	164	21 42	-59	165	20 43	-59	165	19 44	-59	165	18 45	-59	165	17 46	-59
14	23 50	59	165	22 51	59	165	21 52	59	166	20 53	59	166	19 54	59	166	18 55	60	166	17 55	59
13	24 00	59	166	23 01	60	166	22 01	59	167	21 02	59	167	20 03	59	167	19 04	60	167	18 04	59
12	24 09	60	167	23 09	60	167	22 10	59	168	21 11	60	168	20 11	59	168	19 12	60	168	18 12	59
11	24 17	60	168	23 17	59	169	22 18	59	169	21 19	60	169	20 19	59	169	19 20	60	169	18 20	59
10	24 24	-59	169	23 25	-60	170	22 25	-59	170	21 25	-59	170	20 27	-59	170	19 27	-60	170	18 27	-60
9	24 31	60	170	23 31	59	171	22 32	60	171	21 32	59	171	20 33	59	171	19 33	60	171	18 33	59
8	24 37	60	172	23 37	59	172	22 38	60	172	21 38	60	172	20 38	59	172	19 39	60	172	18 39	60
7	24 43	60	173	23 43	60	173	22 43	60	173	21 43	59	173	20 43	59	173	19 44	60	173	18 44	60
6	24 47	60	174	23 47	60	174	22 47	59	174	21 48	60	174	20 48	60	174	19 48	60	174	18 48	60
5	24 51	-60	175	23 51	-60	175	22 51	-60	175	21 51	-59	175	20 52	-60	175	19 52	-60	175	18 52	-60
4	24 54	60	176	23 54	60	176	22 54	59	176	21 55	60	176	20 55	60	176	19 55	60	176	18 55	60
3	24 57	60	177	23 57	60	177	22 57	60	177	21 57	60	177	20 57	60	177	19 57	60	177	18 57	60
2	24 59	60	178	23 59	60	178	22 59	60	178	21 59	60	178	20 59	60	178	19 59	60	178	18 59	60
1	25 00	60	179	24 00	60	179	23 00	60	179	22 00	60	179	21 00	60	179	20 00	60	179	19 00	60
0	25 00	-60	180	24 00	-60	180	23 00	-60	180	22 00	-60	180	21 00	-60	180	20 00	-60	180	19 00	-60

15° — 16° — 17° — 18° — 19° — 20° — 21°

S. Lat. { LHA greater than 180°....... Zn=180—Z / LHA less than 180°.......... Zn=180+Z }

DECLINATION (15°-29

CONTRARY NAME TO LATITUDE

	22°			23°			24°			25°			26°			27°			28°			29°		LHA
	d	Z	Hc	d	Z	Hc	d	Z	Hc	d	Z	Hc	d	Z	Hc	d	Z	Hc	d	Z	Hc	d	Z	
3	47	120	-5 00	48	120	-5 48	48	121	**291**																
9	48	121	-4 27	48	121	-5 15	48	122	-6 03	48	122	**292**													
6	48	121	-3 54	49	122	-4 43	48	122	-5 31	48	123	**293**													
3	49	122	-3 22	48	123	-4 10	49	123	-4 59	48	124	-5 47	49	124	**294**										
1	-48	123	-2 49	-49	123	-3 38	-49	124	-4 27	-49	125	-5 16	-48	125	**295**										
8	49	124	-2 17	49	124	-3 06	49	125	-3 55	49	125	-4 44	49	126	-5 33	49	126	**296**							
6	50	124	-1 46	49	125	-2 35	49	125	-3 24	49	126	-4 13	49	127	-5 02	49	127	-5 51	49	128	**297**				
5	49	125	-1 14	49	126	-2 03	50	126	-2 53	49	127	-3 42	50	127	-4 32	49	128	-5 21	49	128	**298**				
7	50	126	-0 43	49	126	-1 32	50	127	-2 22	50	127	-3 12	49	128	-4 01	50	129	-4 51	49	129	-5 40	50	130	299
8	-50	127	-0 12	-50	127	-1 02	-50	128	-1 52	-49	128	-2 41	-50	129	-3 31	-50	129	-4 21	-50	130	-5 11	-50	130	300
9	50	127	00 19	50	128	-0 31	50	128	-1 21	51	129	-2 12	50	130	-3 02	50	130	-3 52	50	131	-4 42	50	131	301
9	50	128	00 49	50	129	-0 01	51	129	-0 52	50	130	-1 42	50	130	-2 32	51	131	-3 23	50	131	-4 13	50	132	302
9	50	129	01 19	51	129	00 28	50	130	-0 22	51	131	-1 13	50	131	-2 03	51	132	-2 54	51	132	-3 44	51	133	303
9	51	130	01 48	50	130	00 58	51	131	00 07	51	131	-0 44	51	132	-1 35	50	132	-2 25	51	133	-3 16	51	133	304
9	-51	130	02 18	-51	131	01 27	-51	132	00 36	-51	132	-0 15	-51	133	-1 06	-51	133	-1 57	-51	134	-2 48	-51	134	305
8	51	131	02 47	52	132	01 55	51	132	01 04	51	133	00 13	51	133	-0 38	52	134	-1 30	51	134	-2 21	51	135	306
7	52	132	03 15	51	133	02 24	52	133	01 32	51	134	00 41	52	134	-0 11	51	135	-1 02	52	135	-1 54	51	136	307
5	52	133	03 43	51	133	02 52	52	134	02 00	52	134	01 08	51	135	00 17	52	135	-0 35	52	136	-1 27	52	136	308
3	52	134	04 11	52	134	03 19	52	135	02 27	52	135	01 35	52	136	00 43	51	136	-0 08	52	137	-1 00	51	137	309
1	-52	135	04 39	-52	135	03 47	-53	135	02 54	-52	136	02 02	-52	136	01 10	-52	137	00 18	-52	137	-0 34	-53	138	310
8	52	135	05 06	53	136	04 13	52	136	03 21	52	137	02 29	53	137	01 36	52	138	00 44	53	138	-0 09	52	139	311
5	52	136	05 33	53	137	04 40	53	137	03 47	52	138	02 55	53	138	02 02	53	139	01 09	53	139	00 16	52	139	312
2	53	137	05 59	53	137	05 06	53	138	04 13	53	138	03 20	53	139	02 27	53	139	01 34	53	140	00 41	52	140	313
8	53	138	06 25	53	138	05 32	53	139	04 39	54	139	03 45	53	140	02 52	53	140	01 59	53	141	01 06	53	141	314
4	-54	139	06 50	-53	139	05 57	-53	140	05 04	-54	140	04 10	-53	140	03 17	-54	141	02 23	-53	141	01 30	-53	142	315
9	54	139	07 15	53	140	06 22	54	140	05 28	53	141	04 35	54	141	03 41	54	142	02 47	53	142	01 54	54	143	316
4	54	140	07 40	54	141	06 46	54	141	05 52	54	142	04 58	53	142	04 05	54	142	03 11	54	143	02 17	54	143	317
8	54	141	08 04	54	142	07 10	54	142	06 16	54	142	05 22	54	143	04 28	54	143	03 34	54	144	02 40	54	144	318
2	54	142	08 28	54	142	07 34	55	143	06 39	54	143	05 45	54	144	04 51	54	144	03 56	55	145	03 02	54	145	319
6	-55	143	08 51	-54	143	07 57	-55	144	07 02	-54	144	06 08	-55	145	05 13	-54	145	04 19	-55	145	03 24	-55	146	320
9	55	144	09 14	54	144	08 20	55	145	07 25	55	145	06 30	55	146	05 35	55	146	04 40	55	146	03 45	55	147	321
2	55	145	09 37	55	145	08 42	55	145	07 47	55	146	06 52	55	146	05 57	55	147	05 02	56	147	04 06	55	147	322
4	55	145	09 59	56	146	09 03	55	146	08 08	55	147	07 13	55	147	06 18	56	147	05 22	55	148	04 27	55	148	323
5	55	146	10 20	55	147	09 25	56	147	08 29	55	147	07 34	56	148	06 38	55	148	05 43	56	149	04 47	55	149	324
7	-56	147	10 41	-56	148	09 45	-55	148	08 50	-56	148	07 54	-56	149	06 58	-55	149	06 03	-56	149	05 07	-56	150	325
7	56	148	11 01	55	148	10 06	56	149	09 10	56	149	08 14	56	150	07 18	56	150	06 22	56	150	05 26	56	151	326
7	56	149	11 21	56	149	10 25	56	150	09 29	56	150	08 33	56	150	07 37	56	151	06 41	56	151	05 45	56	151	327
7	56	150	11 41	56	150	10 45	56	151	09 48	56	151	08 52	56	151	07 56	57	152	06 59	56	152	06 03	56	152	328
6	56	151	12 00	57	151	11 03	56	151	10 07	57	152	09 10	56	152	08 14	57	152	07 17	56	153	06 21	57	153	329
5	-57	152	12 18	-56	152	11 22	-57	152	10 25	-57	152	09 28	-57	153	08 31	-56	153	07 35	-57	154	06 38	-57	154	330
3	57	153	12 36	57	153	11 39	57	153	10 42	56	153	09 46	57	154	08 49	57	154	07 52	57	154	06 55	57	155	331
1	57	153	12 54	57	154	11 57	58	154	11 00	57	154	10 02	57	155	09 05	57	155	08 08	57	155	07 11	57	156	332
8	58	154	13 10	57	155	12 13	57	155	11 16	57	155	10 19	58	156	09 21	57	156	08 24	57	156	07 27	58	156	333
4	57	155	13 27	58	155	12 29	57	156	11 32	58	156	10 34	57	156	09 37	58	157	08 39	57	157	07 42	58	157	334
0	-58	156	13 42	-57	156	12 45	-58	157	11 47	-58	157	10 49	-57	157	09 52	-58	158	08 54	-58	158	07 56	-57	158	335
5	57	157	13 58	57	157	13 00	58	158	12 02	58	158	11 04	58	158	10 06	58	158	09 08	57	159	08 11	59	159	336
0	58	158	14 12	58	158	13 14	58	158	12 16	58	159	11 18	58	159	10 20	58	159	09 22	58	160	08 24	58	160	337
4	58	159	14 26	58	159	13 28	58	159	12 30	58	160	11 32	58	160	10 34	59	160	09 35	58	160	08 37	58	161	338
8	58	160	14 40	59	160	13 41	58	160	12 43	58	161	11 45	59	161	10 46	58	161	09 48	58	161	08 50	59	162	339
1	-59	161	14 52	-58	161	13 54	-58	161	12 56	-59	162	11 57	-58	162	10 59	-59	162	10 00	-58	162	09 02	-59	162	340
3	58	162	15 05	59	162	14 06	58	162	13 08	59	162	12 09	59	163	11 10	59	163	10 12	59	163	09 13	59	163	341
5	59	163	15 16	59	163	14 18	59	163	13 19	59	163	12 20	59	164	11 21	58	164	10 23	59	164	09 24	59	164	342
6	59	164	15 27	59	164	14 29	59	164	13 30	59	164	12 31	59	165	11 32	59	165	10 33	59	165	09 34	59	165	343
7	59	165	15 38	59	165	14 39	59	165	13 40	59	165	12 41	59	165	11 42	59	165	10 43	59	166	09 44	59	166	344
7	-59	166	15 48	-59	166	14 49	-59	166	13 50	-60	166	12 50	-59	166	11 51	-59	166	10 52	-59	167	09 53	-59	167	345
6	59	166	15 57	59	167	14 58	59	167	13 59	60	167	12 59	59	167	12 00	59	167	11 01	59	167	10 02	60	168	346
5	59	167	16 06	60	168	15 06	59	168	14 07	59	168	13 08	60	168	12 08	59	168	11 09	59	168	10 10	60	169	347
3	59	168	16 14	60	169	15 14	59	169	14 15	60	169	13 15	59	169	12 16	59	169	11 17	60	169	10 17	59	169	348
1	60	169	16 21	59	170	15 22	60	170	14 22	60	170	13 22	59	170	12 23	60	170	11 23	59	170	10 24	60	170	349
7	-59	170	16 28	-60	170	15 28	-59	171	14 29	-60	171	13 29	-60	171	12 29	-59	171	11 30	-60	171	10 30	-59	171	350
4	60	171	16 34	60	171	15 34	59	172	14 35	60	172	13 35	60	172	12 35	59	172	11 36	60	172	10 36	60	172	351
9	60	172	16 39	59	172	15 40	60	172	14 40	60	173	13 40	60	173	12 40	59	173	11 41	60	173	10 41	60	173	352
4	60	173	16 44	60	173	15 44	59	173	14 45	60	173	13 45	60	174	12 45	60	174	11 45	60	174	10 45	59	174	353
8	60	174	16 48	59	174	15 49	60	174	14 49	60	174	13 49	60	174	12 49	60	175	11 49	60	175	10 49	60	175	354
2	-60	175	16 52	-60	175	15 52	-60	175	14 52	-60	175	13 52	-60	175	12 52	-60	175	11 52	-60	176	10 53	-60	176	355
5	60	176	16 55	60	176	15 55	60	176	14 55	60	176	13 55	60	176	12 55	60	176	11 55	60	176	10 55	60	176	356
7	60	177	16 57	60	177	15 57	60	177	14 57	60	177	13 57	60	177	12 57	60	177	11 57	60	177	10 57	60	177	357
9	60	178	16 59	60	178	15 59	60	178	14 59	60	178	13 59	60	178	12 59	60	178	11 59	60	178	10 59	60	178	358
0	60	179	17 00	60	179	16 00	60	179	15 00	60	179	14 00	60	179	13 00	60	179	12 00	60	179	11 00	60	179	359
0	-60	180	17 00	-60	180	16 00	-60	180	15 00	-60	180	14 00	-60	180	13 00	-60	180	12 00	-60	180	11 00	-60	180	360

22°	23°	24°	25°	26°	27°	28°	29°

LAT 50°

CONTRARY NAME TO LATITUDE   LAT 50°

TABLE 5.—Correction to Tabulat

d / '	1	2	3	4	5	6	7	8	9	10	11	12	13	14	15	16	17	18	19	20	21	22	23	24	25	26	27	28	29
0	0	0	0	0	0	0	0	0	0	0	0	0	0	0	0	0	0	0	0	0	0	0	0	0	0	0	0	0	0
1	0	0	0	0	0	0	0	0	0	0	0	0	0	0	0	0	0	0	0	0	0	0	0	0	0	0	0	0	0
2	0	0	0	0	0	0	0	0	0	0	0	0	0	0	0	1	1	1	1	1	1	1	1	1	1	1	1	1	1
3	0	0	0	0	0	0	0	0	0	0	1	1	1	1	1	1	1	1	1	1	1	1	1	1	1	1	1	1	1
4	0	0	0	0	0	0	0	0	0	0	1	1	1	1	1	1	1	1	1	2	2	2	2	2	2	2	2	2	2
5	0	0	0	0	0	0	1	1	1	1	1	1	1	1	1	1	1	2	2	2	2	2	2	2	2	2	2	3	3
6	0	0	0	0	0	1	1	1	1	1	1	1	1	1	2	2	2	2	2	2	2	2	2	2	3	3	3	3	3
7	0	0	0	0	1	1	1	1	1	1	1	1	2	2	2	2	2	2	2	2	2	3	3	3	3	3	3	4	4
8	0	0	0	1	1	1	1	1	1	1	1	2	2	2	2	2	2	2	3	3	3	3	3	3	3	4	4	4	4
9	0	0	0	1	1	1	1	1	1	2	2	2	2	2	2	2	3	3	3	3	3	3	3	4	4	4	4	4	4
10	0	0	0	1	1	1	1	1	2	2	2	2	2	2	2	3	3	3	3	3	4	4	4	4	4	4	4	5	5
11	0	0	1	1	1	1	1	1	2	2	2	2	2	3	3	3	3	3	3	4	4	4	4	4	5	5	5	5	5
12	0	0	1	1	1	1	1	2	2	2	2	2	3	3	3	3	3	4	4	4	4	4	5	5	5	5	5	6	6
13	0	0	1	1	1	1	2	2	2	2	2	3	3	3	3	3	4	4	4	4	4	5	5	5	5	6	6	6	6
14	0	0	1	1	1	1	2	2	2	2	3	3	3	3	4	4	4	4	4	5	5	5	5	6	6	6	6	7	7
15	0	0	1	1	1	2	2	2	2	2	3	3	3	4	4	4	4	4	5	5	5	6	6	6	6	6	7	7	7
16	0	1	1	1	1	2	2	2	2	3	3	3	3	4	4	4	5	5	5	5	6	6	6	6	7	7	7	7	8
17	0	1	1	1	1	2	2	2	2	3	3	3	4	4	4	5	5	5	5	6	6	6	7	7	7	7	8	8	8
18	0	1	1	1	2	2	2	2	3	3	3	4	4	4	4	5	5	5	6	6	6	7	7	7	8	8	8	8	9
19	0	1	1	1	2	2	2	3	3	3	3	4	4	4	5	5	5	6	6	6	7	7	7	8	8	8	9	9	9
20	0	1	1	1	2	2	2	3	3	3	4	4	4	5	5	5	6	6	6	7	7	7	8	8	8	9	9	9	10
21	0	1	1	1	2	2	2	3	3	4	4	4	5	5	5	6	6	6	7	7	7	8	8	8	9	9	9	10	10
22	0	1	1	1	2	2	3	3	3	4	4	4	5	5	6	6	6	7	7	7	8	8	8	9	9	10	10	10	11
23	0	1	1	2	2	2	3	3	3	4	4	5	5	5	6	6	6	7	7	8	8	8	9	9	10	10	11	11	11
24	0	1	1	2	2	2	3	3	4	4	4	5	5	6	6	6	7	7	8	8	8	9	9	10	10	10	11	11	12
25	0	1	1	2	2	2	3	3	4	4	5	5	5	6	6	7	7	8	8	8	9	9	10	10	10	11	11	12	12
26	0	1	1	2	2	3	3	3	4	4	5	5	6	6	6	7	7	8	8	9	9	10	10	10	11	11	12	12	13
27	0	1	1	2	2	3	3	4	4	5	5	5	6	6	7	7	8	8	9	9	9	10	10	11	11	12	12	13	13
28	0	1	1	2	2	3	3	4	4	5	5	6	6	7	7	7	8	8	9	9	10	10	11	11	12	12	13	13	14
29	0	1	1	2	2	3	3	4	4	5	5	6	6	7	7	8	8	9	9	10	10	11	11	12	12	13	13	14	14
30	0	1	2	2	2	3	4	4	4	5	6	6	6	7	7	8	8	9	10	10	10	11	12	12	13	13	14	14	14
31	1	1	2	2	3	3	4	4	5	5	6	6	7	7	8	8	9	9	10	10	11	11	12	12	13	13	14	14	15
32	1	1	2	2	3	3	4	4	5	5	6	6	7	7	8	9	9	10	10	11	11	12	12	13	13	14	14	15	15
33	1	1	2	2	3	3	4	5	5	6	6	7	7	8	8	9	9	10	10	11	12	12	13	13	14	14	15	15	16
34	1	1	2	2	3	3	4	5	5	6	6	7	7	8	8	9	10	10	11	11	12	12	13	14	14	15	15	16	16
35	1	1	2	2	3	4	4	5	5	6	6	7	8	8	9	9	10	10	11	12	12	13	13	14	15	15	16	16	17
36	1	1	2	2	3	4	4	5	5	6	7	7	8	8	9	10	10	11	11	12	13	13	14	14	15	16	16	17	17
37	1	1	2	2	3	4	4	5	5	6	7	7	8	8	9	10	10	11	12	12	13	14	14	15	16	16	17	17	18
38	1	1	2	3	3	4	4	5	6	6	7	8	8	9	10	10	11	11	12	13	13	14	15	15	16	16	17	18	18
39	1	1	2	3	3	4	5	5	6	6	7	8	8	9	10	10	11	12	12	13	14	14	15	16	16	17	18	18	19
40	1	1	2	3	3	4	5	5	6	7	7	8	9	9	10	11	11	12	13	13	14	15	15	16	17	17	18	19	19
41	1	1	2	3	3	4	5	5	6	7	8	8	9	10	10	11	12	12	13	14	14	15	16	16	17	18	18	19	20
42	1	1	2	3	4	4	5	6	6	7	8	8	9	10	10	11	12	13	13	14	15	15	16	17	18	18	19	20	20
43	1	1	2	3	4	4	5	6	6	7	8	9	10	10	11	12	12	13	14	14	15	16	17	18	18	19	20	21	21
44	1	1	2	3	4	4	5	6	7	7	8	9	10	10	11	12	13	13	14	15	15	16	17	18	18	19	20	21	21
45	1	2	2	3	4	4	5	6	7	8	8	9	10	10	11	12	13	14	14	15	16	16	17	18	19	20	20	21	22
46	1	2	2	3	4	5	5	6	7	8	8	9	10	11	12	12	13	14	15	15	16	17	18	18	19	20	21	21	22
47	1	2	2	3	4	5	5	6	7	8	9	9	10	11	12	13	13	14	15	16	16	17	18	19	20	20	21	22	23
48	1	2	2	3	4	5	6	6	7	8	9	10	10	11	12	13	14	14	15	16	17	18	18	19	20	21	22	22	23
49	1	2	2	3	4	5	6	7	7	8	9	10	11	11	12	13	14	15	16	16	17	18	19	20	20	21	22	23	24
50	1	2	2	3	4	5	6	7	8	8	9	10	11	12	12	14	14	15	16	17	18	18	19	20	21	22	22	23	24
51	1	2	3	3	4	5	6	7	8	8	9	10	11	12	13	14	14	15	16	17	18	19	20	20	21	22	23	24	25
52	1	2	3	3	4	5	6	7	8	9	10	10	11	12	13	14	15	16	16	17	18	19	20	21	22	23	23	24	25
53	1	2	3	3	4	5	6	7	8	9	10	11	12	13	13	14	15	16	17	18	19	19	20	21	22	23	24	25	26
54	1	2	3	4	4	5	6	7	8	9	10	11	12	13	14	14	15	16	17	18	19	20	21	22	22	23	24	25	26
55	1	2	3	4	5	6	6	7	8	9	10	11	12	13	14	15	16	16	17	18	19	20	21	22	23	24	25	26	27
56	1	2	3	4	5	6	7	7	8	9	10	11	12	13	14	15	16	17	18	19	20	21	22	23	23	24	25	27	27
57	1	2	3	4	5	6	7	8	9	10	10	11	12	13	14	15	16	17	18	19	20	21	22	23	24	25	26	27	28
58	1	2	3	4	5	6	7	8	9	10	11	12	13	14	14	15	16	17	18	19	20	21	22	23	24	25	26	27	28
59	1	2	3	4	5	6	7	8	9	10	11	12	13	14	15	16	17	18	19	20	21	22	23	24	25	26	27	28	29

Altitude for Minutes of Declination

31 32 33	34 35 36	37 38 39	40 41 42	43 44 45	46 47 48	49 50 51	52 53 54	55 56 57	58 59 60	d / ′
0 0 0	0 0 0	0 0 0	0 0 0	0 0 0	0 0 0	0 0 0	0 0 0	0 0 0	0 0 0	0
1 1 1	1 1 1	1 1 1	1 1 1	1 1 1	1 1 1	1 1 1	1 1 1	1 1 1	1 1 1	1
1 1 1	1 1 1	1 1 1	1 1 1	1 1 2	2 2 2	2 2 2	2 2 2	2 2 2	2 2 2	2
2 2 2	2 2 2	2 2 2	2 2 2	2 2 2	2 2 2	2 2 3	3 3 3	3 3 3	3 3 3	3
2 2 2	2 2 2	2 3 3	3 3 3	3 3 3	3 3 3	3 3 3	3 4 4	4 4 4	4 4 4	4
3 3 3	3 3 3	3 3 3	3 3 4	4 4 4	4 4 4	4 4 4	4 4 4	5 5 5	5 5 5	5
3 3 3	3 4 4	4 4 4	4 4 4	4 4 4	5 5 5	5 5 5	5 5 5	6 6 6	6 6 6	6
4 4 4	4 4 4	4 4 5	5 5 5	5 5 5	5 5 6	6 6 6	6 6 6	6 7 7	7 7 7	7
4 4 4	5 5 5	5 5 5	5 5 6	6 6 6	6 6 6	7 7 7	7 7 7	7 7 8	8 8 8	8
5 5 5	5 5 5	6 6 6	6 6 6	6 7 7	7 7 7	7 8 8	8 8 8	8 8 9	9 9 9	9
5 5 6	6 6 6	6 6 6	7 7 7	7 7 8	8 8 8	8 8 8	9 9 9	9 9 10	10 10 10	10
6 6 6	6 6 7	7 7 7	7 8 8	8 8 8	8 9 9	9 9 9	10 10 10	10 10 10	11 11 11	11
6 6 7	7 7 7	7 8 8	8 8 8	9 9 9	9 9 10	10 10 10	10 11 11	11 11 11	12 12 12	12
7 7 7	7 8 8	8 8 8	9 9 9	9 10 10	10 10 10	11 11 11	11 11 12	12 12 12	13 13 13	13
7 7 8	8 8 8	9 9 9	9 10 10	10 10 10	11 11 11	11 12 12	12 12 13	13 13 13	14 14 14	14
8 8 8	8 9 9	9 10 10	10 10 10	11 11 11	12 12 12	12 12 13	13 13 14	14 14 14	14 15 15	15
8 9 9	9 9 10	10 10 10	11 11 11	11 12 12	12 13 13	13 13 14	14 14 14	15 15 15	15 16 16	16
9 9 9	10 10 10	10 11 11	11 12 12	12 12 13	13 13 14	14 14 14	15 15 15	16 16 16	16 17 17	17
9 10 10	10 10 11	11 11 12	12 12 13	13 13 14	14 14 14	15 15 15	16 16 16	16 17 17	17 18 18	18
10 10 10	11 11 11	12 12 12	13 13 13	14 14 14	15 15 15	16 16 16	16 17 17	17 18 18	18 19 19	19
10 11 11	11 12 12	12 13 13	13 14 14	14 15 15	15 16 16	16 17 17	17 18 18	18 19 19	19 20 20	20
11 11 12	12 12 13	13 13 14	14 14 15	15 15 16	16 16 17	17 18 18	18 19 19	19 20 20	20 21 21	21
11 12 12	12 13 13	14 14 14	15 15 15	16 16 16	17 17 18	18 18 19	19 19 20	20 21 21	21 22 22	22
12 12 13	13 13 14	14 15 15	15 16 16	16 17 17	18 18 18	19 19 20	20 20 21	21 21 22	22 23 23	23
12 13 13	14 14 14	15 15 16	16 16 17	17 18 18	18 19 19	20 20 20	21 21 22	22 22 23	23 24 24	24
13 13 14	14 15 15	15 16 16	17 17 18	18 18 19	19 20 20	20 21 21	22 22 22	23 23 24	24 25 25	25
13 14 14	15 15 16	16 16 17	17 18 18	19 19 20	20 20 21	21 22 22	23 23 23	24 24 25	25 26 26	26
14 14 15	15 16 16	17 17 18	18 18 19	19 20 20	21 21 22	22 22 23	23 24 24	25 25 26	26 27 27	27
14 15 15	16 16 17	17 18 18	19 19 20	20 21 21	21 22 22	23 23 24	24 25 25	26 26 27	27 28 28	28
15 15 16	16 17 17	18 18 19	19 20 20	21 21 22	22 23 23	24 24 25	25 26 26	27 27 28	28 29 29	29
16 16 16	17 18 18	18 19 20	20 20 21	22 22 22	23 24 24	24 25 26	26 26 27	28 28 28	29 30 30	30
16 17 17	18 18 19	19 20 20	21 21 22	22 23 23	24 24 25	25 26 26	27 27 28	28 29 29	30 30 31	31
17 17 18	18 19 19	20 20 21	21 22 22	23 23 24	25 25 26	26 27 27	28 28 29	29 30 30	31 31 32	32
17 18 18	19 19 20	20 21 21	22 23 23	24 24 25	25 26 26	27 28 28	29 29 30	30 31 31	32 32 33	33
18 18 19	19 20 20	21 22 22	23 23 24	24 25 26	26 27 27	28 28 29	29 30 31	31 32 32	33 33 34	34
18 19 19	20 20 21	22 22 23	23 24 24	25 26 26	27 27 28	29 29 30	30 31 32	32 33 33	34 34 35	35
19 19 20	20 21 22	22 23 23	24 25 25	26 26 27	28 28 29	29 30 31	31 32 32	33 34 34	35 35 36	36
19 20 20	21 22 22	23 23 24	25 25 26	27 27 28	28 29 30	30 31 31	32 33 33	34 35 35	36 36 37	37
20 20 21	22 22 23	23 24 25	25 26 27	27 28 28	29 30 30	31 32 32	33 34 34	35 35 36	37 37 38	38
20 21 21	22 23 23	24 25 25	26 27 27	28 29 29	30 31 31	32 32 33	34 34 35	36 36 37	38 38 39	39
21 21 22	23 23 24	25 25 26	27 27 28	29 29 30	31 31 32	33 33 34	35 35 36	37 37 38	39 39 40	40
21 22 23	23 24 25	25 26 27	27 28 29	29 30 31	31 32 33	33 34 35	36 36 37	38 38 39	40 40 41	41
22 22 23	24 24 25	26 27 27	28 29 29	30 31 32	32 33 34	34 35 36	36 37 38	38 39 40	41 41 42	42
22 23 24	24 25 26	27 27 28	29 29 30	31 32 32	33 34 34	35 36 37	37 38 39	39 40 41	42 42 43	43
23 23 24	25 26 26	27 28 29	29 30 31	32 32 33	34 34 35	36 37 37	38 39 40	40 41 42	43 43 44	44
23 24 25	26 26 27	28 28 29	30 31 32	32 33 34	34 35 36	37 38 38	39 40 40	41 42 43	44 44 45	45
24 25 25	26 27 28	28 29 30	31 31 32	33 34 34	35 36 37	38 38 39	40 41 41	42 43 44	44 45 46	46
24 25 26	27 27 28	29 30 31	31 32 33	34 34 35	36 37 38	38 39 40	41 42 42	43 44 45	45 46 47	47
25 26 26	27 28 29	30 30 31	32 33 34	34 35 36	37 38 38	39 40 41	42 42 43	44 45 46	46 47 48	48
25 26 27	28 29 29	30 31 32	33 33 34	35 36 37	38 38 39	40 41 42	42 43 44	45 46 47	47 48 49	49
26 27 28	28 29 30	31 32 32	33 34 35	36 37 38	38 39 40	41 42 42	43 44 45	46 47 48	48 49 50	50
26 27 28	29 30 31	31 32 33	34 35 36	37 37 38	39 40 41	42 42 43	44 45 46	47 48 48	49 50 51	51
27 28 29	29 30 31	32 33 34	35 36 36	37 38 39	40 41 42	42 43 44	45 46 47	48 49 49	50 51 52	52
27 28 29	30 31 32	33 34 34	35 36 37	38 39 40	41 42 42	43 44 45	46 47 48	49 49 50	51 52 53	53
28 29 30	31 32 32	33 34 35	36 37 38	39 40 40	41 42 43	44 45 46	47 48 49	50 50 51	52 53 54	54
28 29 30	31 32 33	34 35 36	37 38 38	39 40 41	42 43 44	45 46 47	48 49 50	50 51 52	53 54 55	55
29 30 31	32 33 34	35 35 36	37 38 39	40 41 42	43 44 45	46 47 48	49 49 50	51 52 53	54 55 56	56
29 30 31	32 33 34	35 36 37	38 39 40	41 42 43	44 45 46	47 48 48	49 50 51	52 53 54	55 56 57	57
30 31 32	33 34 35	36 37 38	39 40 41	42 43 44	44 45 46	47 48 49	50 51 52	53 54 55	56 57 58	58
30 31 32	33 34 35	36 37 38	39 40 41	42 43 44	45 46 47	48 49 50	51 52 53	54 55 56	57 58 59	59

Appendix 8
Traverse Table extract

40°   320° ↑ / 220° ↓   **TRAVERSE TABLE**   040° ↑ / 140° ↓   2h 40m

40 DEGREES.

D Lon Dist	Dep. D.Lat	Dep.	D Lon Dist	Dep. D.Lat	Dep.	D Lon Dist	Dep. D.Lat	Dep.	D Lon Dist	Dep. D.Lat	Dep.	D Lon Dist	Dep. D.Lat	Dep.
1	00·8	00·6	61	46·7	39·2	121	92·7	77·8	181	138·7	116·3	241	184·6	154·9
2	01·5	01·3	62	47·5	39·9	122	93·5	78·4	182	139·4	117·0	242	185·4	155·6
3	02·3	01·9	63	48·3	40·5	123	94·2	79·1	183	140·2	117·6	243	186·1	156·2
4	03·1	02·6	64	49·0	41·1	124	95·0	79·7	184	141·0	118·3	244	186·9	156·8
5	03·8	03·2	65	49·8	41·8	125	95·8	80·3	185	141·7	118·9	245	187·7	157·5
6	04·6	03·9	66	50·6	42·4	126	96·5	81·0	186	142·5	119·6	246	188·4	158·1
7	05·4	04·5	67	51·3	43·1	127	97·3	81·6	187	143·3	120·2	247	189·2	158·8
8	06·1	05·1	68	52·1	43·7	128	98·1	82·3	188	144·0	120·8	248	190·0	159·4
9	06·9	05·8	69	52·9	44·4	129	98·8	82·9	189	144·8	121·5	249	190·7	160·1
10	07·7	06·4	70	53·6	45·0	130	99·6	83·6	190	145·5	122·1	250	191·5	160·7
11	08·4	07·1	71	54·4	45·6	131	100·4	84·2	191	146·3	122·8	251	192·3	161·3
12	09·2	07·7	72	55·2	46·3	132	101·1	84·8	192	147·1	123·4	252	193·0	162·0
13	10·0	08·4	73	55·9	46·9	133	101·9	85·5	193	147·8	124·1	253	193·8	162·6
14	10·7	09·0	74	56·7	47·6	134	102·6	86·1	194	148·6	124·7	254	194·6	163·3
15	11·5	09·6	75	57·5	48·2	135	103·4	86·8	195	149·4	125·3	255	195·3	163·9
16	12·3	10·3	76	58·2	48·9	136	104·2	87·4	196	150·1	126·0	256	196·1	164·6
17	13·0	10·9	77	59·0	49·5	137	104·9	88·1	197	150·9	126·6	257	196·9	165·2
18	13·8	11·6	78	59·8	50·1	138	105·7	88·7	198	151·7	127·3	258	197·6	165·8
19	14·6	12·2	79	60·5	50·8	139	106·5	89·3	199	152·4	127·9	259	198·4	166·5
20	15·3	12·9	80	61·3	51·4	140	107·2	90·0	200	153·2	128·6	260	199·2	167·1
21	16·1	13·5	81	62·0	52·1	141	108·0	90·6	201	154·0	129·2	261	199·9	167·8
22	16·9	14·1	82	62·8	52·7	142	108·8	91·3	202	154·7	129·8	262	200·7	168·4
23	17·6	14·8	83	63·6	53·4	143	109·5	91·9	203	155·5	130·5	263	201·5	169·1
24	18·4	15·4	84	64·3	54·0	144	110·3	92·6	204	156·3	131·1	264	202·2	169·7
25	19·2	16·1	85	65·1	54·6	145	111·1	93·2	205	157·0	131·8	265	203·0	170·3
26	19·9	16·7	86	65·9	55·3	146	111·8	93·8	206	157·8	132·4	266	203·8	171·0
27	20·7	17·4	87	66·6	55·9	147	112·6	94·5	207	158·6	133·1	267	204·5	171·6
28	21·4	18·0	88	67·4	56·6	148	113·4	95·1	208	159·3	133·7	268	205·3	172·3
29	22·2	18·6	89	68·2	57·2	149	114·1	95·8	209	160·1	134·3	269	206·1	172·9
30	23·0	19·3	90	68·9	57·9	150	114·9	96·4	210	160·9	135·0	270	206·8	173·6
31	23·7	19·9	91	69·7	58·5	151	115·7	97·1	211	161·6	135·6	271	207·6	174·2
32	24·5	20·6	92	70·5	59·1	152	116·4	97·7	212	162·4	136·3	272	208·4	174·8
33	25·3	21·2	93	71·2	59·8	153	117·2	98·3	213	163·2	136·9	273	209·1	175·5
34	26·0	21·9	94	72·0	60·4	154	118·0	99·0	214	163·9	137·6	274	209·9	176·1
35	26·8	22·5	95	72·8	61·1	155	118·7	99·6	215	164·7	138·2	275	210·7	176·8
36	27·6	23·1	96	73·5	61·7	156	119·5	100·3	216	165·5	138·8	276	211·4	177·4
37	28·3	23·8	97	74·3	62·4	157	120·3	100·9	217	166·2	139·5	277	212·2	178·1
38	29·1	24·4	98	75·1	63·0	158	121·0	101·6	218	167·0	140·1	278	213·0	178·7
39	29·9	25·1	99	75·8	63·6	159	121·8	102·2	219	167·8	140·8	279	213·7	179·3
40	30·6	25·7	100	76·6	64·3	160	122·6	102·8	220	168·5	141·4	280	214·5	180·0
41	31·4	26·4	101	77·4	64·9	161	123·3	103·5	221	169·3	142·1	281	215·3	180·6
42	32·2	27·0	102	78·1	65·6	162	124·1	104·1	222	170·1	142·7	282	216·0	181·3
43	32·9	27·6	103	78·9	66·2	163	124·9	104·8	223	170·8	143·3	283	216·8	181·9
44	33·7	28·3	104	79·7	66·8	164	125·6	105·4	224	171·6	144·0	284	217·6	182·6
45	34·5	28·9	105	80·4	67·5	165	126·4	106·1	225	172·4	144·6	285	218·3	183·2
46	35·2	29·6	106	81·2	68·1	166	127·2	106·7	226	173·1	145·3	286	219·1	183·8
47	36·0	30·2	107	82·0	68·8	167	127·9	107·3	227	173·9	145·9	287	219·9	184·5
48	36·8	30·9	108	82·7	69·4	168	128·7	108·0	228	174·7	146·6	288	220·6	185·1
49	37·5	31·5	109	83·5	70·1	169	129·5	108·6	229	175·4	147·2	289	221·4	185·8
50	38·3	32·1	110	84·3	70·7	170	130·2	109·3	230	176·2	147·8	290	222·2	186·4
51	39·1	32·8	111	85·0	71·3	171	131·0	109·9	231	177·0	148·5	291	222·9	187·1
52	39·8	33·4	112	85·8	72·0	172	131·8	110·6	232	177·7	149·1	292	223·7	187·7
53	40·6	34·1	113	86·6	72·6	173	132·5	111·2	233	178·5	149·8	293	224·5	188·3
54	41·4	34·7	114	87·3	73·3	174	133·3	111·8	234	179·3	150·4	294	225·2	189·0
55	42·1	35·4	115	88·1	73·9	175	134·1	112·5	235	180·0	151·1	295	226·0	189·6
56	42·9	36·0	116	88·9	74·5	176	134·8	113·1	236	180·8	151·7	296	226·7	190·3
57	43·7	36·6	117	89·6	75·2	177	135·6	113·8	237	181·6	152·3	297	227·5	190·9
58	44·4	37·3	118	90·4	75·8	178	136·4	114·4	238	182·3	153·0	298	228·3	191·6
59	45·2	37·9	119	91·2	76·5	179	137·1	115·1	239	183·1	153·6	299	229·0	192·2
60	46·0	38·6	120	91·9	77·1	180	137·9	115·7	240	183·9	154·3	300	229·8	192·8

| Dist | Dep. | D.Lat | Dist | Dep. | D.Lat | Dist | Dep. | D.Lat | Dist | Dep. | D.Lat | Dist | Dep. | D.Lat |

D Lon / Dep.

50°   310° ↑ / 230° ↓   **50 DEGREES.**   050° ↑ / 130° ↓   3h 20m

Appendix 9
Glossary of terms

AMPLITUDE. The sun's true bearing at sunrise or sunset, measured from E (on rising) or from W (on setting) towards N when sun's decl. is N, towards S when decl. is S.

AZIMUTH. The bearing of a heavenly body measured from N or S.

CALCULATED ALTITUDE. The altitude a body would be if measured at a given lat. and long. (usually the EP) found by calculation (not by sight reduction tables).

CHOSEN POSITION. A chosen lat. and long., normally within $\frac{1}{2}°$ of the yacht's EP, used to find the Tabulated Altitude for comparison with the true alt. found at the actual position.

DR. Dead reckoning position arrived at by reference only to course steered and distance through the water. No allowance for tidal stream, current or leeway.

DECLINATION. The angular distance between a body and the celestial equator, equivalent to the latitude of the body's GP.

DEPARTURE. The distance, measured in miles, between the meridians passing through two places, or the miles which one place is E or W of another. The number of minutes of longitude of the departure depends on the latitude of the position.

DEVIATION. The number of degrees and direction by which the compass bearing or course differs from the magnetic bearing or course. If present, this 'error' will vary according to the yacht's heading when compass is read.

DIP. The angle between a line drawn from the observer's eye to the visible horizon and a line at right angles to the observer's zenith. Varies only with height of eye.

ESTIMATED POSITION. A position arrived at by applying the effects of tidal stream or current, and leeway to the position found by DR. It is the best possible estimate of the yacht's position by reference to course steered and distance run, stream or current and leeway since the last OP or EP.

FIX. A position found by observations of landmarks.

GEOGRAPHICAL POSITION (GP). The point on the earth's surface where a heavenly body is exactly overhead—in the observer's zenith. It is defined by the body's declination (= lat.) and GHA (= long.) at a given moment.

GREAT CIRCLE. Any circle on whose plane lies the centre of the earth. Any great circle bisects the earth into two equal halves. A portion of a great circle which passes through two positions is the shortest distance between them. It cuts every meridian at a different angle (except when it is part of a meridian, or the equator), and appears as a curve, bowed away from the equator, on a mercator chart. It is a straight line on a gnomonic projection chart.

GREENWICH HOUR ANGLE (GHA). The 'longitude' of a body's GP at a given moment, always measured Westward from 0°. It is the angle at the pole between the Greenwich meridian and the meridian on which the body's GP is at a given moment. It can also be measured along the equator.

HORIZON. The line where sea and sky appear to meet.

INTERCEPT. The distance between the chosen position and a point through which the (true) position line runs.

LOCAL HOUR ANGLE (LHA). The angle between the meridian on which the chosen position (or the observer) lies and the meridian on which the body's GP lies at a given moment. It may be measured at the pole or along the equator, always measured *from* CP or observer *TO* the body's GP, always westward.

LIMB. The upper or lower edge of the sun or moon.

MAGNITUDE. The relative brightness of a star or planet. The lower the number (or the greater the minus number) the brighter the body.

MERIDIAN. Any great circle passing through both N and S poles.

MERIDIAN ALTITUDE. Any body is at its greatest altitude when it crosses the meridian on which is an observer. It is then always bearing due N or S (T°).

OBSERVED POSITION (OP). A position found by observations of heavenly bodies.

PARALLAX. The apparent change of an object's position when viewed from a different position.

PRIME MERIDIAN. The meridian on which Greenwich lies, 0°.

PRIME VERTICAL. A vertical circle passing through E and W points on the horizon. A body is crossing the prime vertical when it bears exactly due E or W. Its Zn is then 90° or 270° T.

RHUMB LINE. A straight line drawn between two points on a Mercator projection chart. It cuts every meridian at the same angle, and is not the shortest distance. (See Gt Circle.)

SEMI-DIAMETER (SD). Half the angular diameter of sun or moon at a given time. Moon's SD changes markedly; sun's much less.

TABULATED ALTITUDE (Tab. alt.). The altitude a body would be if measured at the chosen position, given by sight reduction tables.

TRUE ALTITUDE (True alt.). The altitude a body is, as measured at yacht, after all corrections have been applied. Found by sextant.

TRANSIT. The passage of a body across the observer's meridian, then at the body's highest altitude, and bearing due N or S.

TWILIGHT. When sun is below horizon but indirect light still gives some light. Times of beginning (at a.m.) and ending (p.m.) of twilights are listed in Naut. Alm. every third day.
   Nautical twilight when sun is 12° below horizon
   Civil twilight when sun is 6° below horizon
   Star sights are best taken around civil twilight.

VARIATION. The difference at any place between the true bearing or course and the magnetic bearing or course as shown by a compass without any deviation.

ZENITH. The point in the heavens exactly vertically above the observer.

ZENITH DISTANCE (ZD). The angular distance between an observer's zenith and a body. It is the body's altitude subtracted from 90 degrees.

Appendix 10

1
(a) True alt. 10°49'·9.
(b) True alt. 20·05'·0.
(c) True alt. 28°57'·2.
(d) True alt. 20°30'·7.
(e) True alt. 48°41'·8.

2

	GHA	Dec.
(a)	314°12'·2	N 19°52'·7.
(b)	133°49'·8	N 8°38'·2
(c)	114°37'·0	S 11°59'·1
(d)	265°18'·8	S 12°32'·1
(e)	59°33'·1	N 19°56'·5

3
(a) CP W 18°12'·2 N 50° LHA 296°
Dec. N 19°53'.
(b) CP E 165°10'·2 S 50° LHA 299°
Dec. N 8°38'.
(c) CP W 41°37'·0 S 50° LHA 73° Dec. S 11°59'.
(d) CP E 165°41'·2 S 50° LHA 71° Dec. S 12°32'.
(e) CP W 127°33'·1 N 50° LHA 292°
Dec. N 19°56'.

4
(a) Tab. alt. 31°42'   Zn = 097°.
(b) Tab. alt. 11°08'   Zn = 062°.
(c) Tab. alt. 20°03'   Zn = 276°.
(d) Tab. alt. 21°45'   Zn = 277°.
(e) Tab. alt. 29°11'   Zn = 094°.

5
(a) CP S 50° E 165°10'·2, Intercept : AWAY
18'·1, Zn = 062°.
(b) CP S 50° W 41°37', Intercept : TO 2'·0,
Zn = 276°.
(c) N 50° W 129°59'·7, Intercept : TO 18'·2,
Zn = 134°.
(d) N 50° W 127°33'·1, Intercept : AWAY 13'·8,
Zn = 094°.

6
(a) 01^h 14^m GMT obs. lat. 49°28' S.
(b) 20^h 27^m GMT obs. lat. 49°32' N.
(c) 12^h 25^m GMT obs. lat. 50°25'·5 N.

7
(a) Yacht's lat. 49°36' N.   (b) 28°49'·2 N

8

Obs. pos. 50°25'·5 N 6°02' W.

ocean yacht navigator

9
(a) 16-46-38 GMT.
(b) 2000 GMT.
(c) GD 21^d 04-54-13 GMT.
(d)GD 14^d 22-46-48 GMT.

10
(a) CP N 50°, W 3°44'·1, Intercept AWAY 0'·8
      Brg. 282°.
(b) N 50°, W 130°22'·6, Intercept TO 14'·5
      Brg. 173°.
(c) Planned stars:
      Mirfak   21°10'   036°
      ALTAIR   48°04'   166°
      ARCTURUS 24°38'   271°
      OP   49°36' N 6°34' W.
(d) CP 50° S 164°40'·7 E, Intercept TO 17'·6
          Brg. 353°
(e) Moon's mer. pass. 18-54-12 GMT. Lat.
        56°25' S

11
(a) 40°09'·2 N   3°46' E
(b) 39°51'·6 N   6°03'·9 W
(c) 40°28'·5 S   12°09' E
(d) 50°29'·3 S   17°44'·1 W
(e) 50°28'·1 N   174°05'·1 E
(f) 49°36' N   128°27' W
(g) 49°40' S   159°38' E
(h) 50°08' N   38°31' W

12
(a) Total error 11°4 W. Deviation 5°·6, say 6° E.
(b) Total error 22°·8 E. Deviation 2°·2, say 2° W.
(c) Total error 26°·2 E. Deviation 7°·2, say 7° E.

Exercise 13
Answers
1. First sight, 15-52-10 GMT. See Exercise 11f
    for CP and Intercept. Time of mer. pass. 20^d, 20^h
    30^m approx. GMT. OP 49°36' N 128°27' W.
2. Mer. pass. 17^d, 01^h 38^m approx. GMT, lat.
    49°44'·5 S. PM sight, see exercise 11g for
    CP and intercept. OP 49°41 S 159°38 E.
3. See exercise 11h for CPs and intercepts.
    OP 50°08 N 38°31 W.
4. Mirfak, Altair, Arcturus. OP 49°55 N 17°54 W.

Index

ocean yacht navigator

Tropics 96
  sights in the 104

Ursa Major or Plough 59, 74

Variation, checking compass 98
  recording 96
Vernier, sextant 40
Venus 73
Vertical sextant angle, VSA 24
VHF radio 117
Visibility, sights in poor 102
V.m.g. computer 132

Wake course, recording 96
Walker patent log 128
Watch 67, 71
Weather reports 119
Wind direction indicator 132
  prevailing 108
  recording 96
  reports 108
  roses, on charts 108
  speed indicator 132
Winding up deck watch or chron. 71
Wrist watch 67, 102

Yokohama 110

Zenith 17, 18
  distance 18, 19, 20, 21, 55, 57, 83, 84
'Zenith' radio receiver 118
Zone time 68

Abbreviations

A.L.R.S.	Admiralty List of Radio Stations
Alt :	Altitude
A.T.T.	Admiralty Tide Tables
Az :	Azimuth
Cor :	Correction
C.P.	Chosen Position
C.Z.D.	Calculated Zenith Distance
Dec :	Declination
Dep :	Departure
D. Lat :	Difference in Latitude
D. Lon :	Difference in Longitude
D.M.P.	Difference in Meridional Parts
D.R.	Dead Reckoning (position by)
D.W.	Deck Watch
D.W.E.	Deck Watch Error
E.P.	Estimated Position
G.D.	Greenwich Date
G.H.A.	Greenwich Hour Angle
G.M.T.	Greenwich Mean Time
G.P.	Geographical Position
H.M.S.O.	Her Majesty's Stationery Office
H.P.	Horizontal Parallax
I.E.	Index Error (of sextant)
L.H.A.	Local Hour Angle
Lat :	Latitude
Long :	Longitude
L.L.	Lower Limb (of sun or moon)
L.M.T.	Local Mean Time
M	Mile(s)
m	Metre(s)
M.P.	Meridional Parts
Mer : Alt :	Meridian Altitude
Mer : Pass :	Meridian Passage
O.P.	Observed Position
P.L.	Position Line
P.V.	Prime Vertical
R.D.F.	Radio Direction Finding
S.H.A.	Siderial Hour Angle
T.Z.D.	True Zenith Distance
U.L.	Upper limb (sun or moon)
U.T.	Universal Time
Z.D.	Zenith Distance
Z.T.	Zone Time